WORKROOM

CONTEMPORARY SOCIAL THEORY
General Editor: ANTHONY GIDDENS

This series aims to create a forum for debate between different theoretical and philosophical traditions in the social sciences. As well as covering broad schools of thought, the series will also concentrate upon the work of particular thinkers whose ideas have had a major impact on social science (these books appear under the sub-series title of 'Theoretical Traditions in the Social Sciences'). The series is not limited to abstract theoretical discussion – it will also include more substantive works on contemporary capitalism, the state, politics and other subject areas.

Published titles

Tony Bilton, Kevin Bonnett, Philip Jones, Ken Sheard, Michelle Stanworth and
 Andrew Webster, *Introductory Sociology*
Simon Clarke, *Marx, Marginalism and Modern Sociology*
Emile Durkheim, *The Rules of Sociological Method* (ed. Steven Lukes, trans. W. D.
 Halls)
Anthony Giddens, *A Contemporary Critique of Historical Materialism*
Anthony Giddens, *Central Problems in Social Theory*
Anthony Giddens, *Profiles and Critiques in Social Theory*
Anthony Giddens and David Held (eds), *Classes, Power and Conflict*
Ali Rattansi, *Marx and the Division of Labour*
Gerry Rose, *Deciphering Sociological Research*
John Scott, *The Upper Classes: Property and Privilege in Britain*
Steve Taylor, *Durkheim and the Study of Suicide*
John B. Thompson and David Held (eds), *Habermas: Critical Debates*
John Urry, *The Anatomy of Capitalist Societies*

Forthcoming titles

Martin Albrow, *Weber and the Construction of Social Theory*
Clive Ashworth, Chris Dandeker and Terry Johnson, *Theoretical Sociology*
David Brown and Michael Harrison, *Industrial Sociology*
Emile Durkheim, *The Division of Labour in Society* (trans. W. D. Halls)
Boris Frankel, *Beyond the State*
Anthony Giddens, *Between Capitalism and Socialism*
David Held, *Bureaucracy, Democracy and Socialism*
Geoffrey Ingham, *Capitalism Divided*
Jorge Larrain, *Marxism and Ideology*
Claus Offe, *Structural Problems of the Capitalist State*
Michelle Stanworth, *Gender and Class*
John B. Thompson, *Language and Ideology*

CONTEMPORARY SOCIAL THEORY

General Editor: ANTHONY GIDDENS

Theoretical Traditions in the Social Sciences

This new series introduces the work of major figures in social science to students beyond their immediate specialisms.

Published titles

Barry Barnes, *T. S. Kuhn and Social Science*
Julian Roberts, *Walter Benjamin*

Forthcoming titles

Ted Benton, *Althusser and the Althusserians*
David Bloor, *Wittgenstein and Social Science*
Chris Bryant, *Positivism in Social Theory*
John Forrester, *Jacques Lacan*
John Heritage, *Garfinkel and Ethnomethodology*
Athar Hussain, *Foucault*
Bob Jessop, *Nicos Poulantzas*
James Schmidt, *Maurice Merleau-Ponty and Social Theory*
Dennis Smith, *Barrington Moore: Violence, Morality and Political Change*
Robin Williams, *Erving Goffman*

The Upper Classes

Property and privilege in Britain

John Scott

Department of Sociology, University of Leicester

First published 1982 by
THE MACMILLAN PRESS LTD
London and Basingstoke
Companies and representatives throughout the world

ISBN 0 333 28886 6 (hard cover)
ISBN 0 333 28887 4 (paper cover)

Typeset in Great Britain by
THE EASTERN PRESS LTD
London and Reading

Printed in Hong Kong

To my parents, and to Jill, Michael, and Susan

Contents

List of Tables   ix
Acknowledgements   xi
Preface   xiii

1 Property and Privilege in Perspective   **1**
Social stratification and social classes   1
The structure of feudal stratification   6

2 Magnates, Gentry and Bourgeoisie   **12**
Merchants and markets   12
The transition to capitalist agriculture   15
Land, lineage and lordship   22
The monopolisation of social honour   27

3 Rentiers, Farmers and Financiers   **34**
The transformation of the countryside   34
The consolidation of capitalist commerce   42
Fiscal and legitimation problems   48
Oligarchy and patronage: old corruption   53

4 The Rise of the Manufacturers   **67**
Families and firms   67
The capitalist spirit and capitalist surveillance   71

5 Gentlemen of Property   **78**
The city, the lords and the boards   79
Deference and decline   89
Elitism, electoralism and the establishment   96

6 Capital, Wealth and Control   **114**
Wealth and the wealthy   115
The struggle for control   123
Institutional holdings and finance capitalists   130

7   Class, Status and Power   **149**
   Master symbols of legitimation   150
   The old-boy network   158
   The establishment and corporatist politics   179

Bibliography   191
Index   208

List of Tables

2.1	English class structure (1086)	16
3.1	Landownership in England (1436–1790)	35
3.2	Landowners in England and Wales (1790)	37
3.3	Net personal estates of London freemen (1586–1693)	43
3.4	Income distribution in the landed class (1760)	46
3.5	The seventeenth-century status hierarchy	50
3.6	Social orders in England and Wales (1688 and 1803)	59
3.7	Status gradations among gentlemen (1688 and 1803)	59
3.8	Members of the peerage (1688–1789)	60
3.9	New peerage creations (1702–83)	61
5.1	Landed wealth-holders (1809–99)	87
5.2	Top British wealth-holders outside land (1809–1914)	88
5.3	Military participation of peerage and baronetage (1838)	101
5.4	MPs from landowning families (1868 and 1880)	106
5.5	Titles and professions of MPs (1832–1918)	106
5.6	Wealth in parliament (1895 and 1906)	107
5.7	Regimental participation of aristocracy (1883)	108
5.8	Peerage creations (1837–1911)	109
5.9	The grades of knighthood (1830–1914)	110
6.1	Income distribution in the UK (1929–70)	115
6.2	Estimates of top wealth-holding (1911–70)	117
6.3	The share of top wealth-holders (1966–72)	117
6.4	Distribution of income net worth (1968–9)	118
6.5	Size of fathers' estates of top wealth-leavers (1956–7)	120
6.6	Occupation of fathers of large wealth-holders (1924–5)	120
6.7	Landed and non-landed millionaires (1900–69)	121
6.8	Social background and inheritance (1956–73)	122
6.9	Britain's wealthiest families	122
6.10	The ten largest manufacturing companies (1904)	131
6.11	Landownership in Scotland (1970)	134
6.12	Mode of control in top British companies (1976)	140

7.1   Honours awarded (1898–1978)   153
7.2   Peerage, baronetage and knightage (1980)   154
7.3   Background of new peers (1901–57)   155
7.4   Educational background of Conservative MPs
      (1945–74)   163
7.5   Top military officers (1980)   167
7.6   Educational background of top army officers
      (1897–1971)   168
7.7   The senior judiciary (1980)   171
7.8   Social origins of business leaders (1906–70)   174
7.9   Occupational background of Conservative MPs
      (1945–74)   175

Acknowledgements

One of the most pleasurable parts of writing a book is the time when it is possible to thank those who have helped in the production of the book. This pleasure, however, is always dampened by the realisation that it is not possible to mention everybody, and by the fear that others might have to share in the blame for the author's own errors. With these reservations in mind it is still a pleasure to acknowledge the help that I have received whilst writing the book. Leicester University remains one of the most pleasant of institutions at which to work, and my colleagues in the Department of Sociology have been an unfailing source of encouragement. Despite the efforts of the government and the University Grants Committee to destroy the morale of social scientists, Chris Dandeker and Dominic Strinati have always managed to find time to discuss ideas with me.

Although I have spent much time over the last eight years engaged in research into the business enterprise, this research was a detour from my main concern with the structure of the upper class: the business research began because I realised that it was only possible to study the upper levels of the stratification system on the basis of a solid understanding of the structure of corporate property. My current research in this area is financed by the Social Science Research Council under grant HR6992, and some early results of this research appear in Chapter 6. Cathy Griff, the most wonderful of research workers, made a great contribution to this book by allowing me to take time off from the project to complete the book. I am also grateful to my colleagues in the ECPR International Research Group on Intercorporate Structure; they have all helped to make this research such a pleasure.

The SSRC also deserves warm thanks for financing the Cambridge Stratification Seminar, where the participants have been a constant source of stimulation and encouragement. It is rare to find such an unselfish body of academics and I have benefited immensely from my membership of this Seminar since 1974. It is to be hoped that the Seminar, and the SSRC, will survive to continue this role in the future. Some of the ideas developed in this book originated in research carried out for a PhD thesis submitted in 1976, but my concern with the upper classes goes back to my undergraduate days at what was then the Kingston College of Technology. My teachers from those heady days of 1968–71 must, I am afraid, accept responsibility for encouraging me to become a sociologist.

Tony Giddens has been the most assiduous of editors and has read through numerous drafts of the manuscript, giving me the benefit of his friendly and constructive criticism. At Macmillan, John Winckler has been patient and encouraging: the model of a publisher. Doreen Butler typed the whole of the manuscript and I am only sorry that the combined efforts of her and my wife Jill failed to improve my grammar and style as much as they would have liked. I am grateful to Michael and Susan for their friendly interruptions to my work, but I am even more grateful to them for not interrupting too often.

J.S.

Preface

The upper classes in Britain have been unduly neglected in both social research and everyday social imagery. Public opinion tends to reject the relevance of the language of class and to equate such notions as 'upper class' with the remnants of the old peerage. Though such terms as 'working class' and 'middle class' may grudgingly be accepted as having some reference to reality, the prevailing image of the social hierarchy takes on a somewhat truncated form with a 'bottom' and a 'middle' but no top. Social class has, quite rightly, been treated as a central explanatory factor by both sociologists and social historians. But their researches have focused almost exclusively on the working class, a focus dictated by the key assumptions of the Marxian problematic which has structured much of this research. Studies of working-class images of society and political consciousness have recently been complemented by studies of the working class in the labour process and have themselves complemented the older research on working-class patterns of kinship and sociability. Recent attempts to document the characteristics of the 'middle class' have done little to remedy the truncated popular image of society. This relative neglect reflects what might be termed the social anonymity of the privileged class of today. By contrast with the more opulent life-style of their predecessors the members of the dominant class today adopt a low profile and tend to define themselves simply as part of an extensive 'middle class'. Popular interpretations of the distribution of power in terms of 'the powers that be' or 'the establishment' have done little to destroy the anonymity of the privileged class.

The privileged members of society have, of course, figured in the traditional narrative historiography of the British constitution, which has emphasised the actions of kings and courtiers in the flux of politics. But there have been few attempts to place the actions of the kings and courtiers within a class frame of reference. The upper classes have played a crucial role in British social development, and it is necessary to understand the actions of their leading representatives in the context of the overall balance of class forces. A major study which attempted to overcome this neglect of the upper class is, of course, that modern classic of sociological history written by Barrington Moore: *Social Origins of Dictatorship and Democracy.* Moore undertook comparative historical investigations in order to display the dynamics of class relations in social development, emphasising particularly the dialectic of lord and peasant in the making of modern society. It is unfortunate that so few writers have followed Moore's lead in the study of the upper classes.

The one area within which sociologists might have been expected to give some attention to the privileged classes has been the study of political power. But here the main explanatory concept has not been 'class' but 'elite'. To grace the notion of an elite with the word 'concept' may be something of an exaggeration, since the prevalence of elite studies is a pointer to the absence of any worked-out conceptualisation of the real significance of what is being studied. The problems of the elite approach are by now well known: that formal position is not the same thing as actual power and that a common social background is not necessarily an indicator of similarity in policy preferences. But perhaps the fundamental difficulty of the approach lies in the abstractness and generality of the 'elite' notion itself, which originated as an ahistorical alternative to the more specific conceptions of alternative forms of class society. As a result it is generally unclear exactly what claims are being made by those who write about 'power elites' and 'political elites'. Unless the concrete social and political groups which participate in the exercise of power are related to the dynamics of class relations, any analysis remains empty and formal. Where attempts are made to incorporate such notions as 'upper class' into elite studies, this is generally reduced to one characteristic (such as public school education) and is rarely understood as relating to the differential structuring of life chances.

The aim of this book is to draw together the major sources of evidence on the upper classes in British social development and to locate this evidence in a class frame of reference. As such it is a provisional statement of a much larger project, the elaboration of which requires the carrying-out of a great deal more theoretically oriented research into the perpetuation of privilege. In Chapter 1 some of the basic theoretical concepts are outlined and these are used to illustrate the structure of feudal stratification. Chapter 2 shows how the feudal baronage gradually gave way to a differentiation between landed magnates and landed gentry, and how the formation of both these groups was brought about by the development of capitalist agriculture. The bourgeoisie, which emerged in the towns to control the trade in agricultural products, became an increasingly powerful social class and joined the magnates and the gentry at the upper levels of privilege. By the eighteenth century, as shown in Chapter 3, a tripartite division into rentiers, farmers, and financiers had evolved, and the relationship between these groups determined the structure of the political problems of the period. With the industrial revolution of the late eighteenth century a new group of capitalist manufacturers rose to prominence, and Chapter 4 shows how this group introduced new practices of work and supervision and began to extend its influence at the national level. In Chapter 5 it is argued that the three major privileged classes – based in land, commerce and industry – were moving closer together and were increasingly adopting a gentlemanly life-style, the values and practices of this life-style coming to structure their patterns of political participation. Finally, Chapters 6 and 7 show how the economic trends of the twentieth century brought about the formation of a unified business class, still headed by a gentlemanly establishment, which owes its continued existence to its ability to manage the monopoly enterprises of the modern economy. It is shown that the establishment is no longer able to function as the sole support of this system and that new forms of political practice have emerged for the representation of the interests of the business class.

April 1982   JOHN SCOTT
Leicester University

1
Property and Privilege in Perspective

'The history of all hitherto existing society is the history of class struggles.'[1] So wrote Marx and Engels in the *Communist Manifesto*. Since that claim was made there has been much debate and discussion not only about the truth of the claim, but also about the meaning of its central term. What is a 'class'? This is the question which has dogged much sociological and historical writing up to the present. The fact that different writers have given the term varying meanings has resulted in the absence of a true dialogue in research on class. Equally, the attempt to expunge the word 'class' from the sociological vocabulary has only made the confusion worse by the introduction of such vague alternatives as 'elite' and 'mass'. It is for these reasons that my attempt to document the development of the privileged classes in Britain must begin with a discussion of some of the concepts which will be used in this book. I do not pretend to have resolved the many important disputes which have centred on the concept of 'class', but I do feel that it is necessary to make it perfectly clear how various terms are to be used in this book.

Social stratification and social classes

Social stratification has been defined in its most general sense as 'the division of society into strata, or layers, lying one above the other'.[2] This has been usefully specified as involving the 'unequal power and advantage arising out of institutional arrangements'.[3] More specifically, the system of stratification in a society is a system of structured social inequality, a structure of unequal life chances within which more or less definite 'strata' are located in relation to one another. Life chances can be understood as 'the chances an individual has of sharing in the socially created economic or cultural "goods" which typically exist in any given society'.[4] Social strata, therefore, are social categories which stand in relations of advantage and disadvantage to one another with respect to the distribution of wealth, power and prestige.[5]

In his important, though limited, codification of stratification concepts Weber drew a crucial distinction between 'class' and 'status' as distinct aspects of the pattern of social privileges.[6] Agents have a similar 'class situation' when they have in common a specific causal component of their life chances. This causal component is the possession of those goods and skills which give to the agents the capacity to act in such a way as to generate a specific pattern of life chances. Weber generally relates his discussion to the utilisation of such goods and skills in the market; but it is clear from his discussion that the most general feature of class situation is sheer possession, which need not involve the existence of a market at all. What is basic to the notion of class situation is the fact of possession and the capacity to use the object of possession in order to generate wealth. It is for this reason that an agent's class situation can be seen to be determined not only through market forces, but also through such mechanisms as the structure of political power.

By contrast to such 'factual' determination of life chances, Weber uses the concept of 'status situation' to point to the normative determination of life chances.[7] Weber argues that an agent's status situation is that aspect of his or her life chances which is determined by the agent's social standing in terms of some normative order. The central mechanism here is social honour, the estimation of which derives from the normative order and the cultural values which underpin it. 'Status' is derived from the Latin verb _stare_, stand. This root is the common origin of the words 'status', 'standing', 'station', 'state' and 'estate', as well as the German word _Stand_. Weber's exemplar for the analysis of status is the 'Estate' of medieval Europe. The Estate, as a large-scale structured collectivity, is taken as the ideal type of status, in terms of which its constituent elements and processes are analysed as status-like (_ständische_) phenomena.[8] Talcott Parsons is, of course, the theorist _par excellence_ of the normative order and much that he has written is relevant to the analysis of status. Indeed, the major limitation of Parsons's work lies not in the many internal problems of his analysis of normative order, but in his relative neglect of its relation to the 'factual' order. This is apparent from his earliest work, where he analysed stratification solely from the point of view of the differentiation of activities in relation to the normative standards of moral superiority and inferiority.[9] Parsons argues that the normative standards which are current in the society define a 'scale of stratification', which is a measuring device for the estimation of social honour. Social status is determined in relation to this scale of stratification, though the scale may remain implicit in the rankings made by agents and need not be codified into an elaborated image of society.

A normative order identifies certain attributes as being relevant to the following of an 'appropriate' life-style. This life-style rules out certain courses of action and creates a drive towards the monopolisation of other opportunities. In this sense style of life is fundamental to the determination of agents' life chances.[10] Status, therefore, involves claims, and the recognition of claims, in relation to valued attributes. Agents will draw upon the prevailing master symbols of legitimation in order to support what they regard as a justifiable claim. In this way their claims will be phrased in terms of a vocabulary of motive which is acceptable to those from whom they are claiming recognition.[11] Only in this way can agents hope to attain the amount and kind of social honour to which they feel entitled by virtue of their life-style.

Social strata, therefore, are characterised by both 'class' and 'status' components, each having an autonomous effect on life chances. Having discussed these aspects of stratification, it is now possible to continue further along essentially Weberian lines. Weber argues that class situation is generally of primary significance in the structuration of social strata; class situation is a factor which conditions both the social estimation of honour and the material ability to support a particular life-style. It is not necessary for all members of a particular social stratum to have an identical class situation; but it is necessary that their varying class situations generate a similarity in life chances and that they be recognised, and recognise themselves, as being of similar social standing. For this reason, strata may vary in the extent to which they form tightly structured collectivities. This is to say that variations in class situation *within* a stratum may be associated with distinct patterns of social action. Where a stratum is internally divided in this way it will not necessarily exhibit the kind of consciousness and cohesion which is normally regarded as an attribute of social classes. It is for this reason that Weber limits the concept of 'social class' to a particular type of social stratum. A social class is a stratum in which any variations in class situation are such that mobility is relatively frequent between them. That is, when members of the stratum are able easily and frequently to move from one 'sub-situation' to another within the same stratum. To this definition must be added the point that a social class must also be recognised in some conception of social honour which reinforces and legitimates this pattern of mobility. Thus, some but not all social strata can be designated as social classes.

The importance of the above is brought out when it is realised that strata consist of intermarrying families, and not simply of 'individuals' or even 'positions'. That is to say that social classes do not consist of isolated agents or of abstract positions; they comprise a nexus of interconnected families. A particular agent's class situation depends not simply upon his or her 'own' life chances, but also on the class situation of the family of origin and on the life chances which the agent's current family is able to pass on to the next generation. Whilst lifetime mobility, or immobility, is an important determinant of the structuration of a social class, it is important not to neglect the crucial importance of the intergenerational mobility which results from the interweaving of kinship relations with class situation.

Whilst class situation may be of primary importance in social stratification, the role of an agent's status situation must not be underestimated. The social identity and the legitimacy of the various strata in a society derive from the normative standards of that society, and these standards will differentiate and demarcate the strata from one another. When strata are defined in legal or ritual terms they may be designated as 'social orders' with a high degree of social closure.[12] That is, their members are able to restrict 'access to resources and opportunities to a limited circle of eligibles'.[13] Weber's exemplar for the analysis of social status – the medieval estate – can be seen as a social class whose members have their status defined in law:

An estate may be defined as a group of people having the same status. . . . A status in this sense is a position to which is attached a bundle of rights and duties, privileges and obligations, legal capacities or incapacities, which are publicly recognized and which can be defined and enforced by public authority and in many cases by courts of law.[14]

The nobility and the serfs of medieval western Europe, legally described as 'free' and 'unfree' respectively, correspond to this notion of an estate, though the nobility only became fully organised as a classical parliamentary estate in the late middle ages.[15]

It is through the interplay of class situation and status situation that class 'fractions' or 'segments' arise. Social strata, or social classes, bring together agents with relatively distinct class situations, and this is the basis for the segmentation of the strata. Whilst the members of a stratum have a common pattern of life chances derived from similarities in their class situation, there may be differences among them in terms of the specific details of their class situation. A landowning stratum may be segmented into greater and lesser landowners, the differences in class situation between them being outweighed by the similarities. Equally, the similarity of life-style found among members of a social stratum may encompass *internal* status gradations, which may, in turn, correspond to differences in class situation. Thus, the landowning stratum may be constituted as a 'nobility' with an internal hierarchy of titles and ranks. Class fractions, whether distinguished in a hierarchy of status or not, will tend to have specific social characteristics and introduce an element of diversity into the internal structure of a stratum.[16]

This diversity of class and status situation, both within and between social strata, is the basis of the interests, consciousness and actions of agents. To say that an agent has an interest in a particular course of action is to say that this action will facilitate the possibility of the agent achieving his or her wants, even when there is no conscious awareness of these wants.[17] Since both wants and opportunities are associated with the agent's position in the stratification system, it is possible to agree with Dahrendorf's view that interests are 'structurally generated orientations of the actions of incumbents of defined positions'.[18] Interests are 'latent' in social stratification and need not be reflected in the consciousness of agents. When agents do become aware of their interests, or of what they perceive to be their interests, they may form themselves into conscious and cohesive social groups capable of concerted action. Weber analysed such group formation under the rubric of 'party', arguing that parties are self-conscious associations which attempt to influence decision-making processes. He argues that whilst parties may have either a class basis or a status basis, they may also be 'partly class parties and partly status parties'. Indeed, he covers his options even further by adding cryptically that 'sometimes they are neither'.[19] Rex has proposed an account of group formation which successfully avoids Weber's emphasis on formal associations and recognises the possible variations in group organisation. Groups which arise on the basis of common interests evolve a commonly accepted definition of their aims and engage in action which is oriented towards those aims. Where groups have conflicting aims, each will attempt to bring about action on the part of the other which will promote – or at least will not interfere with – its own aims. Conflict groups, therefore, are likely to become involved in a power struggle.[20] Such conflict groups may be recruited from the whole of a particular stratum, from one or more of its fractions or from various classes. Thus, the political rulers in a society may represent an alliance between classes whose shared interests *vis-à-vis* other strata outweigh the differences in their interests.

Having outlined some of the concepts necessary for an analysis of social stratification, it is possible to give a brief account of the position of the privileged class in English feudalism. It is not my intention to give a full account of feudal stratification, an impossible task in such a short space. I shall merely attempt to provide an outline of the basic features of feudal stratification in order to illuminate the development of the essentially capitalist patterns of stratification which will be discussed in the rest of this book.

The structure of feudal stratification

English feudalism was dominated by a privileged stratum of landlords, whose status characteristics defined it as an 'estate'. The landlord stratum had achieved a high degree of social closure on the basis of its ascribed characteristics of 'freedom' as opposed to the unfreedom of the other strata; and its life-style expressed the prevailing values of military chivalry. The determinant element in the life chances of the landlords was political. Since market relations were a relatively unimportant and peripheral feature of feudal society, the landlords' class situation was not based upon an institutionally separate 'economy' of market relations. Having no market situation, the basis of the landlords' possession of the land was the political and military organisation of the society.

The term 'feudalism' in its most general sense describes a particular system of political relations, a system of fragmented power. This system constituted the essential condition of existence for a distinctive set of relations of production which may, by extension, be termed 'feudal'. Property rights in relation to land were of fundamental importance in the determination of life chances, market relations being of very limited importance in relation to landed property. Rather, property rights were integral features of the feudal political order. The legal form of property in feudal society was inextricably involved in the political relations which defined and regulated the possession of land. Property was tied to the appropriation of the means of violence, political power and administration. In this system, the political unit and the production unit coincided in a coercive structure of open and direct exploitation. There was, in short, a 'juridical amalgam of economic exploitation with political authority'.[21]

The Norman conquest of England initiated a social transformation of major proportions. The transplantation of the Norman system to England established a relatively centralised political system and strengthened the institution of hereditary monarchy, all people being defined as subordinates of the king as well as of their immediate lord.[22] The successful invasion of 1066 hastened the process of feudalisation; and the pressing need to consolidate the conquest and to strengthen the country's defences against invasion resulted in a thoroughgoing militarisation of English society. Within this feudal polity 'politics' meant 'war', and political relations were military relations. Although feudalism was institutionally centralised in the monarchy, political power was devolved to semi-autonomous rulers. Feudalism was 'a type of government in which political power was treated as a private possession and was divided among a large number of lords'.[23] Those to whom the crown granted land dominated the direct producers, exercised a monopoly of law and administration within their own territories and headed private and contractual armed forces.[24] The distribution of political power among the landlords resulted in what Anderson has called a 'parcellisation' of sovereignty. The larger the overall territory, the more likely was this system of sovereignty to result in the political fragmentation of the society. This was a condition of 'feudal anarchy' in which there would be 'acute problems of coordination, crises of order and recurrent and apparently anarchic violence'.[25]

The feudal landlords constituted not simply a privileged social stratum, but also a privileged *social class*. They had a unitary class situation, and their position was reinforced by a legitimating system of social honour. As a social class, landlords occupied a definite position in the relations of production. These relations of effective possession of the means of production are the relations within which access to the productive forces, and thereby to their products, is regulated. Feudal relations of production involved a legally codified relationship between 'lord' and 'serf'; and this legal relationship was articulated with legal relationships among the lords themselves. These legal forms, backed by the institutional apparatus of the feudal polity, were the means through which the non-producers drew their support from the producers.[26] The serfs living in a manor were legally dependent upon the protection of their lord and were involved in a mode of production in which the subsistence 'tenement' was separated from the lord's 'demesne'. The legal form which defined the position of the lord himself was that of 'vassalage', a relationship of personal dependence expressed in a formal contract by which land was held in return for the performance of services.[27] Land was held as a benefice or fief, which Bloch has described as 'a property granted not against an obligation to pay something . . . but against an obligation to do something'.[28] It was through the concept of 'service' that the legal form of vassalage was embedded in the military organisation of feudalism: the main service to be performed by the lord – knight service – was the provision of a fixed number of armed and mounted soldiers for the king's wars and campaigns. In his turn, the king's vassal let out the land which he held in separate parcels as 'knight's fees' so as to be able to mobilise the military commitments of his dependent tenantry.[29] Knight service, together with court and administrative services, were the political means through which tenure of land was legally defined. As the formal military function of the landlord diminished somewhat during the twelfth and thirteenth centuries, so court and administrative services increased in importance.

The specific conjunction of social forms in feudal society, therefore, was such as to create a set of underlying relations of production in which those who had *ultimate possession* of the land, as the basic means of production, were separated from those who actually worked on the land. Since land was limited in supply, there was an inherent zero-sum conflict over the distribution of land. Struggle, conquest and war were the most rational and rapid means of increasing income for any lord or group of lords. It was in this sense that the military and political role of the landlord was not simply an essential legal condition of the relations of production; it was also their essential material condition.[30] But the legal title to the land which the landlord held could not be directly translated into control over the conditions of production. The actual producers, the serfs, had *immediate possession* of the land. For the landlord's ultimate possession to be translated into effective control, it was necessary for him to intervene in the social process in order to separate the producer from his day-to-day control over the land. This separation was an object of struggle between landlord and producer: the landlord had to employ force and compulsion in order to be able to appropriate the surplus produce. As Hindess and Hirst have argued:

> title as a right of exclusion enables the landlord to exclude the direct producers from the use of the land if the legal and coercive means of state power are available to act on behalf of its title. The direct producers are therefore forced to pay rent for the right to use the land, to produce their own means of subsistence.[31]

The class situation of the lords, therefore, involved a shared interest in the exploitation of the serfs, for only through this exploitation could they generate the income which sustained their social position. Since there was a distinction between ultimate and immediate possession, this would always be an interest of which the lords were acutely conscious. The energy with which this interest was pursued, however, depended upon the general conditions of class structuration, which varied from time to time and from place to place. The important point is that class struggle was always necessary in order to make separation and exploitation possible. This balance of power between the lords and the serfs was not only essential to effect the separation of the producer from the means of production, it also determined the *rate* of appropriation – and hence determined the productivity of the land. The higher the proportion of the product that was extracted to support the lords' privileged life-style, the lower was the level of technical innovation, and the greater was the tendency towards declining agricultural productivity.[32] To this extent it is true to say that the history of the development of feudal society is, indeed, the history of class struggle.

The privileged social class of English feudalism was defined by its political position as the rulers of society. Their political position was the determinant of their class situation, and this was legally codified in their formal social status. English feudalism was a class-society organised around a privileged social class which was compelled to enter into struggle with the subordinate social class. In the chapters which follow, I shall discuss the fate of this feudal class in the face of capitalist development and the new privileged classes which were associated with it.

Notes to Chapter 1

1.   Marx and Engels (1848) p. 79.
2.   Marshall (1953) p. 187.
3.   Goldthorpe and Bevan (1977) p. 280.
4.   Giddens (1973) pp. 130–1; Dahrendorf (1979) p. 30.
5.   Ossowski (1957) pp. 134–6.
6.   My understanding of Weber's codification is based on various sources, the most important of which are his two incomplete and unintegrated pieces on stratification: (1910), (1918–20). Where other sources are used they are indicated in the text.
7.   Compare Lockwood (1956).
8.   The usual translation of *Stand* as 'status group' is misleading if it is taken to imply small-scale social groups. It is important to be clear that the concept refers to society-wide 'groups' and not simply to

small face-to-face groups. It is also important to distinguish Weber's concept of status from the anthropological usage which contrasts 'status' with 'role'. For an alternative interpretation of Weber see Barbalet (1980).

9. Parsons (1940a) and (1940b). Parsons equates 'stratification' with 'status', so neglecting 'class' in the sense in which it has been discussed in this chapter. Parsons writes this off as a complicating factor under the residual category of 'power', which is analysed little further. The analysis of stratification in Parsons's papers is based on Parsons (1937).

10. Weber (1916–17) p. 405; (1913) p. 300; and (1910) p. 186.

11. Gerth and Mills (1954) p. 115.

12. For Weber on law, convention and custom see his (1920) pp. 312, 319. For the concept of 'social order' see Mousnier (1969). Weber's discussion of 'caste' and 'estate' can be read as an analysis of two types of order: see Weber (1910) pp. 186, 188–9.

13. Parkin (1979) p. 44; Weber (1916–17) p. 408.

14. Marshall (1953) p. 183.

15. See Poggi (1978).

16. Zeitlin *et al.* (1976) p. 1009.

17. Giddens (1979a) p. 189.

18. Dahrendorf (1957) p. 175.

19. Weber (1910) p. 194.

20. Rex (1961) pp. 112–13, 122–3.

21. Anderson (1974a) p. 147.

22. Fourquin (1970) p. 102; Strayer (1965). There is, unfortunately, no space in which to explore the continuity between the early feudal age of Saxon England and the later Norman age. Perhaps the best discussions of this are to be found in Loyn (1962), Stenton (1951) and Stenton (1961).

23. Strayer (1971) p. 63.

24. See Anderson (1974b) p. 407, and Strayer (1965) pp. 12–13.

25. Poggi (1978) pp. 31, 26; Anderson (1974a) p. 148.

26. Painter (1951a).

27. On service tenure and vassalage see Bloch (1940) p. 145; Ganshoff (1944) pp. 66ff and 96ff; Critchley (1978) p. 12; Stephenson (1942); Weber (1920); and West (1975) pp. 52–3.

28. Bloch (1940) p. 167; Anderson (1974b) p. 408.

29. Birnie (1935) pp. 38–9.

30. See Anderson (1974b) p. 31; Critchley (1978) p. 51.

31. Hindess and Hirst (1975) p. 236. See also Anderson (1974a) p. 147; Hilton (1976) p. 14; and Hilton (1975) p. 13.

32. See Brenner (1977a).

2
Magnates, Gentry and Bourgeoisie

Although market relations were never absent from feudal society, they did not constitute a significant factor in class structuration; and so merchants and towns remained peripheral to the main structural forces of feudalism. From the twelfth century, however, rents and services began to be converted into monetary terms under the impact of the expansion of the urban centres. These developments stimulated the commercialisation of agriculture and initiated a self-propelling enlargement of the sphere within which market forces could operate. This process, often described as the 'transition from feudalism to capitalism', resulted in a fundamental transformation of the pattern of stratification. The present chapter is concerned with the consequences of this transformation for the structuration of the privileged strata.

Merchants and markets

Weber's analysis of 'class situation' centres on the role of 'market situation' in the determination of life chances. The emergence of market relations involves the creation of a sphere of action which was separate from the 'public sphere' of political action. Such a separation of 'economy' from 'polity' exists when 'the characteristic modes of participation in one sphere are not determined by those in the other'.[1] This is not to say that political action is uninvolved in economic activities. The important point is that the two spheres of action are institutionally separated and that they operate in terms of different principles. In particular, an institutionally separate economy does not involve the authoritative allocation of work and rewards by a public body; it involves private calculation, contract and profit. In feudal society there was no 'economy' in this sense: the production of goods and services was embedded in the totality of social relations and was not distinguished as a specific system of action.

In a fully developed economy of market relations all goods, including labour, take the form of commodities. The possession and exchange of commodities is the basis of economic interests; and the various opportunities available to an agent in a market constitute his or her 'market situation'. An agent's 'class situation' is determined by the causal impact which this market situation has on life chances. Those with similar economically determined life chances have a common class situation.

In the England of the twelfth and thirteenth centuries such an economy was in the process of formation, and had its major impact in the determination of the life chances of the merchants of the towns. Only as the economy grew in importance did it begin to supplant politics as the major determinant of the life chances of landholders. English feudalism was never totally isolated from international trading activities, and was probably always dependent upon a certain degree of national trade. It remains true, however, that commercial activity could only prosper in places which were relatively immune from feudal impediments. The development of towns involved the creation of relatively autonomous 'non-feudal islands in the feudal seas',[2] within which trade could thrive. From the twelfth century the sale of surplus corn from manors to the neighbouring towns became regularised and the rural 'natural economy' was increasingly supplemented by a money economy.[3] The growth of the towns and of their export trade was incompatible with the persistence of rural self-sufficiency, and the independence of the urban boroughs from the shires hastened the decay of traditional feudal lordship. Fiefs were gradually converted into money rents, and by the thirteenth century the personal 'feudal' nexus had been overlaid and partly supplanted by an extensive network of financial obligations. From the twelfth century a national market system existed for most of the major agricultural products, and the various local markets formed constituent parts of this national system. This system of interlocking markets was the basis of the dominance of the merchants in the main towns, though the county centres formed regional markets where the landed magnates remained the dominant force.[4]

The merchants in each town comprised a distinct social group and described themselves as 'burgesses' or 'burghers'. All the members of this 'bourgeoisie' had a class situation and life-style which separated them from those who depended directly on the land, the main determinant of bourgeois life chances being their trading activities in the market. Within each town the merchants exercised a collective regulation and control over the market through the gilds into which they were organised. Where a town had a number of specialised trades, each was organised into a separate craft gild; and, as well as dominating municipal government, the craft gilds were the means through which merchants could attain citizenship as freemen.[5] Through this gild and freeman system the emergent market relations were contained within elements of the pre-existing feudal pattern of social organisation. Nevertheless, the crucial determinant of bourgeois life chances was market situation, and the bourgeoisie had successfully organised themselves so as to optimise their advantages in the market. In London, the centre of the emergent economy, the merchants were divided into various craft gilds such as mercers, goldsmiths, grocers, and vintners; and the wealthier merchants were able to form themselves into superior 'livery gilds'. The superior wealth and status of the liverymen were expressed in special legal privileges and in a whole panoply of symbolism and pageantry.[6]

This haute bourgeoisie of wealthy merchants also dominated the activities of those merchants who began to be involved in manufacturing. From the thirteenth century the merchant who supplied raw materials or sold the finished product came to dominate the 'independent' craft workshops. This subordination of the producer to the intermediary was due to the growth of the market: the artisan depended upon the middleman who mediated his relation to distant markets, and was often tied to the merchant through indebtedness.[7] The merchants remained separate from those whom they employed and those who were dependent upon them, though dependent workers in London were sometimes able to form themselves into 'yeomen gilds' which functioned very much as medieval trades unions. Although the artisans were, in effect, selling their labour power on the market, they were not yet pure wage labourers since they retained possession of at least a part of the means of production. This formal subsumption of labour under capital was gradually extended through the merchant 'putting-out' work to rural areas which were free from gild restrictions. As well as being involved in production, either directly or by providing finance, the wealthy London merchants operated largely as wholesalers who distributed goods over the rest of the country through the use of 'chapmen' and 'hucksters' who operated at village markets.[8]

The London haute bourgeoisie gradually increased its national and international role and by the end of the fourteenth century they had replaced foreign merchants in the provision of finance for England's foreign trade. Such finance was initially organised through loose merchant syndicates, but these soon gave way to the proto-capitalist merchant companies. The merchants of a town or city would join together to organise external trade through a 'fellowship', 'hanse' or 'company', which would negotiate terms and further the collective interests of the merchants. The wool trade, which was England's largest industry, was organised through the Company of the Staple; and the export of finished cloth was controlled by the Company of Merchant Adventurers of England. The latter was formed through the gradual fusion of the separate companies of the various London gilds dealing in cloth (mercers, drapers, grocers, haberdashers, skinners, etc.). Under the dominance of the mercers the trade with the Low Countries was, with the sponsorship of the crown, formed into a full monopoly as the Merchant Adventurers.[9] By the fifteenth century the London merchants had become part of an international trading and monetary network centred on Antwerp.[10] At the same time they had established strong links with the landowners who dominated England's agricultural production.

The transition to capitalist agriculture

The descendants of the Norman barons had become an hereditary group, as the *de facto* right of fief inheritance became an established legal right.[11] These barons were all the tenants-in-chief of the crown, yet there was much inequality of wealth and power among them. Since some of the greater sub-tenants were also called barons, it is more realistic to regard the baronage as the class of great landholders, with barons and knights together occupying a common class situation. Despite his underestimation of the rising bourgeoisie, Postan has probably exaggerated only slightly in his claim that 'medieval England was a highly stable and wholly polarised two-class community wherein a much elevated class of feudal magnates and knights was confronted with a much inferior mass of rural humanity'.[12]

TABLE 2.1   *English class structure (1086)*

Class		No. of people	%
Lords		9 271	3.5
Free tenants		35 513	12.0
Serfs		197 408	69.5
Slaves		26 362	9.0
Burgesses		7 968	3.2
Miscellaneous		5 296	1.8
	Total	281 818	100.0

Note: 'slaves' were soon converted into 'cottars', a position similar to serf.
Source: Birnie (1935) pp. 50–1, drawing on the Domesday Survey.

The true barony – a fief held as tenant-in-chief – was originally assessed at a value of five or more knights and generally had a chief, inalienable seat.[13] The largest baronies each consisted of 400 to 800 estates spread over many counties, though they were often concentrated in a particular county. There were, of course, variations in the size and dispersal of baronies, with some landholders having two or more separate baronies.[14] There were a number of medium-sized baronies, and the smallest consisted of fifteen to twenty estates each. Table 2.1 shows that these landlords represented 3.5 per cent of the population. In 1066 approximately 170 barons held about a half of the land in England, the remainder being split evenly between the king and the church. By 1166 the number of barons had fallen to about 130, these barons being responsible for the raising of more than 4,000 knights.[15] The spreading of a baron's holdings across a number of counties was an attempt by the crown to prevent the building up of rival territorial powers:

This subtle interlocking of the landed interests of the feudal nobility made for the strength and stability of the new society. It forced the Conqueror's great men to work with him in running the whole land since they could never treat their own estates as a geographical or economic unit. It spread their immediate interests into every county where they held land.[16]

The barons achieved *de facto* control over their estates, the various burdens upon the land being gradually transformed into financial obligations. The increasing importance of the national and international markets for produce led to an agricultural expansion, which led in turn to higher output and higher land values. The major beneficiaries of this were the larger landowners, and throughout the thirteenth century the 100 or so barons improved their position through the purchase of land from smaller landowners. Postan has remarked that 'the smaller men were losing their hold over land and thereby also their collective share in the landed wealth of the country'.[17] Under the impact of an expanding market system, agricultural production became progressively more commercialised. This generated a fundamental shift in the whole basis of landed property. As commercial agriculture came more and more to be the norm, agricultural production began to exhibit capitalist rather than feudal relations of production – and land-holders had to come to terms with the increasingly assertive class of capitalist merchants. It was through such forces that the great feudal barons transformed themselves into capitalist landowners.

The golden age of the demesne farms of the class of landed magnates was the thirteenth and fourteenth centuries. The large family estate generally consisted of scattered holdings which were grouped together into larger blocks in order to be run as an efficient 'business'. Such estates were supervised by stewards and bailiffs and often employed a specialised stock-keeper to supervise the production and marketing of wool in a number of manors within a particular estate. Routinised administrative practices developed and were codified in instructional manuals. The fact that many landholders operated through local agents to whom responsibility was delegated meant that estates became objects of 'management'. In this way, sheep farming cross-cut the traditional manorial structure and began to be organised on a capitalist basis.[18]

The main motivation of the magnate's economic management

was the rational utilisation of resources in order to obtain the material supports of his life-style: leisure and luxury, power and prestige. Centrally important to this life-style was the desire to maintain the family name and estate; and definite family strategies to this end had been evolved by the thirteenth century. The whole panoply of marriage contracts, the specification of portions, jointures and so on, was well-established. Similarly the practice developed of making wills stipulating to whom land should pass in the event of the failure of specified heirs. The survival of a family estate, therefore, depended upon the use of a family strategy to counter the vagaries of demography. Transmission of the estate generally followed the principle of male primogeniture, but heiresses were not infrequent occurrences and so marriage to an heiress, or a co-heiress, was a possible means of enlarging a family's estate. Only if all these tactics failed did land revert to the crown through wardship.[19]

The magnate class had as its central institution the 'lineage'. The lineage comprised those kin who collectively formed a 'house', and was at the centre of a larger 'affinity' – a nexus of relatives, servants, followers, clients and others who were dependent upon their connections to the house. Since marriage was a contractual relation between two families stipulating exchanges of property, a large proportion of first marriages were arranged marriages: 'It was *via* marriages that estates moved to new holders [and] that heiresses brought in the great windfalls so regularly collected by the long-lived houses.'[20] The nuclear family was only weakly separated from the wider kin, 'a loose core at the centre of a dense network of lineage and kin relationships',[21] and the kin exerted a predominating influence over the nuclear family because of the importance of the preservation of the property and status of the lineage. Marriage was a collective decision of family and kin aimed at the maximisation of property, status and power. The head of a family was simply the temporary custodian of the lineal estate, which was normally tied up in legal entails.

Purchase was by no means the most important way of acquiring land. Apart from inheritance and marriage, the single most important source of land was royal largesse, since the crown retained the right to dispose of lands acquired through forfeiture, wardship and other means. Family strategy, therefore, had also to concern itself with the factional and dynastic issues which surrounded the throne. The vagaries of factional politics meant that a family's heritage might be created and enlarged, only to be lost once more when the play of factions moved against them. The constant rising and falling of families meant that a family which lost its estates might nevertheless recover them in subsequent generations, so long as they were in royal favour: 'When a family died out in the main line . . . the inheritance passed either by previous treaty into the hands of another family . . . or into the king's hands to be regranted to his friends or relations.'[22]

From the middle of the fourteenth century the prosperity of the large estates began to falter; a process furthered by the agricultural stagnation of the fifteenth century. At this time of agricultural crisis – sometimes seen as a 'general crisis' – the smaller landowners and the tenant farmers were able to buy and to lease land from the magnates on favourable terms. The numerous tenant farms rose in importance, despite their less efficient and less capitalistic organisation. The magnates let out more and more of their land to tenants, and adopted a 'rentier' position – a tendency in arable farming as well as in sheep farming. The smaller landowners – the 'yeomen' and 'rumplords' – took on tenancies from the bigger landlords and shifted the pattern of their own production towards capitalist farming, with the tenant working the farm himself and the landlord supplying the working capital of seeds, cattle and tools. The capitalist farmers also required cheap wage labour and this pressure hastened the end of serfdom. By the sixteenth century the small landholder had developed into a farmer proper 'who valorizes his own capital'.[23]

The period of the fifteenth and sixteenth centuries was crucial in consolidating the establishment of capitalist relations of production in the countryside. Land was capital only when it was used in relation to the market and in conjunction with wage labour. Despite the early commercialisation of agriculture the producers had retained immediate possession of the means of production until they were finally separated from the land by the ending of serfdom and by their forcible expropriation in the enclosure movement of the Tudor period. Only in this way did the landowners and tenant farmers come to face a stratum of wage labourers. As Marx argues: 'So-called primitive accumulation . . . is nothing else than the historical process of divorcing the producer from the means of production.'[24]

The driving force behind this transformation of agriculture was, of course, the ever-closer relationship between agricultural production and the merchants involved in foreign trade. For most of the middle ages England was the largest and most important source of fine wool for Continental manufacturers, the growth of towns in Italy and the Low Countries having stimulated the English wool trade. In the later middle ages it became advantageous for England to make the cloth rather than simply to export the wool. Thus, England was the only cloth producer which was self-sufficient in its raw material.[25] Although the wool trade remained England's largest industry until the fifteenth century and the staple was heavily involved in government finances, the trade was in decline as England moved from being an exporter of wool to being a producer of woollen cloth.[26] The landed magnates had originally entered into wholesale contracts with export merchants, with whom they traded the wool of small producers in addition to their own wool. During the fifteenth century, trade in the produce of the small landowners and tenants was controlled by local middlemen, who generally dealt in a number of different commodities. These local merchants were separated from the London-based[27] haute bourgeoisie of export merchants and financiers. Men such as William de la Pole, Henry Picard, and Sir John Pulteney were never as wealthy or powerful as the landed magnates. They were, however, the core of a 'group of substantial men, deeply involved in the wool trade but with considerable connection with other branches of commerce as well'.[28] These were the men who organised syndicates to finance both trade and the crown. From the mid-fourteenth century this fraction of wealthy merchants consolidated its position and as the smaller landholders became the focus of capitalist agriculture, so the links between land and commerce solidified. The small landholders, in alliance with the wealthy merchants, became the 'vanguard' of capitalist development.[29]

The growing business links between the small landholders and the merchants were cemented by kinship links between them. During the fourteenth and fifteenth centuries the wealthy London bourgeoisie was barely reproducing its own numbers, partly for demographic reasons and partly because many merchants' sons went into official positions, into the church or the law, or bought land. The haute bourgeoisie, and the merchant class as a whole, had to recruit from outside its own ranks. Although there was a high level of intermarriage of families within the merchant class – the marriages of female heirs to other merchants ensuring that wealth remained within the merchant community – the class had constantly to recruit from the younger sons of lesser landholders, from artisans in the small towns and villages, and from the younger sons of provincial merchants. Many of the merchants who bought land were representatives of cadet branches of landed families which had previously been forced to enter trade, and numerous cousins, grandsons and nephews linked trade and land.[30] Although the merchants had business links with the yeoman landowners, their main business and personal links were with the more substantial of the smaller landholders who came to be designated as the 'gentry'. This interchange between wealthy merchants and the gentry generated an economic and cultural affinity between them and ensured that there was no sharp divide between the two classes. Together the bourgeoisie and the gentry provided a fertile ground for the spread of notions of economic individualism, self-interest and economic freedom.[31]

The landed magnates, however, remained distinct from the other privileged classes. In wealth, power and status the magnates eclipsed both the gentry and the bourgeoisie. In 1436 the great magnates (of whom members of the peerage numbered about 60) had consolidated their estates into a number of great territorial areas of influence. The magnates together held between 15 and 20 per cent of the land in England. The crown, the greatest magnate of them all, held 25 to 35 per cent, leaving 25 per cent held by the gentry and 20 per cent by yeoman landowners.[32] All three privileged classes – magnates, gentry, and bourgeoisie – were now distinctively 'capitalist' classes, though all showed traces of their differing origins. All three classes stood in the same relationship to the means of production, performing different aspects of the function of capital. The magnates, as rentiers, represented the purely 'ownership' aspect of capital, whilst the gentry combined ownership with control over production. To the extent that there was a fraction of the gentry comprised exclusively of tenant farmers, then this was a group which was concerned purely with the productive sphere of capital – though such farmers were perhaps more likely to be operating on a small scale and therefore were likely to be outside the ranks of the privileged classes.[33] The bourgeoisie, of course, had a predominantly distributive or circulatory function in relation to agricultural production, and even their involvement in manufacturing was concerned with the provision of finance rather than with actual intervention in production. By the fifteenth century England was, if not a thoroughly capitalist society, at least a society which was well-advanced on the path of capitalist development. Its privileged social classes found that the market was playing an increasingly significant part in the structuration of their life chances, though their responses to this and many other features of their society continued to show the signs of their feudal past.

Land, lineage and lordship

The period from 1100 to 1600 was the period of European state-building, and the Norman Conquest meant that England early on developed a proto-state with a high degree of internal sovereignty.[34] Within this polity the overriding interest of the crown was to ensure that baronial powers and privileges were directly dependent upon the performance of official services for the crown. By contrast, the interests of the magnates lay in reducing the king to the position of first among equals and in seeking rights which were not dependent upon official services. In support of its strategy the crown frequently sought support from the smaller landholders; and the magnates, in their turn, attempted to control the king by monopolising the great political offices of state. The barons did not oppose royal authority as such, but simply wanted to control it as a focus for their own power. Thus, opposition to the crown expressed itself in disputes over royal succession.[35] The chief barons wished to secure for themselves a position from which they could bargain with a king of their own choice. The smaller landlords supported the magnates in these disputes on a calculative basis: they wished to be well-placed in relation to that magnate who was himself likely to be well-placed in relation to the king.

The chief area in which such disputes arose was in relation to the considerable fiscal problems of the crown. The feudal political system had been supported through the system of military, political and judicial service, though services proper had always been supplemented by casual and occasional financial aid. As services were converted into monetary payments, so the crown was confronted with the problem of fiscal management. Under King John, taxation became both regular and severe, with baronial opposition leading to the Magna Carta agreement as a way of controlling royal finances. If the king wished to carry through policies which required taxation, and if policies went beyond current levels of taxation, it was necessary either to increase the burden of taxation or to offset the budgetary gap by borrowing from the haute bourgeoisie of the City of London.[36] In this way the balance of power between the king and the magnates, and between the two and the bourgeoisie, was structured by the problem of royal finances. More continuous warfare meant a pressing need to finance armies; and as warfare became a regular charge on national finances, so the fiscal problems of the polity were exacerbated. Throughout the fourteenth century the finances of the crown were overstretched in order to pay for expensive wars abroad. The need to resort to heavier levels of taxation and borrowing was perhaps the major cause of the so-called 'wars of the roses' in the fifteenth century.[37]

The immediate origins of these struggles was the attempt by the Duke of York to seek some control over royal finances in response to a debt owed to him by the king. The underlying cause of the conflicts was the relationship between an ineffective central government and increasingly powerful provincial magnates, who were able to mobilise private armies.[38] In such a context power struggles *between* the king and the magnates, and *within* the magnate class itself, concerned personal and factional advantage. The great magnates struggled among themselves for spoils and power, with the gentry taking sides according to their own perceived advantage. Central to the calculation of whether to become involved in disputes, and of which side to support, was the 'affinity' or 'connection' of the magnate lineage. The affinity of a great family comprised its servants, household retainers, client landholders and tenants, and was considered very much as an extension of the lineage itself. Personalised and particularistic loyalties linked together as 'friends' all those who could help one, or on whom one was dependent. Family strategy was aimed at mobilising the support of the 'affinity' in order to defend, and increase, the wealth and prestige of the lineage. The struggle to defend the family's 'honour' was necessarily a struggle *between* families. Politics was not generalised in terms of principles, but remained particularised in relation to the grievances and aspirations of lineages; and resort to violence was regarded as a justifiable expression of the competitive assertiveness of families.[39]

The conflicts of the fifteenth century were an expression of the structural relationship between magnates and gentry, and of the family strategies pursued by members of the magnate class. The marriage policy of Edward III had drawn the normal factional disputes of the magnates into the royal family itself and so factional struggles became embroiled in dynastic issues. This marriage policy transformed the problem of factionalism into a persisting legitimation problem.[40] The autonomous magnate territories with their extensive affinities of dependent gentry and their indentured armies[41] provided the material basis of these conflicts. The alliances and coalitions of lineages shifted according to calculations of self-interest, and this calculative orientation led to the chronic instability of support for both the Lancastrian and the Yorkist factions:

> In the absence of a common motive, each man would choose as his private ambitions and opportunities dictated. The upper classes were already in any case too much divided by local and family feuds to align themselves solidly on any one side. These lesser loyalties now governed their conduct in the wider field of national politics.[42]

Only when the battle at Bosworth in 1485 brought the victory of Henry Tudor over Richard III did the game of musical thrones come to an end. For a time Henry VII seemed even to have resolved the fiscal problems of the feudal polity by limiting government expenditure to the level of income from his own lands. The king's success in this policy reflected the fundamental shift in the balance of power between the magnates and the gentry. As the magnates began to weaken economically in relation to the alliance of gentry and bourgeoisie, so they perceived their interest to lie in 'a displacement of politico-legal coercion upwards towards a centralised, militarised summit'.[43] Through the creation of a centralised state the magnates sought to re-establish the social controls which they had formerly exercised on a local, feudalistic basis. But this strategy of support for royal absolutism proved misguided, since the establishment of such a system under the Tudors led to 'a progressive *dissociation* of the nobility from the basic military function which defined it in the medieval social order'.[44] The Tudors successfully asserted the royal monopoly of violence, and at the same time destroyed the independent power base of the magnates.[45]

The so-called Tudor 'revolution in government'[46] involved far-reaching changes in both the legislative and executive arms of government, as well as a transformation of local administration – though the 'revolutionary' character of these changes has been much exaggerated. The central process was a move away from the *personal* rule of the king and his advisers and towards a distinctly *state* form of rule. In the executive sphere this consisted in the transference of many public functions from the king's household to permanent administrative bodies which could continue to operate smoothly despite changes in ministers and monarchs.[47] Although Henry VII succeeded in reforming his own private finances, the chronic financial insolvency of the medieval polity was not resolved. Once much of the former church land had been sold to raise money, the crown was again dependent on parliament for raising revenue. Although the state achieved a monopoly of taxation, the crown remained fiscally dependent upon parliament. This essentially medieval institution thereby acquired an enhanced importance in the modernised Tudor state.[48] This rendered English absolutism realtively weak by comparison with other European states, and the dependence of the crown upon parliamentary support forced the Tudors to discover techniques of accommodation with both the Lords and the Commons.

Having destroyed the power of the remaining old magnate families, the Tudors raised new peers from among those landowners who had performed political and administrative services for the crown. The episcopal members of the House of Lords, too, were royal appointees after the Reformation. At the same time, those who received a royal summons to attend parliament gradually converted this into an inalienable hereditary right of attendance, and this formalisation of the position of landowners in parliament was associated with their monopolisation of the high offices in the state apparatus.[49] Although representatives of the gentry and the provincial merchants had for some time attended at parliaments, it was not until the Tudors that the balance of power between Commons and Lords was altered. After the Reformation, the crown had massive quantities of land at its disposal, and by the end of his reign Henry VIII had sold two-thirds of the former monastic lands. The bulk of this land had been bought by gentry and merchants, who thus strengthened their allegiance to the crown.[50] At the same time this constituted a stimulus to capitalist agriculture, since those who could afford to buy additional land were those who were making a good profit from their original land – and in order to justify the purchase they had to ensure a good rate of return on the new land. The composition of the Commons reflected the increased importance of the gentry, who generally represented not only the county areas but also the urban boroughs. As a political counterweight to the Lords, the Tudors actively used the Commons as a vehicle for their legislation and developed techniques of parliamentary management through the office of Speaker and through royal placemen.[51]

By filling many of the key positions in the state with members of the gentry, the Tudors solidified the link between parliament and government, and this strategy was employed at the local level as well. As part of the process of internal pacification the crown instituted the office of Lord-Lieutenant to act as the chief commissioner of the county militia, so creating a situation whereby military force was supervised by royal officials. Although the Lord-Lieutenants were normally large landowners, they held military authority by virtue of their office and not simply because they were magnates.[52] The Lord-Lieutenant was also the main arm of central government in the locality, and operated through Deputy Lieutenants and Justices of the Peace recruited from the gentry. In 1595, for example, there were 17 Lord-Lieutenants and 200 Deputy Lieutenants controlling 29 English counties.[53] The cornerstone of Tudor county administration was the institution of the magistracy. The JPs exercised political power at county level, served at Quarter Sessions, were the recipients of tithes and were patrons of church livings. They were responsible within the parishes for the administration of labour and apprenticeship regulations and for 'police' powers over riots and assemblies.

By the beginning of the sixteenth century the changing balance of power between magnates and gentry had been reflected in a transformation of the political system. Running parallel with these developments, and being crucially interdependent with them, was a change in the prevailing conceptions of social honour and the mechanisms through which honour was allocated.

The monopolisation of social honour

The starting-point for an analysis of social honour in the medieval period is Veblen's emphasis on the importance of 'leisure', though Veblen's analysis was intended as a critical commentary on a much later period. The position of the feudal landlord as a warrior and political administrator precluded him from engaging in directly productive labour, and the transformation of the feudal landlord into a capitalist magnate underlined this withdrawal from work. Abstention from productive work became an important indicator of social honour: leisure was the 'non-productive consumption of time'.[54] But if leisure is to function as an indicator of honour it is necessary that it be conspicuous, since there is little point in being leisured if others are unable to see this fact. Honour is granted by others and must be put in evidence. Leisure can be put in evidence through both the *way* in which it is used and through the tangible *results* of its use. The use of leisure for feasts, tournaments, hunting and other entertainments expressed the normative standards of medieval society. As vehicles for the conspicuous consumption of wealth, these leisure activities also signified the material position of the landlord.[55] But honour can also be claimed on the basis of the tangible results of past leisure. According to Veblen there are two types of tangible results of leisure: first, manners and unproductive knowledge; and second, insignia and titles.

The acquisition of knowledge of unproductive accomplishments such as music, classical languages, syntax, and dress was an indicator of the leisure necessary for its acquisition. Similarly, the possession of elaborated social manners indicates that a person has, in the past, had sufficient leisure to acquire and practise polite, decorous and ceremonial usages. Of crucial importance here is the transformation of the dominant normative standards in the direction of 'civilised' behaviour, both manners and unproductive knowledge coming to be seen as components of a civilised life-style. As the territorial state became established, so there occurred a transformation of the royal court. Although the court retained its political functions, the growth of internal pacification strengthened its ceremonial and legitimating functions. The royal court was formally brought together on various occasions, especially for ceremonies at Christmas, Easter and Whitsun, and notions of 'courteous' behaviour arose and became established among the magnates. As the king and principal barons formed assemblies and regular courts around them, so the code of chivalry was transformed into the code of courtesy, which spread through emulation and through the social contacts generated by the consolidation of political power. What Elias has termed the 'compulsive drive' of political centralisation generated, as an unplanned consequence, the gradual 'civilisation' of manners.[56]

The values embodied in the normative standards of courteous and civilised behaviour were derived from the feudal value of chivalry. The root meaning of the concept of chivalry concerned the *chevalier*, the mounted soldier, and this idea was intrinsic to the definition of knighthood. Chivalrous acts were those done in the service of a feudal superior, and the etiquette of chivalry referred to the respect of one warrior for another.[57] The knight had to be a member of a family whose wealth provided for the material equipment and for the leisure necessary for training, and as the landlord evolved into a rentier who hired knights or sub-let his land, so the values of the chivalrous life-style became transformed into the courteous behaviour of the leisured landowner. The proliferation of tournaments enabled the residual notion of knightly chivalry to be expressed in a peaceful context.

The second type of tangible result of past leisure recognised by Veblen comprised insignias and titles. Thus, hunting and sporting trophies indicated the possession of the leisure to engage in such non-productive activities, as well as directly expressing the pacified transformation of chivalrous behaviour. Particularly important as insignia of leisured achievements were ranks and titles, which represented a more formalised and generalised recognition of social honour.[58] Those who were leisured enough to participate fully in politics were accorded titles in recognition of their services, and the title then became an objective indicator of their social standing. The development of an honours system, a formalised set of titles and ranks, was part and parcel of the shifting balance of power between crown and magnates. Although the system was, in part, a consequence of a deliberate royal policy aimed at securing baronial support and legitimating royal power, it was also a reflection of the need for the crown to recognise the *de facto* powers and privileges of the great landholders. Earldoms, for example, ceased to be political offices and came to be simply titular honours granted in recognition of the power position of local landholders: 'to all but a small minority of the barons who received the title, it can have meant little beyond a formal recognition of existing power. In nearly every case this power was based on inherited lands, often combined with local offices which gave their holder influence beyond the circle of his own tenants.'[59] After the mid-fourteenth century the hereditary principle became so strong that titles passed to other male kin in the absence of a direct heir, and titles were brought out of abeyance in the female line to be re-established for the current male owner of the family estate.[60]

The transformation of the system of social honour, therefore, was tied into the competitive struggles of families and factions. The routine of courteous manners and the formalised system of titles were associated with ritualised behaviour which masked the latent violence of the competing families:

> Conflict was least likely to arise when honour positions were clearly defined in terms of those entitled to deference, and those required to accord it. Such visible symbols as graded styles of dress, distinctive manners, and the enforcement of a table of precedence on public occasions, went some way towards ensuring this.[61]

The evolving honours system, however, went beyond the peerage titles of duke, marquess, earl, viscount and baron.[62] From the early fifteenth century, landholders outside the peerage began to describe themselves as 'gentlemen': whilst all landholders felt themselves to be endowed with the quality of 'gentility' (originally meaning the same as 'nobility'), a status division had emerged between the peerage and other gentlemen.[63] The class division between magnates and gentry was reinforced and legitimised by a status division. But the status division was not as sharp as the class division. Just as titular gradations were established within the parliamentary nobility, so the gentry began to discriminate between 'knights', 'esquires' and mere 'gentlemen'. The fact that some landed magnates refused membership of the peerage and remained 'gentlemen' meant that the system of social honour constituted a continuous hierarchy running from duke to gentleman and that the status division between peers and others was by no means an immutable boundary between large and small landholders. Magnates and gentry together pursued a life-style based upon 'the capacity to live idly without undertaking manual, mechanic, or even professional tasks'.[64] The bourgeoisie, however, occupied an ambiguous status. Their way of making a living precluded them from full entitlement to the designation 'gentleman'; but their emulatory life-style, their lack of involvement in the details of productive work, and their many business and personal links with the gentry meant that it was frequently possible for them to usurp the title of 'gentleman' and to be accepted as near social equals by the gentry. Nevertheless, the inferior status position of those engaged in trade must have been an important stimulus towards the purchase of land by merchants.

The status hierarchy became a more and more important feature of English society and pressures towards increased formalisation became an increasingly marked characteristic during the fifteenth century. In the ritualised and routinised aggression of the tournament 'arms' in the sense of weapons gave way to 'arms' in the sense of insignia. The chivalrous code of honour was supported by heralds who acted as recorders and judges of a body of heraldic law. This law was separate from both civil and canon law and had an independent authority of its own, with the heralds constituting an informal judiciary of honour. The bearing of heraldic arms came slowly to be recognised as a mark of gentility and by 1300 there were more than 3,000 armigerous families.[65]

The shift in the balance of power in favour of the crown with the accession of the Tudors had important implications for the system of honour, as Henry VIII successfully initiated a monopoly of honour alongside the monopolies of violence and taxation. Whilst previously the royal heralds had no established precedence over private heralds, from the sixteenth century the crown was officially defined as the 'fount of honour'. This monopoly of honour was expressed in the requirement that 'honourable status needed to be granted or confirmed by state-authenticated and state-supported heraldic visitations'.[66] The Royal College of Arms was given precedence in heraldic matters and operated through the Court of Chivalry, which regulated claims to arms and titles. From 1530 these institutions were reinforced by the periodic 'visitations', whereby royal heralds travelled to all parts of the country to record arms and pedigrees with the express purpose of suppressing the usurpation of status.[67] This attempt at the monopolisation of honour, together with the Tudors' attempts to reduce the independent military and political power of the magnates, was part of the process through which the transformation of the major landholders from feudal lords to royal courtiers was completed.[68]

Notes to Chapter 2

1. Giddens (1973) p. 286.
2. Postan (1972) p. 239.
3. See Birnie (1935) p. 36.
4. See Barlow (1955) p. 67.
5. See Thrupp (1948) pp. 53ff.
6. See Postan (1972) p. 243.
7. See Landes (1969) pp. 43–4.
8. See Postan (1972) p. 234; and Thrupp (1948) p. 7.
9. See Carus-Wilson (1954) p. 143.
10. See Tawney (1926) and Wallerstein (1980).
11. See Stenton (1951) p. 69; Critchley (1978) pp. 14–15.
12. Postan (1972) p. 174.
13. See Painter (1943) pp. 351–2.
14. See Duby (1962) pp. 197ff; Postan (1966).
15. Painter (1943) p. 26; Bolton (1980).
16. Stenton (1951) p. 66; Stenton (1960) pp. 57–63.
17. Postan (1972) pp. 182, 178ff; Postan (1966) p. 593.
18. See Power (1941) pp. 28, 35.
19. See Holmes (1957) p. 43; Rosenthal (1976) p. 58. Macfarlane (1978) has put forward the contentious thesis that land tenure in England was based on individual rather than family ownership. Although his argument relates specifically to the existence or non-existence of a 'peasantry', it has implications for the analysis of large landowners. Whilst it may be the case that tenure was individual in law, it is nevertheless the case that the perpetuation of the estate was part and parcel of a definite family strategy.
20. Rosenthal (1976) p. 88.
21. Stone (1979) p. 69.
22. Holmes (1957) p. 9.
23. Marx (1867) pp. 905, 877; Fourquin (1970) p. 204; Bremner (1977a); Tawney (1912) pp. 27ff.

24. Marx (1867) pp. 874–5; Neale (1975b); Wallerstein (1974a).
25. See Power (1941) p. 16.
26. See Power (1933).
27. Although London was undoubtedly the most important English trading centre, a number of the Bristol merchants were important in foreign trade.
28. Power (1941) p. 117.
29. Moore (1966) p. 15.
30. See Thrupp (1948) pp. 203–6, 232, 256ff, 279ff; McFarlane (1973) p. 11; Hexter (1950).
31. See Tawney (1926).
32. Mingay (1976a) p. 59, table 3–1.
33. The yeomen also combined ownership with control, but were actively involved in the performance of labour on their own farms. As such, the yeomen occupied what has recently been termed a 'contradictory class location' in the context of the 'new middle class'. See Wright (1978) pp. 61–2.
34. Elias (1939b).
35. See Stenton (1961) pp. 218–19.
36. See Ardant (1975); Myers (1952).
37. The notion of the 'wars of the roses' was a romantic invention of Sir Walter Scott, who based his own stories on the romanticised Shakespearian conception of history aimed at glorifying Tudor achievements. The struggles of the period were not 'wars' at all. Rather the struggles were simply sporadic intensifications of the endemic disorder of fifteenth-century England. See the works of Lander (1965) and (1969), and see also Williams (1936).
38. See Dockray (1979).
39. See James (1974) pp. 184ff and (1978) p. 1; Heers (1974) pp. 8, 20, 23.
40. Myers (1952).
41. ‘McFarlane (1936) has termed this system 'bastard feudalism', using the latter term in its political sense.
42. McFarlane (1936) p. 411.
43. Anderson (1974b) p. 19.
44. Ibid. p. 126.
45. See Stone (1967) pp. 96ff.
46. Elton (1953).
47. Ibid. pp. 415ff.
48. See Hill (1967) p. 102; Braun (1975).
49. See Stone (1967) p. 30.
50. See Birdoff (1950) pp. 115–16.
51. Ibid. p. 214. See also Neale (1949).
52. See Finer (1975) and Hexter (1958).
53. Rowse (1950) p. 340; Scott-Thomson (1923).
54. Veblen (1899) p. 46.
55. Ibid. p. 65.
56. See Elias (1939a and b); Bendix (1964) and (1968); Bloch (1940) pp. 312ff.

57. See Critchley (1978) pp. 38–9.
58. Veblen (1899) pp. 46–7.
59. Stenton (1961) p. 234.
60. See Rosenthal (1976) pp. 25–6.
61. James (1978) p. 6.
62. 'Earl' and 'baron' go back to Saxon and Norman times and later continued to have a political meaning, but as patented ranks they date from 1328 and 1387 respectively. Of the other peerage ranks, the first non-royal duke was created in 1351, the first marquess in 1386, and the first viscount in 1440.
63. See McFarlane (1973) p. 275; Denholm-Young (1969). In the rest of Europe this distinction was generally made between 'greater' and 'lesser' nobility, the latter being accorded titles in their own right. This accounts for the apparently larger nobilities found outside England.
64. Stone (1967) p. 27.
65. McFarlane (1973) pp. 7, 144.
66. James (1978) p. 18.
67. See Pine (1963) p. 62; Wagner (1975) p. 40, and (1972).
68. See Stone (1967) p. 183. The destruction of the independent power of the peerage has often been seen as a consequence of massive casualties in the wars of the roses. McFarlane has argued against this, claiming that the shrinkage in the size of the peerage in the fifteenth century can be explained in purely demographic terms: the peerage declined in size at the rate of one in four families extinct every 25 years, and new peerage creations failed to keep pace with extinctions. See McFarlane (1973) pp. 15, 143, 146–7; Lander (1965) p. 28 and (1976) pp. 307–8, 127ff.

3
Rentiers, Farmers and Financiers

The period from the sixteenth to the eighteenth centuries saw the culmination of many of the trends traced in the previous chapter. The magnates and the gentry were forged into a unified class of landed rentiers which made itself the dominant economic and social force in the country. Together with a class of active capitalist farmers, the landed class revolutionised the countryside, both economically and physically. In the sphere of commerce, the haute bourgeoisie split off from the rest of the merchant community and became the core of a commercial class centred on London, but with offshoots in a number of provincial cities. As allies of the dominant fraction of landowners, the financial fraction of this commercial class monopolised the exercise of political power. But this was not simply a smooth process of evolution. Two major political revolutions punctuated the period – three revolutions if the American war of independence is included – and it was only through the means of these revolutions that the state and the economy were so thoroughly modernised.

The transformation of the countryside

By the end of the eighteenth century English agriculture was thoroughly capitalist in form. A restructuring of the agrarian classes and a series of innovations in both the techniques and the scale of agricultural production consolidated the establishment of capitalist farming. Following the Tudor destruction of the old magnate families, members of the gentry were able to acquire a substantial proportion of the former monastic lands as the crown sold this land to generate additional revenue. The number of large landowners increased significantly and the new magnate families were not so sharply distinguished from the smaller landowners as their predecessors had been. This process of economic assimilation meant that magnates and gentry have to be considered as fractions within a unified landed class rather than as distinct classes. Both fractions were essentially rentiers and were separated from the lesser landowners who were forced to engage in active farming on their own account. Parallel with the 'rise of the gentry' was the rise of the owner-occupying yeomen farmers who also acquired more land and, together with the tenants of the rentier landowners, were at the forefront of capitalist farming. Table 3.1 shows clearly the rise in importance of 'gentry' and yeomen at the expense of the church and the crown between 1436 and 1690.

TABLE 3.1 *Landownership in England (1436–1790)*

Category	Percentage of land held in		
	1436	1690	1790
Magnates	15–20	15–20	20–25
Gentry	25	45–50	50
Yeomen	20	25–33	15
Crown and Church	25–35	5–10	10

Note: figures for 1436 relate to England and Wales.

Source: Mingay (1976a) p. 59, table 3.1.

The rise of the gentry can be seen as the first stage in the monopolisation of land by a rentier class. The 'agricultural revolution' of the eighteenth century brought about the second stage: a concentration of land in the hands of the magnates and gentry at the expense of the yeomen freeholders. The sixteenth century saw the beginning of a long process of agricultural 'improvement' through enclosure and technical innovation, the major burst of improvement coming in the last half of the eighteenth century. Under the influence of such prominent Norfolk landowners as 'Turnip' Townshend and Thomas Coke, the centre of improvement and innovation spread throughout Essex, Suffolk, Norfolk, Hertfordshire and Leicestershire. In the north of the country improvement was concentrated in Northumberland and the Scottish lowlands, especially East Lothian. From these areas the wave of improvement spread to other parts of the country.[1] The main characteristics of the agricultural revolution were clearance and enclosure of land through the parcelling up of the old open fields and common pastures, together with land reclamation, crop rotation, better implements for working the land, and the improved breeding of livestock. The extent of enclosure in England can hardly be underestimated: between 1760 and 1801 alone more than 10 per cent of the land area was enclosed, mainly through Acts of Parliament.[2]

This whole period of 'agricultural revolution' consolidated the capitalist relations of production in the countryside and led to the emergence of 'farming' as the regular source of the nation's food. Agriculture was no longer simply a way of life but became an 'industry'. In particular, the distinction between 'landowner' and 'farmer' was sharpened. As shown in Table 3.1, the rentier landowners increased their hold over the land after 1690 as the smaller owners were forced to sell land in the face of the failure of their incomes to meet rising expectations.[3] The large rentiers generally had a managed home farm but let out the rest of their land under leasehold, the whole estate often being operated through employed managers. The growth of the large estate was associated with the consolidation of tenancies into large agricultural units, the average English farm being considerably larger than agricultural units in continental Europe. The decline of the small farm meant that the agricultural industry was focused around the tenants and owner-occupiers who led the expansion of capitalist farming.[4] In particular, those who held tenancies faced competitive pressures towards the adoption of the most profitable forms of agriculture. Those farmers who could not keep their costs down to a level at which they could sell their output at the going market price were unlikely to be able to meet their rent payments and so faced the prospect of losing their tenancies.[5] For this reason, tenant farmers were active improvers, and many of the landowners who promoted Bills for enclosure did so at the instigation of their prosperous tenants.

In analysing the ownership of land and its significance for social class structure it is necessary to draw out the dimensions in terms of which its most important features can be discerned. In considering land as divided into 'economic units' it is possible to identify two dimensions which characterise the relations of persons to the land

TABLE 3.2 *Landowners in England and Wales (1790)*

Category	No. of families	Income (£ p.a.)	% of non-common land
Magnates	400	5 000–50 000	20–25
Gentry			
(i) Wealthy gentry	700– 800	3 000–5 000 ⎫	
(ii) Squires	3 000– 4 000	1 000–3 000 ⎬	50–60
(iii) Gentlemen	10 000–20 000	300–1 000 ⎭	
Freeholders			
(i) Wealthy	25 000	150–700 ⎫	
(ii) Lesser	75 000	30–300 ⎭	15–20
Total	114 100–125 000		

Note: approximately 25 per cent of total land was common land.

Source: adapted from Mingay (1963) p. 26.

as a means of production as capital. The first dimension is that of ownership in its legal sense: rights of use, benefit and disposition. By the eighteenth century the concept of absolute private property had more or less fully crystallised, feudal tenures having been formally abolished in 1646. Rights over parcels of land were transferable from one person to another, and so the contrast between 'ownership' and 'non-ownership' was fundamental to what Giddens terms the 'institutional mediation of power'. But in so far as land was capital, a second dimension of analysis is whether the individuals concerned participated in the performance of the function of capital or the function of labour. It is clear that ownership by itself is insufficient to characterise effective possession of a unit of capital. The landlord who had legal rights of ownership to a unit of land may have directly controlled its use as capital himself or he may have delegated this task. This delegation – 'the mediation of control' – involved either the employment of managerial agents, such as bailiffs, stewards, estate agents, etc., or the leasing-out of land to tenant farmers. In either case effective possession of capital was shared among rentiers, agents, and tenants.[6]

Table 3.2 shows the relative importance of the freeholding farmers who combined legal ownership with participation in the function of capital. Although numbering 100,000 families, this group had declined from 150,000 one hundred years previously.[7]

Although it is difficult to put a precise acreage figure to it, it is clear that the freeholders' farms must be of some considerable size before the land can truly function as capital. The unit of production must be large enough to generate a sustained marketable surplus and not merely a periodic surplus over and above subsistence requirements. Those freeholders whose landholding was too small to function as capital were not capitalist farmers but subsistence peasants, who differed from labourers only in that they owned sufficient land to produce their own subsistence without having to sell their labour power to another person. Tenant farmers numbered a further 100,000 and, like the freeholding farmers, lived on the actual profits of farming rather than on rentals from land. Indeed, far from letting-out land, many freeholders rented additional land from a landlord. For both the tenant and the owner-occupier the primary significance of land lay in its function as a revenue-generating unit of production; and this similarity overrode the legal differences between them. Thus, Mingay has commented: 'In discussing the life of the lowest ranks of landed society there is little point in distinguishing between owner-occupiers and tenant-farmers.'[8] From the Restoration up to the middle of the eighteenth century the small freeholders were losing out in the struggle for land, as the owners of the large estates increased the size of their holdings. Throughout the early part of the eighteenth century the large landowners and newcomers to the land (generally rich merchants) gained at the expense of the owner-occupiers and the smaller landlords. Large accumulations of landed capital emerged in this period and Halévy has pointed to the role of market forces in the process through which the separation between owners and cultivators was economically crystallised and the yeomen disappeared:

> In the open market with its rapid fluctuations of value the small cultivator who lacked capital was powerless to resist for long the fall of prices. The great landowner, on the other hand, and the big farmer, were able to resist, and would then buy up, at the first good harvest, the land of the small cultivator who had been brought to ruin.[9]

It was the extension of the market for land which led to the concentration of ownership and control in the hands of the rentiers and capitalist farmers and their complete separation from a landless rural proletariat.

The magnates comprised a small group of about 400 families, most of whom were peers or baronets. Their estates ranged in size from 10,000 acres upwards, and the social rank of the magnate generally corresponded to the size of his estate. Many of the peers had immense estates spreading over a number of counties, and these estates exceeded in size many of the German principalities. Indeed, Plumb has described the English dukes as 'agrarian millionaires'.[10] Below the magnates in size of estate stood the 15–20,000 gentry families: about 1,000 of the heads of these families were baronets or knights, and here again social rank was correlated with size of estate. The wealthy gentry (see Table 3.2) were mostly baronets, and together owned about 15 per cent of the land area of England and Wales. The total proportion of land held by the squirearchy of lesser gentry was 12–15 per cent, with the country gentlemen – that massive group of clergymen, army officers, etc. – owning about 25 per cent of the land, generally in small estates of one or two farms.[11]

Capitalist farming during the eighteenth century involved an increasing *technical concentration* of capital into large, physically contiguous farms. Alongside this technical concentration there was an increasing *financial centralisation* of capital through the grouping together of discrete physical estates under unified ownership. The rentiers, as the agents of financial centralisation, were partially separated from the stewards, tenants and freeholders who constituted the main focus of technical concentration. Although both classes – rentiers and farmers – participated in the exercise of the capital function, there remained this important separation; and this precluded any general move towards effective co-ordination between the financial and technical levels. Dominant within this economic 'partnership' of rentier and farmer was, of course, the rentier landlord, who ran the landed estate as an object of economic management. There were, however, important limits to this practice of management. That is to say that although individual large *farms* were compelled to compete with one another on the market, this was not true of *estates*.[12] The economic management of the landed estate was an integral part of a broader family strategy.

The basis of the existence of the landed class was the family estate, which provided both revenue and residence for the landowner and his family. As a family estate the landed estate provided the material basis for the lives of the whole landed family.[13] Crucial to the reproduction of the landed class, therefore, was the family strategy adopted by its members, and central to family strategy was the adoption of an appropriate marriage strategy. Because marriage ensured the continuity of the estate and the revenues which depended upon it, marriage could not be left to the personal choice and decision of the parties involved. Marriages were a family affair and had to be put on a secure legal basis. When something as important as the family patrimony was involved, it was necessary that the marital agreement be clearly defined and legally circumscribed. Contractual relations between the potential spouses were simply one of the many legal relations among the families involved. The marriage settlement was the basis for defining and re-defining the incomes which would provide the whole family with a more or less secure life. As Mingay remarks:

> The grand object of family policy . . . was to secure the continuance and enhance the wealth and position of the family, and to this end the succession to the property and the marriage of the children, particularly the marriage of the heir or heiress, were carefully regulated.[14]

During the sixteenth and early seventeenth century an important transformation in the nature of the landed family had occurred. Magnate and gentry families moved away from the earlier 'open lineage' structure, in which the nuclear family was simply the core of an affinity of kin and 'friends', and moved towards the domesticated nuclear family.[15] The family turned inwards, away from the broader affinity, and so the kinship system became a network of nuclear families, each being concerned with preserving intact the inherited property of the family.[16] Although the landed family was still patriarchal in form, there had been an important reduction in the power of the father. The rights of all members to an income from the family estate were set out as annuities, dowries, jointures, pin-money and portions, and were legally defined in a trust or settlement.

The central legal institution in eighteenth-century family strategy was the strict settlement, which had evolved in the course of the seventeenth century.[17] Marriage strategy was decided in terms of the conditions of the legal settlement through which the land was held. Under the strict settlement the rentier was, in law, a life-tenant of the whole estate and so had to submit to limitations on his rights to alienate or mortgage parts of the estate. This was, of course, a legal fiction; the estate was resettled in each generation and so the sale of land and the distribution of income could be agreed at that time by the landowner and his heir. Just as the joint-stock company was to permit industrial activities to be regulated through a legal device which made the capitalist manufacturer a *de jure* employee of the company, so the strict settlement made the capitalist landowner a 'tenant' of his own estate. Mingay has estimated that by the eighteenth century about half of the land of England and Wales was held under strict settlement.[18]

Family fortune depended, to a considerable extent, upon demographic factors which determined the number of jointures and portions to be paid out to members of the family. The strict settlement enabled mortgages to be arranged in order to meet those demands which were in excess of current revenue. Similarly, when revenue exceeded outgoings to family members, wealth could be accumulated and mortgages redeemed. Whilst the fluctuations of demography over the generations might ensure that some families could use surplus revenue to pay off mortgages, other families were inevitably forced into severe financial difficulties through the accumulation of demographic accidents and the inability to repay mortgages.[19] Mortgage finance was also closely linked to agricultural improvement. So long as revenue from the estate was sufficient to meet the interest payments, the mortgage itself could acquire a more long-term character, and so landowners were better able to provide for their dependants and were able to increase the size of their estate. The growth of an institutionalised credit system was an essential precondition for this. Thus, there was a tendency for *credit* to become a more central feature of estate management as the burden of debt grew in importance. Such credit was essential if the estate was to function as a viable unit, but it became all the more important that a stable and rising revenue be generated from the use of the land. The drive to improve revenue became a drive to improve agriculture. The 'agricultural revolution' was, in many respects, a response to the institutionalisation of mortgage finance for settled estates.[20] Landowners could not simply adopt a passive role, but had to take on a more active function in agriculture through the use of bailiffs, through control over tenants, and through the provision of capital to tenants.

The consolidation of capitalist commerce

I have argued that mortgage finance on landed property was dependent upon the establishment of a credit system, and the key agents in the establishment of the latter were, of course, the merchants and financiers of the City of London who formed the core of a prosperous commercial class. The sixteenth century saw the establishment of a true world market for agricultural produce, and this capitalist world economy was consolidated during the seventeenth and eighteenth centuries. At the core of this international economy was north-western Europe, and for much of the seventeenth century Dutch merchants dominated world trade. After a period in the first half of the eighteenth century when English and French merchants successfully challenged Dutch hegemony, English merchants eventually achieved a position of dominance in the international circulation of commodities.[21] In its rise to world power the English commercial class developed and exploited links with the state. The state policy of mercantilism was expressed in such protectionist measures as the Navigation Acts, which began to superimpose a national economic policy upon the more privatised interests of the old regulated companies.[22] The increasingly powerful machinery of the state was utilised to protect and enhance the position of English merchants in the international economy, in return for which the flow of trade was to expand national wealth.

Whilst the aggregate wealth of the business community was small in comparison with that of the landed class, the wealthy men of business had the great advantage of the liquidity and flexibility of their wealth. Commercial capital could take the form of commodities, bullion or securities, and could easily be converted from one form to another. At the heart of the commercial class were the London foreign traders and domestic wholesalers, though the provincial ports such as Glasgow, Bristol and Liverpool were also producing wealthy merchant dynasties.[23] Whilst most businessmen had some basis in commodity trading, the larger fortunes depended more upon financial dealings and capital gains: the manipulation of money was rather more important that the distribution of goods.[24] Table 3.3 shows the distribution of fortunes among London freemen from 1586 to 1693.

TABLE 3.3 *Net personal estates of London freemen (1586–1693)*

	1586–1614		1666–1677		1678–1693	
Value (£)	No.	%	No.	%	No.	%
0	235	14.86	264	23.12	155	19.82
up to 500	927	58.63	449	39.32	302	38.62
501 –1000	167	10.57	147	12.87	110	14.06
1001–5000	199	12.59	228	19.96	174	22.25
over 5000	53	3.35	54	4.73	41	5.25
Totals	1 581		1 142		782	

Source: adapted from Grassby (1970b) table 3, p. 224.

The differences in the form of commercial capital meant that there was a tendency for different fractions to appear within the commercial class. In particular there was a tendency for the active merchant who invested his own capital to be distinct from both the passive investor and the active financier who speculated for capital gains. Equally, specialist goldsmiths and private bankers could often be distinguished from other members of the class. The distinctions among these fractions within the commercial class, however, were not sharp: the categories shaded over into one another and mobility between them was frequent. Following the reconstruction of the public finance system at the end of the seventeenth century, however, there was a tendency for a fraction of extremely wealthy government financiers to be separated from the rest of the commercial class.[25] This fraction – the so-called 'monied interest' – entered into a profitable alliance with the landed magnates for the purpose of political rulership.

The English economy remained essentially 'a *congeries* of local or regional economies rather than a genuinely unified whole'.[26] The localised and uncoordinated nature of the market is especially clear in the development of merchant involvement in manufacturing. Merchants were particularly involved in those industries which were connected with overseas trade: tobacco and sugar-processing, textile-making and dyeing, and shipbuilding. While some of this production necessarily occurred in centralised 'mills' or 'workshops', most manufacturing was organised through the handicraft or putting-out systems. In the latter the merchants organised finance, but did not supervise production. Merchant capital subsumed an existing labour process and did nothing actively to transform that labour process. The capitalist remained, in an important sense, extraneous to the actual process of production; instead of working solely on his or her own account, the worker worked for a capitalist. The various stages of production were farmed-out to home workers by merchants and their agents, the whole being articulated into a network of credit and debt.[27]

This network of credit was highly fragmented, and the absence of a developed capital market was only partially rectified during the eighteenth century as the capital needs of the landowners began to grow and as public finance underwent reform. Of crucial importance in this formation of an adequate capital market, therefore, was the relationship between the landed and commercial classes. As has been seen in the previous chapter, landowners entered early on into economic relations with the merchants who controlled the sale of wool and cloth. By the sixteenth century the landowners had also begun to take an investment interest in such allied activities as shipping. The growth of agrarian capitalism through the seventeenth and eighteenth centuries created stronger links between land and commerce. The raw materials produced by the farming industry had to be processed before they were sold to the final consumer, so food-processing and transport took on a capitalist character. As Thompson remarks: 'Ascendant agrarian capitalism involved not only rent-rolls, improvement, enclosures, but also far-reaching changes in marketing, milling, transport, and in the merchanting of exports and imports.'[28]

Thus, capitalist landowners and capitalist farmers had to seek more extensive economic relationships with capitalists in other spheres of activity. Particularly important were those links which involved the exploitation of minerals such as coal and iron. Minerals were, in law, the property of the owner of the land under which they lay; and therefore landowners had the right to revenue from them so long as they were willing to exploit them. Minerals could be exploited directly by the landowner through his bailiff, but more normally they were exploited in the same way that land was used for agriculture: mining rights were leased-out to men willing and able to exploit them. In many respects there was a logical progression of economic diversification from farming to timber-planting and mineral exploitation. Once this progression had been made it was but a short step to involvement in such things as ironworks which, like mines, tended to be leased-out to those willing to undertake the enterprise. The development of industry and the growth of trade led to a great demand for transport and housing, and those who owned land in areas ripe for urban development or where roads and canals were to pass were able to move in this direction. In all these activities, from farming to urban development, the link between the landlord and the actual process was a rentier relation, except in the very few cases where direct exploitation occurred.[29]

Perhaps the major way in which landowners came into contact with members of the mercantile class was through the use of mortgages on their property, a practice that was encouraged by the growth during the eighteenth century of an effective capital market. Landowners with surplus wealth, together with wealthy individuals from the professions and the army, could make funds available to other landowners through a London banker or lawyer who acted as an intermediary seeking out suitable mortgages. These kinds of links between land and commerce were reinforced by the marriage strategies of landowners and the social aspirations of merchants. Through appropriate marriages it was possible for someone to establish social relationships which would increase the 'social assets' of the family.[30] The location of a person within the network of kinship and 'friendship' which structured the upper levels of the stratification system determined his or her ability to benefit from the resources which were distributed through these relationships. The possession of social assets was an important condition of social mobility. Marriage strategies, however, generated not merely social assets, but also economic assets, since marriage was central to the production and reproduction of land as capital. Landowners in need of a transfusion of money capital into their estates could tap the immense reservoir of mercantile wealth by securing an appropriate marriage for their sons or daughters – and whether a landowner had a son or a daughter as his heir was crucial to the continuity of the estate as a family patrimony. In turn, the merchants who secured the marriage of themselves or their children to landed families could climb the social hierarchy and obtain such social assets as the contacts necessary for a political career.

The movement of commercial elements into land had important implications for estate management. The merchants who entered the land in the eighteenth century brought with them mercantile practices of accounting and profitability. Agrarian capitalism came into contact with the more 'professional' forms of business practice which had evolved in the merchant community. This may be seen as one of the main stimulants to the practice of employing stewards, secretaries and accountants, which was a concomitant of the agricultural revolution.[31]

The principle of *primogeniture*, according to which the estate passed to the eldest son, meant that the landowner inherited both the means of his own security and the obligation to support the remaining members of his family. The revenue from the estate was generally insufficient to support all the male members of the family and some means for supplementing income was essential. Thus, the movement of merchants and bankers into landed society through marriage or through the purchase of small estates was complemented by the movement of the younger sons of landed families into commercial occupations as financiers, traders, planters and shippers. The cliché that the younger sons of members of the landed class went into commerce, the law, the army and the church is a close approximation to the truth.[32]

TABLE 3.4   *Income distribution in the landed class (1760)*

No. of families	Total income (£000)	Annual income per family (£)
10	200	20 000
20	200	10 000–19 999
40	320	8 000– 9 999
80	480	6 000– 7 999
160	640	4 000– 5 999
17 760	6 880	200– 3 999

Source: adapted from Mathias (1957) table 9.1, pp. 186–7. The data are based on contemporary estimates by Joseph Massie.

Though this movement from commerce to land occurred primarily at the level of the gentry fraction, it was by no means limited to that level. It has been found, for example, that a majority of peers married outside the peerage, and that the younger sons of peers showed a particularly strong tendency to marry outside their own status group. In the period 1710–35 there was a particularly sharp decrease in the homogamy of peerage marriages. Whilst much of this decrease was due to marriage with gentry families, a proportion would have been marriages to merchants or to gentry who had themselves 'risen' from the commercial class.[33] Table 3.4, which should be compared with Table 3.2, shows the distribution of income among members of the landed class. There were, therefore, close personal and financial relationships between land and the commercial world. Many of the merchants and lawyers with whom the landowners dealt were themselves the younger sons of landed families or were descendants of younger sons. Many of these men would eventually marry into the gentry and establish new landed branches of their own family. Throughout the seventeenth and eighteenth centuries the high mortality rates of the rentier class meant that family lines had a relatively high probability of disappearing. For this reason, strict endogamy was impossible. Much of the mobility into the landed class was 'semicircular', involving the acquisition of family land by descendants of a cadet branch of the family. Mingay has argued that 'the history of most rising families was one of . . . gradual progress based on marriage and the incorporation of the wealth of other families and of their own junior branches'.[34] The consequences of this pattern for the internal structure of the landed class have been described by Cole:

> there are usually a small number of great families, extending through the households of younger sons and the marriages of daughters outside the inner circle, so that the feeling of kinship to the great extends far beyond the reality of greatness. Side by side with these great houses are the families of lesser landowners – anglicé; squires; and these in turn throw off shoots of aristocratic sentiment, and sometimes intermarry with the less eligible members of the great families.[35]

The changing relations between the rentier class, the farmer class and the commercial class were not without their consequences for the structure of political power. The patterns of struggles and alliances amongst these classes and their fractions generated both a situation of civil war and, eventually, a new constitutional settlement.

Fiscal and legitimation problems

As the state became relatively more bureaucratised, a regular source of state revenue became more and more imperative. The absence of both a system of long-term government credit and effective direct taxation meant that the crown was dependent upon parliament for raising revenue. Any attempt by the crown to raise the level of taxation encountered opposition from the landowners in parliament:

> By 1603 the propertied classes had become accustomed to avoiding taxation, and efforts by the Stuarts to tighten things up and to tax the rich at a realistic level by means of impositions, fines for wardships, forced loans or ship money inevitably ran into serious legal and political obstacles. The early Stuart monarchy was financially boxed in at all points, since it could only achieve fiscal solvency and an equitable distribution of the tax burden at the cost of a political crisis.[36]

That is to say, the fiscal dependence of the crown on parliament meant that the king had constantly to come to terms with the demands of the interests represented in parliament. In order to forestall the need to resolve the problem of the crown–parliament relationship the Stuart kings adopted various expedients such as the sale of offices and honours. The key role in these revenue-raising efforts was played by the king's political manager and a host of other courtiers, to whom the king delegated rights to offer titles, offices, and concessions. These brokers, of whom the Duke of Buckingham was the most important, enabled the king to supplement the direct income he was able to generate through his own trafficking and through the sale of lands and the farming-out of the right to collect customs duties. Eventually the scale of this revenue proved insufficient and Charles I was forced to call a parliament in 1640, by which time his fiscal problems had generated a legitimation crisis.

Intervening between the fiscal problem and the legitimation crisis was the political and administrative structure of the Stuart state, which generated increasingly difficult problems of efficiency and 'rationality'.[37] The archaic state was sufficiently mercantilist to promote capitalist development, but it was incapable of responding to the dislocations which this generated.[38] In particular, the gentry and tenant farmers, together with provincial and lesser merchants, were unable to impress their demands on the rulers. At the centre of this problem was the royal court and the 'court group' which clung to it. Courtiers, royal officials, the higher clergy and lawyers, and wealthy merchants all competed for royal favours and participated in an extravagant life-style of conspicuous consumption.[39] The Stuart monarchs promoted the formation of this court group around such families as the Cecils, Howards, Herberts and Villiers, and the group became the essential allies of Stuart rule. The increased power and wealth of the court group relative to the country gentry and lesser merchants was an important factor in generating the legitimation crisis of the state, since the opposition of the increasingly resentful gentry and lesser merchants was exacerbated by a slump in the prestige of the court group. The key to this slump in prestige was the nature of the honours system.

The honours system was part and parcel of the organic, hierarchical image of society which permeated seventeenth century society. Political representation emphasised the part of each local community in the national society, within which each rank was to perform its own function. Genealogy and formal titles were important mechanisms of social integration in that a family's ancestry emphasised its continuity in the community and its social standing was embodied in its social rank. Equally, formal honour served to set the seal of official recognition on those who had been socially mobile.[40] It was on this basis that an elaborated system of formal honours had begun to evolve. Table 3.5 shows the structure of the evolving status hierarchy, with its authoritatively established and generally recognised gradations. Whilst the most important divide was that between all 'gentlemen' and the commonalty of yeomen, labourers and so forth, the category of 'gentlemen' was divided into peerage and non-peerage grades.[41] These ranks carried varying legal privileges and were associated with conventional distinctions of clothing and mode of address. It was this evolving status hierarchy which was put at risk by the internal difficulties of the Stuart state.

TABLE 3.5 *The seventeenth-century status hierarchy*

Peerage grades:	Other gentlemen:
Duke	Baronet
Marquess	Knight
Earl	Esquire
Viscount	Gentleman
Baron	

Note: all titles of baronet level and above were legally inheritable, knighthoods disappeared with the death of their holders, and the remaining titles were conventional only.

Source: adapted from Laslett (1971) p. 38.

The undermining of the status system and the social integration which it brought about was a direct consequence of the fiscal difficulties of the state. The number of knights had been constant and relatively low under the Tudors, but King James's urgent need for revenue led to the number doubling in the first few years of his reign. Direct sales and the granting of knighthoods for other favours increased the number of knights and so reduced the prestige of knighthood. The title rapidly fell into disrepute.[42] In response to this devaluation of knighthood, the king introduced the title of baronet in 1611. The baronetcy was introduced, not without controversy, as an exclusive, hereditary knighthood, and was supposed to be linked with the financing of the Ulster settlement. Baronetcies, however, were soon treated in the same way as knighthoods, and by 1641 the baronetage was twice as large as the original limit on numbers. The inflation of honours was simply exacerbated. The introduction of the baronetcy, however, was only a prelude to the trade in peerages themselves. The number of peers doubled before the sale of peerages began in earnest in 1615. Irish peerages and viscountcies were particularly popular, but numerous dukedoms were created after 1623.

This expansion in the numbers of titled people, for what were widely seen to be pecuniary reasons, led to a debasement in the value of individual honours and generated an inflationary spiral in the allocation of prestige. The sale of hereditary honours was particularly crucial in this process: whilst the number of knighthoods depended on whether new knights were created to replace those who died, hereditary honours had a cumulative effect over the generations. The result of this inflation was a slump in the prestige of the peerage[43] which alienated the peerage from the crown and, more importantly, finally broke the remaining bonds of deference between peers and other privileged classes. Those who were excluded from the court and its privileges saw their own honours decline in importance and their sense of relative deprivation was increased. The final destruction of the bonds of affinity and deference between the magnates and the gentry led to the latter perceiving themselves as 'independent' men of substance. In this way the gentry came to regard themselves as being a 'country party' opposed to the 'court party'. As Stone remarks: 'By 1640 the gentry were neither faithful retainers of a local earl nor obedient servants of the political faction in control of power at court.'[44] The 'independence' of the gentry was enhanced by the fact that county politics had continued in the absence of regular parliaments, so inculcating in the gentry a sense of their own power and importance. These, then, were the structural forces underlying the legitimation crisis which the English state experienced in the middle of the seventeenth century.

The Civil War can be seen as a consequence of the attempt to contain capitalist development within the framework of an archaic form of state. Indeed, Anderson has argued that the Civil War can be seen as a bourgeois revolution 'by proxy'[45] – that is to say that the class in whose interest the war was fought was not prominent among the protagonists. But the coexistence of an archaic state with a capitalist economy cannot be considered as a sufficient condition for civil war. Without the intransigence and ineptness of the Stuart monarchs, no legitimation crisis would have arisen; and without the legitimation crisis, war was unlikely. Stuart mishandling of politics, particularly after 1629, translated the underlying structural conditions into a highly unstable conjuncture. When parliament was called in 1640, the king had destroyed the power bloc on which his rule depended, and he lost the support of court and country alike. The gentry in the House of Commons chose to pursue their interests and express their 'independence', and an almost united Commons faced a crumbling royal government.[46] It was this almost unanimous opposition to the king which pushed the conflict towards the brink of civil war. As the conflict progressed, however, the king was able to rebuild a strong royalist party as many gentry and merchants split away from the parliamentary forces out of fear of the popular radicalism which had been unleashed. In the City of London most mercantile opinion had been against the king from 1640 because of his disregard for the business interests of the wealthy merchants. The swell of radicalism which shook the City in 1641, however, led to a growing fear of social chaos, in the face of which antipathy to the crown waned into insignificance.[47] The royalist party was formed on the basis of this counter-revolutionary sentiment in the towns and the countryside. Thus it was that the outcome was civil war rather than simply the deposition of the king. The Civil War, however, was not a straightforward conflict of classes. The conflict groups involved – the royalist and parliamentary parties – overlapped in the social composition of their membership, and, whilst there was a tendency for the smaller landowners and merchants to support the parliamentary side, this was far from universal. It is this which has led Hill to suggest that the war was about principles, and that the parliamentary group was centred on puritan religious ideas which embodied political criticisms.[48]

The parliamentary cause was directed by an army council operating through a purged and much diminished 'rump' parliament. When the king had been captured and the parliamentary group were established as the rulers, this rump parliament was responsible for the trial and execution of the king and for the proclamation of a republic. Cromwell, as head of the ruling military junta, abolished the House of Lords and the legal privileges of peers, but failed to produce any constitutional alternative to the archaic state which had been taken over.[49] It was this constitutional vacuum which decided the parliamentary leaders to restore the Stuart monarchy soon after Cromwell's death. Thus it was that Charles II came to the throne in 1660 and was able to rule in the same manner as his father. The king was initially able to rely on the support of the old court party, though the king and his supporters were held together in a precarious relation of mutual dependence and suspicion. The court party, essentially based on the landed magnates and rich merchants, used the powers of influence and patronage to mobilise parliamentary support for the king, the House of Lords having been restored and the whole status hierarchy of Table 3.5 being re-established with a vengeance. The social tensions of the first half of the seventeenth century continued after the restoration, but the experience of civil war and regicide had fundamentally transformed the way in which these tensions were expressed politically. The country gentry had always been opposed to the court rather than simply to the king, and when differences emerged between king and court the country party could be mobilised in support of the monarchy. The label 'Tory' emerged to describe the Carlist gentry who constituted an effective parliamentary counterweight to the great 'Whig' landowners and merchants who dominated the court.[50] Whigs and Tories, as the main participants in the exercise of political power, were not formally organised associations but were 'loose groupings of men who found it convenient to work together in Parliament'.[51] The Stuart kings continued to rely on *ad hoc* techniques of parliamentary management, failing to resolve the constitutional issue of the relationship between parliament and the executive powers of government. As Plumb has argued: 'To bring the independent country gentry into some ordered relationship with government, or to diminish their role in it, became an absolute necessity if political stability was ever to be achieved.'[52]

The attempt by James II to force through measures to remove restrictions on Catholics led to the destruction of the parliamentary bloc which his brother had built up. Whigs and disaffected Tories withdrew their support for the king and once more the parliamentary struggle spilled over into social conflict. This time the king was unable to mobilise a royalist bloc and was unable to prevent the Whig-sponsored usurpation of the throne by William of Orange.[53] Although the so-called 'Glorious Revolution' can be understood as an attempt by the landed and mercantile classes to establish a monarch favourable to a constitutional settlement with parliament, this attempt was only partially successful. The main area in which advance was secured was the establishment of new fiscal mechanisms. These included the introduction of excise and land taxes under parliamentary control and the establishment of the Bank of England, the Stock Exchange and a new East India Company, all of which contributed to the regularisation of government borrowing and to controlling the money supply.[54]

Oligarchy and patronage: old corruption

In the wake of the 'Glorious Revolution' of 1688 ultimate political power was, in effect, transferred from the king to the so-called

'Whig oligarchy'. A highly integrated ruling group recruited from the landed magnates and the moneyed interest became the principal force in the state. Fewer than 200 families personally dominated national affairs for much of the eighteenth century. The Whigs were the party of large-scale capital in both land and commerce,[55] and to be a Whig was to be a supporter of the existing constitution and the Hanoverian succession. The main opposition to the Whigs came from the independent country gentry, who were formed around the rump of the old Tories and were still dominant in the counties and parishes. The form of state in which the Whig oligarchy were dominant was not an impersonal bureaucratic state operating through paid employees, but was what Nairn[56] has termed a 'patrician state': the major positions in the state apparatus were occupied personally by the Whigs and their allies. The 'policy' pursued by this patrician state was the expansion of national power through the expansion of national wealth. The aggrandisement of the state itself was the fundamental aim of Whig politics; the economy and foreign policy were subordinated to the pragmatic, acquisitive and aggressive strategy of the patrician state.

As seen from the outside, the Whig oligarchy and its patrician state was described by its opponents as 'Old Corruption'. The patrician state comprised a 'complex of predatory interests'.[57] The Whigs and the whole court party milked the state for their own benefit, and used its power to consolidate and enlarge their already large estates. Plumb has characterised the oligarchy as follows:

> What the Revolution did was to confirm the authority of certain men of property, particularly those of high standing . . . whose tap-root was in land but whose side-roots reached out to commerce, industry, and finance. And their authority was established not so much because Parliament became a continuous part of government but because they settled like a cloud of locusts on the royal household and all the institutions of executive government.[58]

Thompson has argued that, paradoxically, the state could be used in this 'irrational' way because its patrician form meant that it was essentially a *weak* state. Because the state did not interfere in the normal run of business and was responsive to the demands of the great Whig merchants, it could retain its corrupt, predatory features.

The key to Old Corruption was the system of patronage, whereby wealth, prestige and political power were structured. Patronage was not simply a tool of government for securing political support, it was a general principle of social organisation. The patronage system was a particular type of 'market', in which social and cultural assets were mobilised in order to determine the monopolisation and closure of opportunities for access to valued social positions. When one agent recognises that another, with whom he has personal contacts, has some legitimate claim upon him, he is operating in such a 'market'. Parsons has argued that this is analogous to the economic market: money is the generalised medium through which physically incommensurable goods can be compared as 'commodities', and 'recognition' is the medium through which the various collectivities in which an agent participates can be compared in order to arrive at a composite assessment of his or her prestige. An agent's personal contacts – his social and cultural assets – are the determinants of the agent's chances of entering valued social positions.[59] In this way, marriage, offices, votes and so on were all objects of property rights, and so were quasi-commodities: although they could often be translated into a monetary equivalent, they were not fully marketable. 'The property assumed its value . . . only within a particular structure of political power and influence, interest and dependency.'[60]

Government patronage involved numerous social honours and public offices; private patronage related to a mass of lesser things such as church livings, local offices, clerkships to merchants and lawyers, tutorships and posts as domestic servants. The social assets available to a member of the landed or commercial/mercantile classes – his network of friends and relatives – determined his chances of participating in politics. Recruitment to positions of benefit and importance was from that category of persons referred to as 'friends': relatives, members of the household, tenants, political supporters and general acquaintances. Appointment to a position depended upon the ability to mobilise one's immediate social network in such a way that some kind of contact could be made with the social network surrounding the person who had the power to make the appointment: an acquaintance, a relative or an employer might be persuaded or might offer to write to someone known to him who might, in turn, make further approaches.[61] The social and economic assets acquired through an effective marriage strategy could be converted into the benefits and advantages of a political career or a government sinecure. These political assets could, in turn, be 'reconverted' into social and economic assets in the form of a marriage, land or a commercial investment.

The bonds of patronage stretched upwards to the Whig oligarchy itself, which had control of the major public positions and social honours. At this level patronage became part and parcel of the mechanisms of political rule. Within the state the balance of power had shifted away from the crown, even if Halévy exaggerates somewhat in his claim that the first two Georges were the well-paid figureheads of aristocratic power.[62] It is nevertheless true that the ruling oligarchy of magnates and financiers collectively exercised many of the powers of the monarchy, especially the political management of parliament through bribery, coercion and other forms of influence.[63] Although the king retained the formal power to select ministers and to influence parliament, in practice the king accepted as ministers those who were able to construct and mobilise a parliamentary majority.[64] There was, therefore, a finely tuned balance in the state, whereby the king was one of the larger magnates himself but had certain additional powers by virtue of his occupancy of the throne. The king was a member of the ruling group rather than being separate from it. The king worked through political managers to construct his parliamentary majority from among the overlapping factions and groups of which parliament consisted. Namier has argued that the picture of the Commons 'is one of many small, loosely knitted, shifting groups of which hardly any is of a uniform character, but must show some predominant characteristic, and can be described accordingly as bearing an oligarchic, territorial, professional, political, or a family character'.[65] In the first half of the eighteenth century governments headed by Walpole and Chatham (Pitt the Elder) purged the executive of those whom they defined as Jacobite 'Tories', and appointed the Duke of Newcastle as their political manager. Newcastle built up a massive political machine whose sole purpose was to sustain Whig dominance.[66] Newcastle and his henchmen used influence, patronage and bribery to mobilise various parliamentary factions and a large enough number of independent country gentry in order to ensure the necessary majority to carry government business. Walpole headed what was effectively a one-party state; all political competition occurred within the Whig consensus. This one-party patrician conservatism was maintained through the system of patronage and parliamentary control which Walpole and Newcastle had refurbished. A whole hierarchy of patrons and sub-patrons formed overlapping parliamentary cliques, and Hill has remarked that 'the "natural rulers" had to group themselves in packs, united by kinship or geography, in order to hunt down the spoils of office':[67] 'Everybody in politics wanted to become the King's friend, for though the King had no independent power, the major spoils of office were distributed in his name and often with his direct participation.'[68]

The Commons in 1761 comprised 558 seats of which 24 were Welsh, 45 Scottish and 489 English. Both counties and boroughs were represented, 12 of the Welsh and 15 of the Scottish seats being borough seats.[69] Whilst Scottish and Welsh representation was through single-member constituencies, English representation was more complex. The 489 English seats represented 245 constituencies, there being 80 county seats, 4 university seats and 405 city and borough seats. Thus, English voters elected almost 88 per cent of the House of Commons, the English boroughs electing almost 73 per cent. More than half of all MPs came from seats in London and south-east England.[70] Namier estimates that in 1761 the government had 30 borough seats under its more or less immediate patronage and had significant influence over a further 25 or 30. In addition, 55 peers had influence over 111 borough seats, and 56 commoners had influence over 94 borough seats. Thus, 235 borough seats, about half of all English seats, were subject to the influence of patrons. In the counties the major landowners generally had control, though the outcome at elections depended upon the balance of power among the various landowners active in the county.[71] In the parliament of 1761 a total of 119 seats (22 per cent) were held by the magnates: 81 MPs were sons of English peers, 10 were sons of Scottish peers and 28 were Irish peers or sons of Irish peers.[72] Thus the magnates who had hitherto formed the court party were highly successful in using their electoral patronage to further the parliamentary careers of their own immediate families. It is, of course, likely that magnate influence spread wider than this, since many of the remaining members of the Commons, titled and untitled, would have been family members or nominees of the magnates. A total of 182 members were in paid employment, including 59 army officers, 21 naval officers, 50 'merchants' and 40 lawyers. These men would have included many of the younger sons of the magnates, together with the gentry and their sons.[73] For example, Namier claims that half of the army officers sitting in parliament were the sons of peers.

The accession of George III disrupted this stable Whig oligarchy. George III had pretensions to reassert royal power and began his task by dispatching the Whig government and appointing the Marquess of Bute as his political manager. The king attempted to break the single-party system of government and the consensus with which it was associated, and in the resulting confusion the manœuvering of rival factions and interests became all important. The removal of the Whigs from unchallenged power broke up the old corps of political rulers into its constituent elements of overlapping factions.[74] In the face of this diversity of interests the king and Bute were unable to construct a new power bloc. It was not until the 1780s that some semblance of stability returned with the construction by Pitt of a parliamentary majority led by men who called themselves 'Tories'.

Pitt, like his eighteenth-century predecessors, used social honours, and especially peerages, to exercise control over parliament. In order for such a strategy to be successful, it was necessary that the various titles and decorations form part of a widely accepted hierarchy of status. The hierarchy depicted in Table 3.5 had been seriously undermined by the actions of the early Stuart kings, but the Restoration re-established the move towards an elaborate and formalised hierarchy. The various privileged social classes stood in complex hierarchical relations to one another, the gap between the most privileged classes and the mass of the working population being bridged by those defined as the 'middle ranks' or 'middle orders'. The latter included many freeholding and tenant farmers, as well as lesser merchants. Such people were not quite acceptable as 'gentlemen', though many usurped this status or adopted the title 'Mr'. Their standing was certainly higher in the local status systems than in the national hierarchy, and Halévy has rightly remarked that the farmer was a 'gentleman of the second rank', the landlords and farmers together forming the dominant social and political force in the counties.[75] Table 3.6 shows the relative importance of these groups in the status hierarchy, and Table 3.7 shows the hierarchy among gentlemen.

TABLE 3.6   *Social orders in England and Wales (1688 and 1803)*

		1688		1803	
Social order		% families	% income	% families	% income
Gentlemen		1.2	14.1	1.4	15.7
Middle ranks		31.7	59.0	31.6	59.4
Lower orders		67.1	26.9	67.0	24.9
	Totals	100%	100%	100%	100%
		(1.4m.)	(£44.64m.)	(2.0m.)	(£209.53m.)

Note: Perkin takes the figures for 1688 from the work of Gregory King and those for 1803 from Patrick Colquhoun.

Source: Perkin (1969) pp. 20–1.

TABLE 3.7   *Status gradations among gentlemen (1688 and 1803)*

		Number of families	
Status category		1688	1803
Sovereigns, peers, and bishops		186	314
Baronets and knights		1 400	890
Esquires and 'gentlemen'		15 000	26 000
	Totals	16 586	27 204

Source: as Table 3.6.

In terms of formal titles the order of gentlemen was divided into three grades, each of which was itself divided into various levels. The peerage (including the sovereign and the bishops) was the smallest in terms of numbers, but included the largest number of subdivisions (see Table 3.5). Each level of the peerage was hierarchically ordered according to the date of creation of the title and whether it was a peerage of the United Kingdom, Great Britain, England or Scotland. Interleaved with these titles were the courtesy titles of widows, sons and daughters, and the Irish peerage which, regardless of grade, ranked below all other peerages.[76] Table 3.8 shows the slow but steady expansion in the size of the peerage between 1688 and 1789. The various Orders of Knighthood were normally divided into subsidiary categories such as 'Companion', 'Member' and 'Officer', which carried no title of distinction, but which were important in differentiating among the esquires and 'gentlemen' to whom they were awarded. The eighteenth century witnessed the culmination of the formal status hierarchy which had been evolving since the fourteenth century. This complex status hierarchy carried important political and economic functions for the powers of the privileged classes.

TABLE 3.8   *Members of the peerage (1688–1789)*

Year	Number
1688	150
1704	161
1726	179
1760	174
1780	182
1784	200
1789	250

Note: the various sources are not always clear, but it is likely that the figures for 1688 and 1704 are English peers, whilst figures for later years are both English and British peers together with Scottish representative peers. Irish peers are not included.

Source: 1704 and 1780 from Habakkuk (1962) p. 17; 1688 and 1760 from Halévy (1913) p. 193; 1784 and 1789 from Sampson (1965); 1726 from Plumb (1950).

In political terms, formal social honours were used for the purpose of political management, and not to raise revenue. In general, to qualify for membership of the peerage it was necessary to be a landed magnate (with the grade of peerage generally reflecting the size of the estate), but this was not a sufficient condition. The grant of a peerage was consistently used as a reward for political services, the ruling group using the desire for honours as a way of building up parliamentary support.[77] Whilst peerages were normally given in order to build up support in the House of Lords, Irish peerages (which conferred no seat) and other honours could be used to reward those who were not wanted in the House of Lords and those who had performed lesser political services. Those with the largest estates and who performed key political roles were created dukes and marquesses, with the latter category expanding considerably from the time of Pitt. 'Promotion' was possible within the peerage according to alterations in political services, but there was generally no means of removing an honour once conferred, except under extreme circumstances. In general, the rate of creation and promotion depended upon political needs, the initiative in the creation of honours having passed from the king to the Prime Minister. The rate of creation of new peerages was generally moderate until 1783 (see Table 3.9), when Pitt built up a parliamentary majority through a massive expansion of the peerage. In the course of his ministry Pitt created a total of 300 peerages, including many Irish peerages.[78] In 1688 there had been

TABLE 3.9   *New peerage creations (1702–83)*

Monarch	Period	No. of creations
Anne	1702–14	30
George I	1714–27	28
George II	1727–60	39
George III	1760–83*	47

Note: * George III remained king until 1820, latterly with a Regency; the figures for his reign refer to the period prior to Pitt's first ministry.

Source: Habakkuk (1962) p. 17.

800 baronets and 600 knights, these numbers declining over the period to 1803. Pitt did, however, expand the size of the older Orders of Knighthood such as the Garter and the Bath, as well as introducing the Irish Order of St Patrick. Most importantly, Pitt expanded the number of companionships and similar honours – so increasing the total number of honours without devaluing the title of knight itself. These lesser honours became particularly important as alternatives to pensions and offices, the widespread acceptance of the status hierarchy making them an acceptable form of recognition. Peerages, other social honours, military positions and public offices were brought together through the system of patronage to form a complex political machine, the purpose of which was to maintain the existing pattern of social arrangements and to defend British national interests.

The economic function of the status hierarchy was to facilitate interchange between land and commerce, but at the same time to define commerce as inferior to land. The motive for entering trade was generally to accumulate the kind of wealth which would enable oneself or one's successors to enter landed society and to participate in the institutions of the landed class and its life-style.

Profit-seeking was a means rather than an end; economic activity was entered for non-economic reasons. As Perkin remarks:

> The pursuit of wealth *was* the pursuit of status, not merely for oneself but for one's family. In the last resort the ultimate motivation . . . was a dynastic one: to found a family, to endow them splendidly enough to last for ever, and to enjoy a vicarious eternal life in the seed of one's loins.[79]

This pursuit of status within the dominant set of values lay behind the conversion of wealth from commerce into land, and the 'reconversion strategies' which have been described throughout this chapter.

Of what then did the desirable life-style of the gentleman consist? The gentleman's life was essentially leisured, the only really serious activity permitted to him being national or local politics. This life-style was neither exclusively urban, nor purely rural. The centrepiece of the rural features of this life-style was the estate and its great house.[80] Through such county activities as entertaining, hunting and Quarter Sessions the landed class could express its leisure and consumption in a conspicuous way. The importance of competitive emulation in country-house entertaining has been emphasised by Veblen:

> The competitor with whom the entertainer wishes to institute a comparison is . . . made to serve as a means to the end. He consumes vicariously for his host at the same time as he is witness to the consumption of that excess of good things which his host is unable to dispose of single handed, and he is also made to witness his host's facility in etiquette.[81]

The mass of servants who ran the country house was also an important aspect of the gentleman's life-style: not only was a servant an indicator of the master's leisure and wealth, but his livery and demeanour showed that he conspicuously knew his place.[82] The larger the number of servants, the grander their livery; and the greater the degree of hierarchy among them, the better did they serve as indicators of status.

The urban features of the gentleman's life-style centred on London 'Society' and its associated 'season' of activities. This

Society had its regional counterparts in such places as Bath, Harrogate and Scarborough, where the rich would periodically gather for a myriad of social activities.[83] The social scene of the London season was an integral part of the parliamentary year and of the need to visit London to see lawyers and bankers on estate affairs. The season comprised a round of balls, dinners and race meetings through which potential marriages could be discussed and arranged, and where social and cultural assets could be accumulated and used. Though an important part of Society, the court was no longer the sole arbiter of manners and acceptability. Rather, Society as a whole took on these functions. The town house was an important arena for conspicuous consumption in an urban setting, and for those who could not afford to buy or rent a town house, or preferred not to, the London clubs grew in importance: solidly 'country' clubs such as Brooks's and Boodle's were established, as well as political, anti-trade clubs such as White's and the Carlton

Halévy rather understated the significance of London when he remarked that 'London was no more than a huge business centre where the representatives of the nation assembled yearly for a limited number of months, and that rather to dictate to the capital the wishes of the country than to issue orders to the provinces in the name of the central government.'[84] Nevertheless, he correctly brings out the fact that London was the meeting-place for those who lived in the country rather than existing as a totally separate urban enclave.

By the end of the eighteenth century, therefore, national political power was firmly in the hands of the dominant fractions of the landed and commercial classes. At the local level capitalist farmers joined the landed gentry in the monopolisation of country and parish politics, though lesser merchants often played a role in the urban areas. The three most privileged classes – landed, farming and commercial – divided political power among themselves. In the last quarter of the century, however, a new class of manufacturing capitalists was in the process of formation, and this was soon to challenge the prevailing balance of class forces.

Notes to Chapter 3

1. See Halévy (1913) p. 228; Rudé (1972) p. 39; Wilson (1965a) pp. 152–3.
2. See Chambers and Mingay (1966) ch. 4; Tawney (1912) pp. 213ff.
3. This argument has been put in a number of papers by Habakkuk. See particularly his (1939), (1950), (1953), (1960), and (1962). For critical discussions see Clay (1974), Slater (1976), and Bonfield (1979).
4. Chambers and Mingay (1966) pp. 20, 92.
5. Brenner (1977b) p. 76.
6. On the 'mediation of control' see Giddens (1973) ch. 9.
7. Chambers and Mingay (1966) p. 18; Neale (1981) p. 74.
8. Mingay (1963) p. 233.
9. Halévy (1913) p. 220.
10. Plumb (1950) p. 18; Rudé (1972) pp. 45–6.
11. Mingay (1976a) pp. 59ff., and (1963) pp. 10, 19ff.
12. See Pollard (1965) pp. 26–7.
13. See Namier (1930) p. 22.
14. Mingay (1963) p. 32.
15. See Stone (1979) and James (1974) p. 182.
16. See James (1974) pp. 188ff, and Trumbach (1978).
17. Stone (1967) p. 274.
18. Mingay (1976a); Habakkuk (1962); Macpherson (1973a) p. 131.
19. See Habakkuk (1962) p. 9.
20. Mathias (1969) p. 58.
21. See Wallerstein (1980) p. 20 and (1974b) pp. 399, 402.
22. See Wilson (1965a) pp. 57–8.
23. See the discussion of Glasgow colonial merchants in Devine (1971) and (1975), and in Smout (1968).
24. Grassby (1970a) p. 103.
25. Ibid. p. 106.
26. Wilson (1965a) p. x.
27. See Coleman (1975) pp. 15, 24; Marx (1866) pp. 1021–3.
28. Thompson (1965) pp. 42–3.
29. See Hobsbawm (1962) p. 67.
30. See Mingay (1963) pp. 28–9, 76. On the notion of 'social assets' see Bourdieu (1971).
31. Mathias (1969) p. 52.
32. Perkin (1969) p. 60.
33. Hollingsworth (1964) pp. 8–9; Thomas (1972).
34. Mingay (1963) p. 76; Laslett (1971) pp. 199–202.
35. Cole (1955) pp. 82–3.
36. Stone (1972) p. 62.
37. Habermas (1973) discusses the notions of fiscal, rationality, and legitimation problems in the context of late capitalism. In using these terms I am not, of course, implying that these problems reflect the translation of 'economic crisis tendencies' into the structure of the

state. The latter situation is specific to the growth of state intervention in an industrial capitalist economy.

38. See Trevor-Roper (1959).
39. See Stone (1967) ch. 10.
40. See ibid. pp. 16, 37.
41. See Laslett (1971) p. 23.
42. Stone (1967) p. 43.
43. Ibid. p. 350.
44. Stone (1972) pp. 74–5.
45. Anderson (1964) p. 14. A considerable literature has arisen over the causes of the civil war, mainly centred around the debate over 'the rise of the gentry'. Unfortunately, each writer seems to use the term 'gentry' in a distinct way and so much confusion has arisen. See, in particular, Tawney (1941); Trevor-Roper (1953) and (1959); Hexter (1958); Hill (1958); Hobsbawm (1954); Manning (1956); and Stone (1972).
46. See Stone (1972) p. 126.
47. See Ashton (1979) p. 219.
48. See Hill (1958) pp. 30–1.
49. See Ashley (1952) p. 97.
50. See ibid. p. 146.
51. Bulmer-Thomas (1965) p. 8.
52. Plumb (1967) p. 22.
53. William had married Mary, a daughter of James II, and the two reigned jointly.
54. See Hill (1967) pp. 184–5.
55. See ibid. p. 213, and Plumb (1950) p. 14.
56. Nairn (1977).
57. Thompson (1965) p. 50. See also Thompson (1978b) pp. 139, 141.
58. Plumb (1967) p. 69.
59. See Parsons (1953) pp. 401–11, and (1970) pp. 38, 40, 50ff.
60. Thompson (1978b) p. 138.
61. See Perkin (1969) pp. 46–9; Dandeker (1978) p. 302.
62. Halévy (1913).
63. Rudé (1972) pp. 147–8.
64. Namier (1930) p. 58.
65. Ibid. p. 237.
66. See Plumb (1950) pp. 116–17.
67. Hill (1967) p. 217.
68. Ibid. p. 219. See also Brewer (1976) p. 5.
69. Although the succession of James Stuart brought about a union of the crows of England and Scotland, parliamentary union did not occur until 1707. Unfortunately I have not been able to discuss the distinctiveness of Scotland prior to the Union.
70. Namier (1928) p. 62.
71. Ibid. pp. 142ff.
72. Namier (1930) p. 262.
73. Ibid. p. 262.

74. See Brewer (1976) pp. 43–4.
75. Halévy (1913) pp. 235, 239.
76. No separate Scottish or English peerages were created after 1707, both being superseded by titles in the peerage of Great Britain. Irish peerages were limited in number by law after 1801, when titles in the peerage of Great Britain gave way to those in the peerage of the United Kingdom.

Inheritance of titles by women was unusual but not unknown. Slightly more frequent was male inheritance of titles through the female line. The clergy were accorded distinct rank according to their position in the church: whilst bishops ranked with barons, archbishops ranked with dukes, and parish clergy ranked with mere gentlemen.
77. See Namier (1928) p. 14.
78. See McCahill (1981).
79. Perkin (1969) p. 85. See also Coleman (1973) p. 95.
80. See Girouard (1978).
81. Veblen (1899) p. 65.
82. Ibid. p. 56.
83. See Thompson (1965) p. 43.
84. Halévy (1913) p. 222.

4

The Rise of the Manufacturers

For most of the eighteenth century Britain remained an agrarian society; for much of the nineteenth century it was an industrial society. In a relatively short period of time British society underwent a fundamental transformation and a new class of manufacturing capitalists rose to prominence. During the course of the nineteenth century this manufacturing class successfully challenged the power of the landed class and began to make itself felt as an important economic and political force. In order to understand the relationship between the various privileged classes in the nineteenth century, it is necessary to know a little more about the rise of the manufacturing class itself.

Families and firms

For most of the eighteenth century, industry remained a relatively unimportant activity and continued to be organised in much the same way as in earlier centuries. Manufacturing was the preserve of merchants who controlled the production process through their control over the buying and selling of goods and through their ability to offer credit.[1] Industrial production had first become of any real significance during the period 1540–1640, but this spurt of activity was limited in both scope and extent and the rate of development was not maintained through the following century. A specific conjunction of factors in the 1740s – the growth of international markets, a substantial increase in population, and an unusual run of good harvests – led to a further spurt of industrial expansion which lasted through to the 1760s.[2] Then, in the 1770s, the expansion of industrial production accelerated and a series of technical innovations were taken-up and led to the revolutionary technologies of cotton and iron production.[3] The merchants who had accumulated both wealth and experience in industrial production were able to take up the opportunities offered by the growth of trade and so could invest surplus capital to meet the demand which had been stimulated by the growth in the population. Foster has shown that the many cotton mills built in Oldham were mainly set up by people who had already accumulated capital in areas such as coal-mining, banking and trading. Not only did these people have the necessary capital required to set up the expensive factories, they also tended to own land on which factories could be built.[4] For these reasons, rapid industrialisation occurred under the aegis of well-established business families which had been incrementally accumulating capital on a small scale for a number of generations. From about 1780 – the date is both conventional and spurious – there occurred a rapid move towards larger-scale production with great numbers of workers assembled together in one mill or workshop. Production became 'self-sustaining': 'the shackles were taken off the productive power of human societies, which henceforth became capable of the constant, rapid, and up to the present limitless multiplication of men, goods, and services.'[5]

This so-called 'industrial revolution' was not a conscious creation of those involved in manufacturing; indeed its significance was not, at first, realised by those involved. The industrial revolution evolved out of the archaic constraining structure of eighteenth-century Britain as an 'unsought, unplanned, unprecedented phenomenon'.[6] The technical aspect of this process involved an improvement in the getting and working of raw materials and the substitution of mechanical devices for human skills and powers.[7] This rapid and fundamental change in the organisation of human productive powers was the result of the unplanned and unco-ordinated activities of many small producers.

The first phase of the industrial revolution was centred upon textiles, especially cotton, but from 1815 this industry was characterised by a falling rate of profit. As a consequence, the capital which had been generated in textile manufacturing sought more profitable outlets and much of the capital went abroad. The expansion of the cotton industry had led to the 'growth of a class of *rentiers*, who lived on the profits and savings of the previous two or three generations' accumulation'.[8] Fortuitously, the declining profitability of textiles coincided with the early promotion of the railways, and railway investment became the 'irrational passion' of the rich with surplus capital to invest. The railway 'manias' of the 1830s, 1840s, and 1860s punctuated an almost uninterrupted process of railway development which lasted into the 1870s. Railway promotion enabled the problem of economic growth to be resolved, since the capital requirements of the nascent railway system soaked-up much of the free-floating capital in the economy and substantially increased the demand for the products of the iron and related industries.[9]

The industrial revolution was based essentially on family enterprises. The legal form adopted was normally the one-person business or the partnership. The 'Bubble Act' of 1720 had placed legal restrictions on the formation of joint-stock companies extremely difficult, but there is no evidence that there was any great demand for joint-stock organisation among manufacturers. The amounts of capital which needed to be mobilised were generally not sufficient to make joint-stock enterprise necessary. The local country bankers might, if the entrepreneur was well-known to them, make some short-term credit available to the firm – and this could sometimes be 'rolled-over' into what was, in effect, a long-term loan. Similarly, merchants who had dealings with the manufacturer might be willing to make goods available in advance of payment or might enter into partnership with the manufacturer. Manufacturers were generally dependent upon the merchants who handled the wholesale distribution of their products; and many of the prominent manufacturers themselves carried on businesses as merchants. The various families involved in manufacturing frequently had overlapping business ventures and partnerships among themselves, and these contacts led to further help with credit, materials and so on. At the local level, therefore, merchants and manufacturers did not occupy totally distinct class situations. The merchants of the larger provincial cities, and of course those in London, remained rather more distinct from those who were involved in manufacturing; and the manufacturers would often be dependent on these City merchants. For example, the cotton manufacturers of Rochdale and Oldham were linked through such dependence on the wealthy merchants of Manchester.[10]

The raising of capital, therefore, was dependent upon the personal resources of the entrepreneur and on his ability to draw upon his social assets of kinship, friendship and business contacts. Through such personal relationships it was possible to raise capital, secure markets and recruit reliable partners and managers. The normal patterns of informal interaction could be drawn upon in order to buttress the requirements of a business – and in such situations of relatively high trust, it was relatively easy to restructure partnerships. Mathias has claimed that 'Recruitment to enterprise so often came as nephews were sent to learn a trade with an uncle, cousin with cousin, or the cadets of one family joined with the businesses of their wives' families.'[11]

The connection between business and kinship was, in fact, mutual. Business formation and growth depended upon the mobilisation of kinship networks, and marriage partners were frequently chosen from among the families of business partners. When manufacturers were drawn from nonconformist religious minorities, such as the Quakers or the Unitarians, which prescribed or encouraged endogamy, then the overlap between business links and kinship links was particularly strong. In such cases the personal ties of kinship and friendship were reinforced by a shared sense of social identity, and this whole complex of factors provided important material and cultural supports for business development. To quote Mathias once more:

A bond of confidence in business was very commonly reinforced by kinship: marriage partners were chosen from the same charmed circle. Recruits for partnerships were also to be found from the cadets of other families in the clan. Ownership, capital, succession to partnerships, extensions of enterprises all tended to run within the same social and religious enclave and often [to] be sealed by a kinship link. This could become self-reinforcing, particularly when the values protected in these enclaves encouraged a higher propensity to work and invest than in the echelons of society above these groups and below them in the social structure. By such a mechanism a high rate of investment and expansion could be achieved in such firms.[12]

Quaker families, for example, adopted a system of 'visiting', whereby families in one part of the country would receive members of families from elsewhere for short or long visits. Such visits would often lead to new business or kinship links between the families. As a consequence a dense 'cousinhood' of Quaker families extended over much of Britain during the eighteenth and nineteenth centuries. Families such as Barclay, Lloyd, Truman, and Gurney were involved in numerous overlapping businesses in brewing, banking, iron and other areas. The various families were involved in one another's businesses either because they were kin or because they were personally known to one another, and the practice of 'visiting' encouraged this reliance upon close friends in choosing marital, political and business partners.[13]

The Quaker cousinhood was but an extreme consequence of the normal practices of family-based manufacturing firms. The market for industrial capital was both localised and personalised, and there was no direct link between individual producers and specialised national credit institutions. Capital was mobilised through personal contacts and local intermediaries. But as the capital needs of firms grew, so the number of intermediaries in the particularistic capitalist market was increased. In this way, manufacturing firms were gradually integrated into a nation-wide system of capital mobilisation which ran from the individual firms through lawyers, bankers, merchants, goldsmiths and brokers to the London and provincial stock exchanges.[14] Business decisions were made by families and alliances of families within the loose constraints of this decentralised and particularistic capital market. The markets for the sale of finished goods were similarly decentralised, with each of the separate firms having only a limited power over the market because of the competitive pressures exerted by rival producers in the atomistic market.

The capitalist spirit and capitalist surveillance

The manufacturing class which rose to prominence in the eighteenth century cannot be understood simply in terms of the family character of their enterprises. The new manufacturing firms took to a high level of development a radically new form of capitalist enterprise. In the seventeenth and eighteenth centuries, prior to the burst of rapid industrialisation, this new form of economic organisation evolved out of the more traditional forms of capitalist undertaking. Adopting this new form of enterprise, the manufacturers became far more intimately involved in the actual process of production than their merchant predecessors had been.

In the seventeenth century a traditionalistic orientation towards economic activity was the primary characteristic of both the landed rentiers and the mercantile community. Traditionalism was certainly not incompatible with capitalism, but it did prevent capitalist practices being pursued in a 'rational' way. This traditionalistic structure of customs and norms which constrained economic activities had to be broken before a sustained economic take-off could occur. Although some of the early manufacturers were able to operate within the framework of traditionalism, a complete break with traditionalism was necessary when the scale and technology of production required new habits of work and 'good' labour discipline.[15]

The key factor in this break has been described by Weber in his account of the role of the rational ethic of ascetic Protestantism in generating the 'spirit' of capitalism. The latter is the specific distinguishing characteristic of the emergence of modern capitalism and involves the recognition of a duty to engage in the rational and systematic pursuit of profit as an end-in-itself. During the seventeenth century ascetic forms of Protestantism, especially Quakerism, were the seedbeds for the cultivation of this capitalist spirit. The specific theological character of Quakerism, in association with other social characteristics of the Quaker community, ensured that many of the early successful manufacturers were Quakers.[16]

The emergence of the ethos of modern capitalism permitted the adoption of new habits of work on the part of the capitalist – who thereby became an 'entrepreneur' – and encouraged the inculcation of new strategies of labour discipline. In this way capitalist manufacturing began to take on fundamentally new characteristics. As the manufacturing system became established the production unit came to involve a clear functional division between the employer as the representative of capital and the employee as a wage labourer. Just as the forces of market competition constituted the nexus *between* firms so the contract of employment was the link between 'master' and 'men' *within* the firm. The employment relationship, as a cash nexus, was an important condition for the real subsumption of labour to capital. Whereas labour is formally subsumed under capital when the labour process is subordinate to the valorisation process of capital, the general form of every capitalist process of production, the real subsumption of labour under capital is specific to particular modes of capitalist production.[17] With the emergence of manufacturing proper, where a number of wage labourers were made to co-operate, 'the command of capital develops into a requirement for carrying on the labour process itself, into a real condition of production'.[18] That is to say, control over the valorisation of capital became a necessary condition of the social labour process itself. The real subsumption of labour under capital existed where labour was forced to submit to the authority of the capitalist, who thereby became an active agent in the process of production. The organisation of capitalist enterprise came to involve a practice of control and surveillance over the labour process, a practice which was inextricably linked with the technical work of co-ordinating the labour of the large numbers of workers who were brought together in the factories.[19]

The capitalist entrepreneur, therefore, had a twofold role in the process of production. On the one hand he played a technical role in bringing-together and co-ordinating a complex division of labour within the factory. On the other hand he was involved in the mobilisation of capital for productive purposes. It was this dual role of the manufacturer which differentiated his class situation from that of the merchant, whose involvement in production had always been at one remove and had not involved direct intervention in the technology of production. The class situation of the manufacturer was integrally involved with the technology of factory production and its associated division of labour. For this reason the new role of the capitalist was related to a transformation in the role of the worker. As the division of labour was increased within the workshop, so the individual labourer became simply a part of the collectively organised workforce. Labour was performed collectively because each of the craftsmen who were brought together performed merely a small part of the total process of production. The individual workers were organised into a hierarchy of skills, with a corresponding hierarchy of wages, and could function as workers only in relation to the capital owned by their employers. The worker was separated from the means of production by virtue of the capitalist's possession of these means;

the worker could exercise his or her skills only as part of a co-ordinated production process supervised by the capitalist: 'Not only is the specialised work distributed among the different individuals, but the individual himself is divided up, and transformed into the automatic motor of a detail operation.'[20]

The industrial revolution led to simple manufacturing giving way to what Marx called 'machinery and large-scale industry', and in this process the real subsumption of labour under capital was further developed. The instruments of labour were transformed from 'tools' into 'machines', people were subordinated to the power and pace of these machines, and the hierarchy of skills was progressively undermined by the attempted reduction of all work to the level of the machine minder.[21] Mental and manual labour were increasingly separated from one another, and the former was assimilated to the power exercised by the manufacturing capitalist over the worker. It was this which led Adam Smith to remark that the market situation of the entrepreneur was such that his income comprised a 'profit' element in return for his entrepreneurial activities and a 'wages' element in return for his work of control and surveillance. This latter 'mental labour' could, of course, be delegated to a salaried manager, though the predominant pattern until the late nineteenth century was for production to be directly controlled by a 'working capitalist who both owned and managed his own enterprise'.[22]

The manufacturing enterprise, therefore, possessed charac-teristically 'modern' features: the 'business' was clearly separated from the 'household', rational methods of book-keeping were used, and production was oriented towards the requirements of a regular market. The work of control and surveillance, which had become a part of the function of capital, involved 'the rational capitalistic organisation of [formally] free labour'.[23] The workforce had to be disciplined to the patterns and rhythms of work required by capitalist production, and this discipline was built into the social structure of the factory itself through the establishment of close supervision, rule enforcement, incentives and punishments and so on.

In the early stages of industrialisation, industrial management was perceived not simply as a technical problem, but also as a means of promoting industry in the face of the indifference of the landed class and the resistance of the workers. The rational, calculative orientation of the entrepreneur ran counter to the traditionalistic patterns of action which permeated the society. The generation of a capitalist spirit among entrepreneurs, therefore, also involved an aggressive assertion of the legitimacy of modern capitalist practices. By the middle of the eighteenth century the religious basis of this spirit had died away and the ethos had, of course, spread beyond the nonconformist sects.[24] This transformation in economic orientation was a key factor in permitting the rapid take-off which had occurred in the industrial revolution, and in providing a moral justification for the new business practices. Once the take-off had occurred, however, the new practices were no longer dependent on the capitalist spirit. Once firms had been set up along modern capitalist lines and began to compete with one another, the competitive pressures of the market forced the entrepreneurs to conform to the new practices. Put simply, those firms which failed to adopt the new methods or which departed from them would go out of business. Survival in a competitive market became the constraining force over entrepreneurial behaviour: 'The Puritan wanted to work in a calling; we are forced to do so.'[25] Calculative techniques of labour discipline and of control over the labour process became external and constraining social facts for the entrepreneur and, therefore, became embedded in the organisational form of the capitalist enterprise:

> The capitalistic economy of the present day is an immense cosmos into which the individual is born, and which presents itself to him, at least as an individual, as an unalterable order of things in which he must live. It forces the individual, in so far as he is involved in the system of market relationships, to conform to capitalistic rules of action.[26]

It was still necessary, however, for the manufacturer to justify these practices to himself and his workers, and for him to defend his actions against the criticisms and opposition of groups wedded to the old values. Bendix has documented the gradual formulation of an entrepreneurial ideology which could take on this legitimating role. The central tenets of this ideology were elaborated in the works of political economists such as Malthus and Ricardo, in the radical political doctrines of Cobden and Bright, and in the homely hagiography of Samuel Smiles.[27] This entrepreneurial ideology was formulated as a moral claim to leadership on the part of the capitalist manufacturers, and presented the rational managerial activities of the employers as the source of national wealth and as the pattern which all should follow. Smiles, in particular, popularised the idea of 'self-help', through which success was held to be available to all who chose to pursue it through their own efforts.

The emergence of new forms of capitalist enterprise, the industrial revolution and the formulation of an entrepreneurial ideology produced a large and important class of manufacturers headed by a group of wealthy industrialists who could begin to compete in terms of money with the landowners and merchants. This class was distinguished from the most privileged classes by its active, directing role in economic activity, a characteristic which it shared with the capitalist farmers. The industrial revolution created such wealthy manufacturers as Josiah Wedgwood, Richard Arkwright, John Guest and Robert Peel, who were amongst the most prominent members of the new men who 'emerged distinctively as a middle class, conscious of their difference both from the gentry and from the main mass of the people below their economic level.'[28]

In asserting their identity and power, members of the manufacturing class became involved in municipal and parliamentary politics and began to voice their shared interests in a political form. This forced the class into confrontation with the landed class, but the common interests of the privileged classes *vis-à-vis* the working classes prevented this struggle from being pushed too far. As will be shown in the next chapter, the politics of the nineteenth century can best be understood as a reflection of the complex patterns of alliance and opposition which were to be found among the privileged classes.

Notes to Chapter 4

1. See Mathias (1969) pp. 126–7.
2. There has, of course, been endless discussion as to the causes of the industrial revolution. My aim here is simply to point out the more important conditions of industrial take-off.
3. See Deane (1969).
4. Foster (1974) pp. 9–11.
5. Hobsbawm (1962) p. 43.
6. Perkin (1969) pp. 7–8; Habsbawm (1968) p. 64.
7. Landes (1969) p. 1.
8. Hobsbawm (1968) p. 119.
9. See Hobsbawm (1962) pp. 61, 64; Gourvish (1980).
10. Foster (1974). See also Briggs (1963) ch. 3.
11. Mathias (1978) p. 102; Hobsbawm (1975) p. 282.
12. Mathias (1969) p. 161.
13. See Perkin (1969) pp. 82–3.
14. See Mathias (1973) p. 93.
15. See Sombart (1913) pp. 356–7; Tawney (1926) p. 45; Bendix (1956) pp. 47, 60.
16. Weber (1904–6) p. 180.
17. Marx (1866) p. 1019.
18. Marx (1867) p. 448.
19. Ibid. p. 449; Carchedi (1975) p. 63.
20. Marx (1867) p. 481.
21. Ibid. pp. 492, 545.
22. Perkin (1969) p. 112.
23. Weber (1904–6) p. 21.
24. It is for this reason that critiques of Weber's protestant ethic thesis which refer to the religious affiliations of eighteenth- and nineteenth-century businessmen are totally beside the point. Weber's thesis was specifically related to the seventeenth century; and Weber recognised the important changes which occurred after this time. For a good discussion of this see Marshall (1980).
25. Weber (1904–6) p. 181.
26. Ibid. p. 54.
27. Bendix (1956) pp. 100–1.
28. Cole (1955) p. 84.

5
Gentlemen of Property

Between the end of the eighteenth century and the first world war, manufacturing industry grew steadily in importance to become the dominant element in the economy. Britain became the self-styled 'workshop of the world' and was pre-eminent politically and economically in the world economy. At the beginning of the period the vagaries of the climatic variations which determined the quality of harvests were still the major determinants of the pace and level of economic activity. By the middle of the nineteenth century a trade cycle of 'booms' and 'slumps' was a well-established feature of the world economic system. Britain stood at the centre of this international economy, increasingly being forced to share its central position with France, Germany and the United States of America.[1]

These economic changes were reflected in the structure of class relations. The altered significance of agriculture in relation to industry tilted the balance of power in favour of the manufacturing class, and the landed class was forced to come to terms with its changed circumstances. Similarly, the central position of Britain in the international flow of commodities and money ensured the continuing importance of the financiers and merchants of the City of London. But by the end of the century the landed, manufacturing and commercial classes had moved closer together in economic, cultural and political terms. Though not forming a unified social class, the three classes could no longer be considered as totally distinct from one another. The classes were on the verge of forming a single propertied class, but the differences in their market situations continued to separate them. This chapter will examine the degree of unity and disunity among these classes and will trace out the patterns of struggle and collaboration between them in the political system.

The city, the lords and the boards

At the beginning of the nineteenth century three different types of banks together formed the British banking system. These were the London private banks, the chartered banks and the country banks. At the heart of the London financial system were the private banks such as Hoares, Childs, Coutts and Martins, which had often developed out of older goldsmith businesses. The private banks of the West End tended to have many landed clients and were often heavily involved in the long-term mortgage business of the landed class. By contrast the private banks of the City itself were mainly concerned with the provision of short-term credit for merchant firms and, to a much lesser extent, manufacturing concerns. The Bank of England and, perhaps less importantly, the Scottish chartered banks were particularly concerned with the management of government finances, but also carried out some private banking transactions for the merchant houses which comprised its major shareholders.[2] The Bank was by no means a central bank which regulated the rest of the banking system; its main role was perhaps to facilitate the formation of the financial syndicates which purchased government stock. The third type of bank to be found in Britain was the country bank – a private bank located outside London. The country banks had often arisen as adjuncts of mercantile concerns and had strong banking links with both local landowners and local industrial concerns. Although their businesses were highly localised, the country banks were tied into the national system of capital mobilisation through their use of London agents and correspondent offices – generally one or other of the London private bankers.

A major change in the financial system began with the repeal of the 'Bubble Act' in 1825 and the two Companies Acts of 1856 and 1862. These changes in the law made limited liability and transferable shares[3] more easily available to businesses and did much to stimulate the establishment of joint-stock banks in London and the provinces. The country banks were often involved in the formation of joint-stock banks, a number of these being in London. Agency arrangements between London and country banks were, in many cases, formalised in mergers to form large joint-stock banks. This tightening up of the banking system enabled it to become more closely involved in capital mobilisation:

agricultural wealth filtered through the country banks to London, from where the money went to finance the industries of the north and to finance landowners' mortgages.[4]

By the 1860s and 1870s the City of London had become the hub of an international monetary system, with a particularly important group of 'merchant banks' specialising in the financing of foreign trade and in funding foreign government loans. Such prominent merchant bankers as Rothschild and Baring, together with others such as Göshen and Hambros, were generally based around the businesses of *émigré* merchants and bankers and often continued with their merchant businesses alongside their banking activities. The merchants and merchant bankers of the City of London formed a tightly integrated group with numerous overlapping business activities: they joined together to syndicate loans, they dominated the board of the Bank of England and they coalesced to run the major dock, canal and insurance companies. These business links were reinforced by kinship links among the families involved, and the Jewish bankers in particular constituted a closely knit cousinhood within the City.[5] Indeed, the private bankers, merchant bankers and merchants formed a distinct fraction within the broader commercial class. This City fraction was united through the bonds of business, kinship and friendship, and its cohesion was enhanced by the frequency and informality of face-to-face contacts in the exchanges, coffee-houses and other meeting-places of the square mile itself.

During the eighteenth century the distinction between the class of landed rentiers and the class of capitalist farmers had become sharpened as a result of the continuing process of agricultural improvement. By the middle of the nineteenth century the enclosure movement was all but complete, and a class of agricultural wage labourers had been created.[6] The trilogy of landlord, farmer and labourer characterised Victorian rural society and formed the basis of both contemporary and current images of the rural world. The landlord was the undisputed chief figure in terms of wealth, power and prestige; and the class of farmers had fallen below the levels of privilege attained by both merchants and manufacturers. The rentier landowners at this time held about three-quarters of the land in England, and a considerably higher proportion in Scotland.[7] Running a large landed estate, as has been seen, was very much a form of economic management: the estate was treated as a unit of capital and was administered through various rules, procedures and routines similar to those used in the larger mines and ironworks.[8] The estate was managed by the landowner through agents and stewards, to whom general executive responsibilities had been delegated and who undertook the collection of rents, kept the accounts and supervised the tenants. Spring has used the case of the Duke of Bedford's estate to show that the distinguishing feature of the very large and complex estate was not simply the employment of a resident land agent with delegated authority, but was the employment of a chief agent with a subordinate staff to handle such specialised tasks as timber, minerals and so on.[9]

There existed in the landed estates a partial separation of ownership from control: the legal relation of ownership was entwined in a complex mediation of control whereby general supervision of the affairs of the estate – strategic control – remained the responsibility of the landowner, and day-to-day administration was the responsibility of a managerial staff.[10] Where land was let out to tenants, strategic control was shared between the landowner and the tenant. The landowner and his agents exercised a supervision over the tenants and made decisions over the renewal of tenancies, as well as contributing to some of the capital requirements of the farms. The tenant was not only the active day-to-day manager of his farm, but also participated in strategic control. This relationship between landowner and tenant was cemented in the financial arrangements whereby the farmer received the profit generated by the farming activities and used it to pay his rent to the landowner. These various arrangements had become so complex by the middle of the nineteenth century that estate management was taking a much greater amount of the landowners' time than was formerly the case.[11] Although estates did not enter into competitive relationships with one another as units of capital, many features of modern capitalist practice had been introduced to estate management. These activities, however, continued to be structured in terms of the family strategies adopted by the landowners. The landed rentiers formed a system of intermarried extended families, each ranging over several generations and degrees of cousinhood, and each dependent upon the fortunes of a particular estate. Family strategy was an important structuring mechanism in economic life, and the highly regulated marriage market helped to ensure both the maintenance of the traditional family life-style and the perpetuation of the family estate.

It was under the continuing influence of such family strategies that the landowners began to diversify their interests. During the nineteenth century farming offered a relatively poor rate of return when compared with the investment opportunities which had been opened up by the progress of industry. For this reason many landowners supplemented their agricultural earnings by diversifying into investments in minerals, in urban property, in railways and docks, and in overseas mining and pastoral concerns. Many great landowners, for example, began to develop those parts of their estates which were well-sited for urban growth. Until the mid-nineteenth century the urban areas, apart from London, were relatively small and localised, but the pace of development soon increased. In London the major landowners included the Duke of Portland, the Duke of Westminster (in Pimlico, Belgravia, and Mayfair) and the Duke of Bedford (Bloomsbury and Covent Garden). In smaller cities and towns prominent landowners included: the Duke of Norfolk and Earl Fitzwilliam in Sheffield; the Marquess of Salisbury and the Earls of Derby and Sefton in Liverpool; the Marquess of Bute in Cardiff; and the Calthorpes in Birmingham. As fashion drifted away from the Spa towns to seaside resorts in the 1880s and 1890s, landowners such as the Duke of Devonshire profited from the growth of such holiday centres as Eastbourne, Brighton, Hastings and Scarborough. In 1886, 69 out of 261 provincial towns were largely owned by great landowners; and a further 34 towns were owned by smaller landowners.[12] Similarly, the Duke of Sutherland, the Marquess of Bute and the Earl of Dudley were prominent as mineral developers. Railways offered gains not only through investment but, more importantly, through the sale of land to railway companies and through compensation money. Where landowners did invest heavily in railways, this tended not to be in the main-line companies but in the secondary lines which connected their mineral interests to the main arteries of the railway network. In this way, landowners saw railway investment as a way of improving the yield earned from the agricultural and mineral resources of their own estates.[13]

Landowners complemented their estate business with interests in industrial and commercial ventures, the already close business links between the rentiers and the City financiers easing this diversification. The City financiers were also important in their own right as promoters of business ventures, especially railway companies. The railways were, from the beginning, giant enterprises whose capital requirements outweighed those of all other businesses together. London bankers, especially Glyn Mills, acted as active promoters for the railway companies and brought together the masses of 'anonymous' investors, many from the professions and many 'widows and orphans', who provided much of the railway capital. The railway boom of the 1840s led to the situation in which the 15 largest companies controlled 75 per cent of all railway revenue, and the boom of the 1860s strengthened the position of the top 4 companies with 44 per cent of revenue.[14] From the 1860s many landowners began to take portfolio investments in the big main-line railway companies, having formerly restricted their attention to those lines which would help their own estates. The railway booms, therefore, brought together some of the interests of the financial community and the landowners. But the development of the railways also had an important indirect impact on industrial funding. Limited liability had rarely been thought necessary by industrial entrepreneurs, and those who found a need for this or for transferable shares were generally able to adapt the principal of the 'trust' to their undertakings.[15] As the capital requirements of some industries increased, the trust and the partnership began to give way to the joint-stock company. This enabled manufacturers to draw on a wider pool of capital and to provide for the various members of their families by issuing shares to them. By the mid-1860s about 1000 new joint-stock companies were being registered annually, though the majority of manufacturing concerns were still run as partnerships. The spread of railway shareholdings encouraged the growth of the London and provincial stock exchanges, and so made it easier for expanding industrial enterprises to raise capital. Specialised stockbrokers and stockjobbers in these exchanges joined with bankers, lawyers and accountants in the promotion and underwriting of share issues by industrial undertakings.[16]

The move towards joint-stock capital was associated with an increase in the level of economic concentration. It has been estimated that in the 1880s the 100 largest industrial firms accounted for less than 10 per cent of the total market,[17] but a spate of company amalgamations led to greater concentration from the 1890s as the increased merger activity outpaced the growth of the market. Companies were floated on the stock exchange and might then grow by taking over their competitors; or rival firms might join together to float a common holding company. The families whose firms were floated or merged at this time often retained the ordinary, voting, shares for themselves and allowed debentures and non-voting shares to be sold to the wider public. Thus, family control could be maintained on the basis of a relatively small capital investment.[18] The flotation of firms allowed capital to be raised from outside the family circle; and the joint-stock form allowed family wealth to be diversified and so made more secure. Large amalgamations of family firms occurred in a particularly rapid burst between 1898 and 1900, but the rates of flotation and merger continued at high levels until 1914. The amalgamations, however, were often hamstrung by attempts to maintain the autonomy of the constituent family firms, leaving the large firms as mere holding companies with no real control over their subsidiaries. In such cases the holding company functioned as little more than a joint marketing organisation. The desire to maintain family control was often of overriding importance and could lead to passionate struggles amongst the families whose firms had joined together. In the fusion of 59 firms which produced the Calico Printers' Association in 1899, each of the 84 directors on the unwieldy board 'was determined to safeguard the interests of his original company which, in the majority of cases, was still under his own management'.[19] The founding families struggled with one another to defend and enhance the position of their own firms in the amalgamations; and those large companies which succeeded in adopting a more centralised structure were generally either those in which one constituent firm was considerably larger than the others, or those in which a particular family managed to subordinate its fellows in the struggle for control. Because of the growing concentration of economic activities in a smaller number of firms, there were fewer positions of control in the commanding heights of the manufacturing sector. The families who lost-out in the struggle for these positions were faced with the choice of either retiring into land or politics (the gentleman's route) or moving into new business ventures (the so-called player's route).[20]

Families who wished to leave business often decided to sell out to

a company promoter prior to the stock exchange flotation. Although such families sometimes retained a stake in the firm, they were not involved in active control. Controlling shareholdings were often transferred to syndicates of businessmen who collectively controlled recruitment to the company boards. In this way a number of the wealthier manufacturers and their families came to control many of the larger companies, often in close association with the second-rank bankers and promoters who handled the mechanics of share-issuing. These promoters were often keen to recruit peers to the boards of the companies which they floated, feeling that a 'lord on the board' would enhance the saleability of the shares. From the 1870s landowners joined the boards of joint-stock companies, particularly the large amalgamations. By 1896 a quarter of all peers had directorships; though not all of these were in manufacturing concerns, and a number of men would be ennobled manufacturers. Many of these men would have been invited on to the boards for decorative purposes, but many landowners found their directorships to be a significant supplement to their income. They may even have performed a useful function for the companies since the managerial problems of delegated administration which they faced on their estates were similar to those faced by the directors of the large amalgamated companies, and it is not inconceivable that companies may have benefited from the 'managerial' experience of the landowners.

The changing fortunes of the various social classes and class fractions were dependent upon the general economic trends of the period. As the balance of economic activity between industry and agriculture changed in favour of the former, so a growing proportion of national income was spent on manufactured goods rather than on food, and so the returns to agriculture tended to decline as a proportion of returns to the economy as a whole. This trend was aggravated by the agricultural depression of 1873–96, which hit the smaller landowners far more severely than the larger landowners who had been able to diversify into non-agricultural activities.[21] The squeeze which this exerted on the smaller landowners exacerbated the growing awareness and criticism of the accumulation of wealth in land, commerce and industry. The concentration of landownership generated the most heated controversy, and so the government eventually set up an official investigation to scotch the claim that the bulk of British land was owned by 30,000 people. In fact, this attempt backfired: the investigation discovered that the land was owned by a much smaller number of people.

The results of the investigation were published in the *Return of Owners of Land* (the 'New Domesday Book'); and, although there is some confusion in the various summaries of the *Return*, certain general conclusions are clear. In 1873 – the year to which the survey relates – four-fifths of the land was owned by 7,000 people, of whom 4,200 in England and Wales and 800 in Scotland held 1,000 acres or more. Among these people a total of 363 held 10,000 acres or more, 44 having 100,000 acres or more.[22] In total the large landowners held about 24 per cent of the land, the smaller rentiers held about 55 per cent and the owner-occupiers held a further 10 per cent, with the church and the crown holding a similar amount.[23] This national pattern was repeated at the local level: in East Anglia, for example, 350 people owned 55 per cent of the agricultural land of Norfolk, Suffolk and Cambridgeshire.[24] Most of the largest estates were in Scotland: there was a total of 35 estates larger than 100,000 acres, of which the 25 Scottish estates accounted for a quarter of the Scottish land.[25]

Of the 2,500 people with an annual rental income of £3,000 or more in 1873, 866 received an income of £10,000 or more and 76 received £50,000 or more.[26] Sixteen people received a rental income in excess of £100,000, the largest income-recipients being the Dukes of Norfolk and Buccleuch, and the Marquess of Bute. Any attempt to construct a list of Britain's richest people is complicated because there was not a perfect correlation between income and acreage. Only 7 people had both 100,000 acres and £100,000 annual income: the Dukes of Buccleuch, Devonshire, Northumberland, Portland and Sutherland, the Marquess of Bute, and the Earl Fitzwilliam. The survey did not extend to the rental income derived from urban land, and the wealth of men such as the Duke of Westminster was underestimated. To identify Britain's richest landowners more closely it is necessary to include the Dukes of Norfolk and Westminster, who had large incomes from relatively small estates, and 6 men with massive estates though receiving less than £100,000 rental: the Duke of Richmond, the Earls of Breadalbane, Fife, and Seafield, Alexander Matheson, and Sir James Matheson.[27] These 15 people constituted the core of the British landed class – and it is worthy of note that the two Mathesons were from families which were involved in far-eastern commerce. The continuing overlap between the rich and the peerage is obvious. Out of the 363 people with both £10,000 income and 10,000 acres, together holding almost a quarter of Britain's land, 246 were members of the peerage; and a further 350 peers had smaller estates.[28]

Table 5.1 shows a recent estimate by Rubinstein of the numbers of landed millionaires and half-millionaires – that is, those leaving

TABLE 5.1   *Landed wealth-holders (1809–99)*

		No. of deceased wealth-holders in each period		
		1809–58	1858–79	1880–99
Millionaires		75	33	32
Half-millionairs		150	50	n.a.
	Totals	225	83	–

Note: n.a. = not available.

Source: Rubinstein (1974a) pp. 149–53.

land valued at £500,000 or more on their death. It is clear that the number of landed millionaires fell considerably between the first and the second half of the nineteenth century. It is important to recognise that the holding of land through settlements and trusts tended to result in an underestimation of landed wealth in studies based on land held at death. The position of landowners in relation to wealthy merchants and manufacturers was deteriorating significantly. In his researches for *Capital*, Marx tried to assess the number of industrial millionaires by analysing the returns for Succession Duty so as to discover the number of personal estates of more than £1m. For the ten years 1815–25 he found no deceased industrial millionaires, in the thirty years 1825–55 he found 8 and in the three years 1856–9 he found 4.[29] More recently Perkin has estimated that there were, in 1850, 2,000 businessmen with profits of £3,000 or more; 338 of these people received £10,000 or more, and 26 received £50,000 or more.[30] In 1867 the wealthiest 0.5 per cent of the population received 26.3 per cent of the total income.[31] By 1880 the number of businessmen with Schedule D profits of £3,000 or more had risen to 5,000, of whom 987 received £10,000 or more and 77 received £50,000 or more. The figures in Table 5.2 show that the commercial and manufacturing classes had, by 1880, overtaken the landed class in economic terms. Despite the

TABLE 5.2   *Top British wealth-holders outside land (1809–1914)*

	No. of deceased wealth-holders in each period			
	1809–58	1858–79	1880–99	1900–14
Millionaires	9	30	59	75
Half-millionaires	47	102	158	181
Totals	56	132	217	256

Source: Rubinstein (1977) p. 604.

methodological problem of changes in the value of money over the period, the broad pattern is clear. The financial sector consistently accounted for between one-fifth and two-fifths of all non-landed millionaires. Within the manufacturing sector, textiles consistently accounted for about one-tenth (rather more in the earliest period), and metals accounted for one-tenth in both of the earlier periods and then fell away. It can be concluded that both of the main industries of the industrial revolution were well-represented among millionaires. In the later periods the food, drink and tobacco industries together accounted for about one-fifth of all non-landed millionaires, and from 1858 the distributive trades accounted for one-tenth.

The wealthy men of land, commerce and manufacturing were drawing closer together during the Victorian period, though the landowners still tended to deprecate merchants and manufacturers as 'middle class' and concerned with 'trade'. This status exclusion was made easier by the existence of a vast number of clerks, shopkeepers and tradesmen who were oriented towards the commercial and manufacturing classes and appeared to form a continuous social category with them. The wealthy millowner could be derogated as being the status equal of a small shopkeeper. In fact, the economic gulf between them was immense. The increase in the scale of activity in business and the emergence of the joint-stock company as the major form of business enterprise brought into existence a group of salaried managers and administrators who occupied an important position in the class structure. Structurally distinct in class situation from manual workers by virtue of their higher earnings, the 'career' nature of their work and their participation in the control and surveillance of the labour process, they were nevertheless distinct from the capitalists themselves. As aspects of the function of capital were delegated to a specialised administrative hierarchy, so the clerks who manned this hierarchy felt some sense of identity with the entrepreneurs. As industry became more complex the number of such clerks expanded and they achieved a degree of status unity with the tradesmen and small employers in the towns. At the same time, the administrative servants of the state and the older professions of medicine, law and church were joined by newer 'professional' occupations.[32] These diverse groups formed a 'massive social tail'[33] to the manufacturing class. They constituted a loose middle stratum below the main areas of privilege, but enjoyed superior life chances to the majority of the population. The members of this stratum were dependent upon the business and private actions of the manufacturers and merchants, and were also direct beneficiaries of the new form of property which the joint-stock company represented. The savings of this stratum were an important source of capital for the large business enterprises; by becoming 'investors' in these companies they acquired an obvious material interest in the business system and were able to boost their annual incomes to a level of between £60 and £200.[34] These small investors acquired 'a share in the ownership, as distinct from the control, of large-scale industry'.[35] Strategic control, of course, remained with the capitalists themselves.

Deference and decline

The three privileged classes were drawing closer together as the nineteenth century proceeded. The involvement of landowners on the boards of manufacturing and commercial companies was complemented by the continuing movement of industrial and commercial wealth into land. At the same time the extent of intermarriage between the classes increased. London bankers and merchants such as Lloyd, Baring, Drummond and the Rothschilds, brewers such as Barclay, Hanbury and Whitbread all bought into land, as did many wealthy lawyers, West India plantation owners and shippers. Although entry into land through purchase or through marriage continued at very much the same rate as in the previous century, alternative and more profitable investment outlets were far greater than formerly, and so it must be presumed that land was still being bought mainly for status reasons.[36] Later in the century industrialists such as Tennant, Armstrong, Coats and Wills bought into land. This move into land was matched by increased movement in the opposite direction. Erickson discovered that late Victorian steel executives tended to marry into the landed class or into the higher professions more often than they married the daughters of other businessmen; and 13 per cent of the executives in the steel industry were recruited from a landed background.[37]

The movement of the privileged social classes towards one another was marked culturally by the emergence of a particular conception of the status of the 'gentleman' and its associated life-style. The notion of the gentleman had for a long time marked the fundamental status divide in society; and as the number of manufacturers and merchants increased, so this social status took on an increased significance in social control. The relatively small size of the peerage in relation to the large manufacturing and commercial classes meant that even the admission of their most wealthy representatives into the peerage could only operate as a mechanism of social control if the peerage continued to be associated with the more informal and flexible concept of the gentleman.[38] Acceptance as a gentleman by those who were already recognised as gentlemen defined a person as someone who mattered socially and politically. The fact that the status could be accorded or withdrawn at will by influential social circles without having to be justified in terms of any explicit, formal criterion, made it a curiously subtle and effective mechanism of social control.

The life-style of the gentleman, therefore, had to be accommodated to the practices of the manufacturing and commercial classes. The round of dining and visiting in the great country houses, the meetings of the Quarter Sessions, and rural pursuits such as foxhunting and racing were already integrated into a London-based 'Season' of activities in which all members of 'Society' participated. During the course of the nineteenth century this became steadily more formalised and acquired a new authority over those who regarded themselves as gentlemen. The rise of wealthy men from outside the ranks of the landed class meant that the traditional institutions of 'Society' had to be altered in such a way that their legitimate claims could be recognised without upsetting the traditional order completely. Davidoff has correctly argued that 'Society can be seen as a system of quasi-kinship relationships which was used to "place" mobile individuals during the period of structural differentiation fostered by industrialisation and urbanisation.'[39] In a period in which Society was rapidly growing in size, directories listing the families of gentlemen found a ready market. In 1833 John Burke published the first edition of his genealogical directory of county families. Initially entitled *Burke's Commoners*, this volume was subsequently given the more acceptable title of *Burke's Landed Gentry*. The 1833 volume listed 400 county families, the qualification for inclusion being possession of at least 2,000 acres of land. The volume for 1906 had grown to include 5,000 families, of whom 1,000 were from industrial backgrounds.[40] Entry into this semi-official social register of the exclusive status levels required the ownership of at least 2,000 acres, a condition which continued until the twelfth edition of 1914. Burke's *General Armory* was published in various editions from 1842 and listed all those families claiming the right to bear heraldic arms. Most of the 60,000 families included in the definitive 1884 volume owned little or no land. The existence of these and other registers of social acceptability[41] is an important indicator of the changes which Society was experiencing.

This formalisation of the institutions of Society can also be seen in the changing nature of court presentation. The royal court was considered to be the greatest of the great houses, with presentations to the crown occurring at important points in the life of a gentleman and his family. By the middle of the nineteenth-century presentation had become an essential entry into Society, and the needs of the newcomers to Society were met by the publication of manuals of instruction and by the issuing of Certificates of Presentation.[42] The London Season, together with such events as yachting at Cowes and grouse-shooting on the Scottish moors, were central features of the life-style of the gentleman, but undoubtedly the most important institution in forging a cultural unity between the landed class and the newcomers was the Victorian 'public school'.

Through these essentially private educational institutions the landed meaning system was diffused to the other privileged classes. The educational revolution initiated by Thomas Arnold at Rugby in the second half of the nineteenth century was intended to produce 'Christian Gentlemen', an amalgam of the traditional notion of the gentleman with the romanticism and humanitarianism of evangelical Christianity.[43] Prior to the 1850s schools had not been particularly significant, and only Oxford and Cambridge were at all important for professional positions. This changed with the public school reforms of the 1860s, which eventuated in the formation of the 'Headmasters' Conference' as the central forum through which the major schools[44] could exert control and influence over the lesser schools. By the 1870s the public school to Oxbridge route to top positions had been systematised. The rise of new men aspiring to social leadership, the expansion of the number of suitable posts in government service and the increasing use of competitive examinations for recruitment, all lent force to the benefits of a public school education. The moral and leadership training deemed necessary for a gentleman played a key role in mediating the relations between economic changes and the cultural and political order:

> The recruiting needs of a new, expanding bureaucracy demanded middle-class participation in government. The public schools met this need by opening their gates to the commercial and professional classes. They took the fees of the textile magnate and the lawyer, and in return they exposed their sons to the full public service traditions of the aristocrat and the country squire. . . . They perpetuated the political supremacy of the landed classes by 'capturing' talent from the rising bourgeoisie and moulding that talent into 'synthetic' gentlemen.[45]

The code of gentlemanly behaviour which was passed on through the public schools defined what was 'done' and what was 'not done'. Its central assumption was that the gentleman had certain definite rights and obligations towards other members of society. The latter were regarded as having a corresponding obligation to defer to the 'natural' superiority of the gentleman. Deferential behaviour was expected from subordinates as a sign of the legitimacy of the prevailing patterns of inequality; and the economic dependence of farmers and rural workers on the local gentleman provided a fertile ground for at least an outward show of deference.[46] Whilst there may have been problems in translating such notions to the urban context, where force had been the normal and frequent sanction of authority in the first half of the nineteenth century, the code of the gentleman was eagerly adopted by the rising class of manufacturers. Although developed, in part, as a response to the reforms of recruitment and promotion in the civil service, the law and the army, the public school ethos ran counter to the rationality, efficiency and functionality of trade and industry. Such manifestations of the capitalist spirit were regarded as ungentlemanly in the extreme. The gentleman eschewed any rigorous practical application to instrumental matters and sought to temper any necessary involvement in economic affairs with the traditional gentlemanly virtues. The need to provide at least some 'practical' knowledge meant that the public schools came to represent 'a balance between rationalized organisation and traditional power', with their curriculum caught 'between the reward of intellectual merit, on the one hand, and the reward of hereditary privilege, on the other'.[47] This compromise between landed and entrepreneurial ideas modernised the gentleman ideal. The notion of the public school gentleman was an expression of the *modus vivendi* between the landed class and the newcomers; as such, it legitimised their expectation of deference from the middle stratum and working class below them.[48]

The hegemony of the values of the gentleman and the associated cult of amateurism have frequently been cited in the context of the thesis of 'entrepreneurial decline', which claims that Britain's relatively poor economic growth after 1870 was due to the pursuit of traditional status by manufacturers. The constant outflow of successful businessmen from the ungentlemanly fields of trade and industry to the more acceptable fields of politics and the land, is held to have resulted in a 'haemorrhage of talent' from industry.[49] It is certainly true that many manufacturers had for a long time seen the creation of a successful family business as but the first step in a long-term strategy of establishing a landed family. Members of the rising manufacturing class found a set life-style waiting for them once they had accumulated sufficient wealth. The successful manufacturer 'would become a ''gentleman'', doubtless with a country house, perhaps eventually a knighthood or peerage, a seat in Parliament for himself or his Oxbridge-educated son, and a clear and prescribed social role'.[50] Coleman has argued, however, that the exit from industry for the landed life created opportunities for the entry of new dynamic entrepreneurs. The industrial revolution itself, argues Coleman, was in part due to the constant opening-up of opportunities for the practical men (the 'players'), as the gentlemen who had established businesses left the field. For this reason, he claims, the same process in the late nineteenth century can hardly be taken as an explanation of entrepreneurial *failure*:

> because manufacturing business was not seen as an occupation fit for gentlemen and because successful businessmen regularly withdrew their children from the business world by sending them through the gentlemanly educational process, the field was constantly being cleared for a succession of thrusting ambitious Players.[51]

Although McCloskey has thrown some doubts upon the existence of any kind of entrepreneurial failure, arguing that the relative industrial slowdown was a sign of economic maturity,[52] there is some evidence that the post-1870 generation of manufacturers failed to take up investment opportunities in the new industries such as cars, chemicals and electrical engineering. Perhaps the main explanation for this is not the 'haemorrhage of talent', but the attempt by heads of family firms to keep their firms under family control. Because most business families wished to keep control of their own businesses, there were positive incentives *not* to grow: once a certain level of income had been achieved, maximum growth could be traded-off against the pursuit of leisure or a political career. The following of the gentlemanly life-style was part and parcel of a family strategy aimed at maintaining control over the family business. It was for this reason that family firms often did not want to follow the path towards large-scale organisation and new technology. Those which did grow through take-overs and amalgamations often did so as a defensive response to threats from domestic and foreign competition; only through amalgamation could they seek to retain some control over their firms.[53] This family strategy was reinforced by the fact that investment in new technology was often not in accordance with economic rationality. So long as satisfactory profits could be earned from the old, perhaps obsolete plant, there was no incentive to take the risk of investment in new technologies which would not yield significantly higher earnings.[54]

The transformation of the gentleman ideal was, therefore, a consequence of the changing balance of power between the various privileged classes. As they moved closer together economically, the concept of the gentleman was adjusted so as to reflect the partial merger of landed, commercial and manufacturing interests. The landed meaning system was accommodated to the entrepreneurial ideology, and Victorian society came under the sway of this hybrid system of values. Bendix has recognised one important aspect of this in his claim that Victorian morality

> identified the pursuit of self-interest with the cultivation of the minor Christian virtues such as hard work, frugality, and prudence. In his attempts to develop these virtues in himself each man was on his own – under the hard, but beneficient pressure of economic necessity. These virtues of moral self-reliance and self-development became a national creed.[55]

But to these essentially individualistic ideas were added communal, solidaristic ideas drawn from the traditional landed meaning system. The public school ethos emphasised that the individual was part of a group and part of an historical tradition. The school as a 'historic community', a living chain which grows but never dies, generated the attitude of mind which permitted loyalties to house and school to be transferred to groups such as the Regiment, the House of Commons and the Nation.[56] Individualism and group loyalty were united in the ideals of gentlemanly behaviour.

Victorian society was characterised by this move towards unity among the privileged social classes, in terms of both class situation and status situation. But the classes did not achieve complete integration. Whilst the landowners and the City fraction had certainly come very close to one another, manufacturers and provincial merchants remained apart. By the last half of the nineteenth century autonomous and assertive industrial dynasties were firmly entrenched in areas such as Glasgow, Liverpool, Manchester, Birmingham, Cardiff and Newcastle. It was at this provincial level that manufacturers and merchants had grown closest together, and by the end of the century the terms 'merchant' and 'manufacturer' were often used interchangeably. The three privileged classes could no longer be clearly distinguished from one another. Although each class was based around a particular kind of property, they entered into ever more extensive business and personal relationships with one another. Each class also included people who were not active participants in the control and use of property, but who drew an income from this and had family links with the core of their class. Such people were to be found in politics, the professions and the intelligentsia; and these occupations constituted major areas of overlap between the fringes of the three privileged classes.

Elitism, electoralism and the establishment

It was in the field of politics that the new patterns of class alignment were to be found at their clearest. For the first part of the nineteenth century the national political rulers were drawn exclusively from the landed class and the City fraction of the commercial class, with the manufacturers and provincial merchants pursuing their interests in the towns and cities. From the middle of the century the old patrician style of national politics began to break down as the changing balance of power between the privileged classes led to changes in the composition of the political leadership. In the 1780s Pitt began the creation of a new Tory group in parliament, and this group remained in power until 1830. Although drawing on monarchist traditions, the Tories presided over the final achievement of parliamentary dominance over the crown. Just at the point when the Tories had consolidated their hold over the government, the sanity of George III finally failed, and the government were forced to continue with only a figurehead monarch. The Tories were able to complete the subordination of the crown which the Whigs had begun in the early eighteenth century. Whilst the Tories had, in effect, taken over many of the old Whig ideas and practices, the Whigs had themselves undergone a thorough transformation. For a while during the early years of the reign of George III the Newcastle–Rockingham group of Whigs, whose spokesman had been Edmund Burke, had allied themselves with John Wilkes's extra-parliamentary reform movement. The majority of the old Whigs, however, had become simply the parliamentary opponents of Tory government. Halévy has aptly summarised the paradoxical situation which existed in 1819: 'It was the Tories . . . who secured the triumph of the old Whig doctrine of the supremacy of Parliament. . . . It was the leaders of the Whig opposition who . . . were batering to pieces the old edifice of Whig aristocracy.'[57]

The policy of the ruling Tory group was essentially a negative protection of the established social order: no parliamentary reforms and no concessions to labour radicalism. The changing balance of power between the landed class and the manufacturing class meant that some economic reforms were eventually forced on the government. In 1813–14 the state finally abandoned the Elizabethan wage and apprenticeship regulations, but a number of import and export controls were maintained. More economic controls were dismantled during the 1820s, but the pace of economic reforms was not as rapid as the manufacturers wanted. It was not until the change of government in 1830 that this changed. The Whig government, faced with the tension between maintaining the political power of the landed class and satisfying their commercial and manufacturing supporters, speeded-up the move towards a *laissez-faire*, facilitative state and succeeded in forcing the 1832 Reform Bill through parliament.[58] The major area of political activity for the manufacturing class was at the local level. Although many urban areas were not recognised as municipalities or borough constituencies until the reforms of the 1830s, local politics were often seen as more important than national politics. The major line of division within the towns was between a county group of merchants and manufacturers, generally Anglican and Tory and oriented towards the local gentry, and a metropolitan group of newer manufacturers and merchants who were often dissenters and were oriented towards the national Whig leadership.[59] Within the urban areas the two groups struggled to dominate the council and the magistracy, and to determine the choice of MP. Foster, for example, has shown that in Oldham there was a separation between the cotton capitalists who were oriented towards the merchant dynasties of Manchester, and the older capitalists (especially colliery-owners) who were oriented to the local landowners.[60]

Until the 1860s the dominant form of political representation was what may be termed 'elitism'. Elitism is that system of representation in which the interests of a privileged social class are mediated through their position as a dominant status group. In the early nineteenth century the notion of the gentleman was the means through which the landed class defined itself as the natural rulers of society. The patrician values of the landed class, the basis upon which that class defined itself as an 'elite',[61] justified their monopolisation of political power through personal participation in the apparatus of the state. Landowners regarded themselves as having a right, indeed an obligation, to exercise such power and to speak on behalf of those who were not entitled or competent to participate in the exercise of political power. This elitist conception of political representation was essentially a revamped version of the more parasitic, oligarchic representation of old corruption. Elitism constituted a comprehensive system of political representation running from the level of the national government, through county politics, to the level of the parish; the magnates, of course, were dominant at the national level, and the gentry dominated the local level.

From the 1840s a rival principle of 'electoralism' became more and more important. Electoralism involved a fundamentally different principle of political representation. Class interests were to be represented in the state not through a personalistic, elitist system, but through those who were elected to decision-making positions by those who wished to have their interests represented. Politics was to be based on an open and critical dialogue in the 'public sphere', where public opinion could be formed and decisions arrived at. Parliament and parliamentary elections were, ideally, at the centre of this public sphere. Despite their 'individualism' in business, the manufacturers introduced the idea of combination for political purposes. In order to further their common interests in the face of the local county oligarchies, the metropolitan groups formed numerous 'Societies', 'Unions' and 'Leagues'.[62] The political interests of business, for example, were expressed in the Chambers of Commerce which were formed in the large cities of Manchester, Birmingham, Glasgow, Belfast, Edinburgh and Leeds, and which spread to other areas in the 1830s and 1840s. Such chambers were widespread in urban areas by the 1850s and a national federal association was set up in 1860. In addition to the business-related organisations, manufacturers formed numerous voluntary associations and campaign groups, the most successful of which was perhaps the Anti-Corn Law League. This social innovation of the formal association did not spread to the other privileged classes until later in the century; but the 1830s saw a step in this direction when the Tories, still based in White's

Club, set up the Carlton Club as their political centre and began to adopt the name 'Conservatives'. Four years later, in 1836, the Whigs branched-out from their base at Brooks's Club and set up the Reform Club. The Carlton and the Reform functioned as headquarters for the party activists and handled electoral registration, selection of candidates and liaison between local and national leadership. As such, they marked the first real break with the old system of political representation; the first step towards party organisation.

The period from the 1840s to the 1860s was a period of confrontation between elitist and electoral principles of political representation. Prior to this period the elitist principle was in an almost undisputed position. After this period formal party organisations were rapidly established, but the outcome was not simply the replacement of elitism by electoralism. Rather, the landed class had to come to a compromise with the manufacturing class, and the structure of political representation reflected the nature of this compromise. The changing balance of power among the social classes was reflected in a characteristic pattern of political representation. Before this can be looked at in more detail it is necessary to examine the structure of politics in the period 1840–60.

At the heart of the elitist system of representation was the notion of deference. Bagehot has analysed the political significance of deference in relation to the 'dignified' aspects of the state apparatus: 'those which excite and preserve the reverence of the population'.[63] Bagehot argued, as has Habermas much more recently, that the purposive social action which constitutes the 'efficient' working of the state cannot generate its own legitimation. In order to legitimate the state it was necessary to draw upon certain 'non-efficient' or 'theatrical' elements which embody claims and ideas which transcend immediate practicalities. These theatrical elements constitute a residue of tradition 'inherited from the long past'.[64] Central to legitimation, argued Bagehot, was the existence of the monarchy and the peerage. Although both performed certain real political functions, a peerage culminating in a royal family gave a 'sacred' quality to the laws and practices of the state. The royal family, which 'sweetens politics by the seasonable addition of nice and pretty events', cast an aura of sacredness on the machinations of the magnate political families.[65] The landowners' assumption of *noblesse oblige*, the obligation to shoulder responsibilities for others, was an integral part of this pattern, since deference was expected to be shown to those who carried out these obligations. But deference was a consequence of specific social relationships in the particular groups and networks of the traditional agrarian community. Deference could not easily be transferred to an expanding urban context, and so could not be relied upon to provide an effective guarantee for the continuing political rule of the landed class.[66] Elitism, therefore, came under an increasing strain as urban influences grew.

The system of deference and its associated elitist mode of representation is apparent from evidence on the social background of the political rulers in the period. Within the state the continuing predominance of the House of Lords over the House of Commons meant that the restricted electoral franchise of the Commons remained subject to constraint from the non-elected Lords, who exerted control and influence over parliamentary elections. Although the 1832 reforms opened up the system a little, the elitist pattern of representation was not substantially affected. Of the 13 Cabinets which were formed between 1830 and 1868, peers and commoners were each dominant in 6 and the two Houses were equally balanced in 1. Those Cabinets in which the Lords had a majority tended to be the relatively short-lived Conservative governments, and this might seem to indicate that the Commons were of greater importance in the nineteenth century than in the eighteenth century. To a certain extent this is true, but it must not be assumed that those who entered the Commons were a totally distinct group from those in the Lords. Of the 103 men holding Cabinet offices in the period 1830–68, 68 were major landowners, 21 were merchant bankers and 14 were drawn from the legal and medical professions.[67] In the parliament of 1833 there were 217 MPs who were the sons of peers or who were themselves baronets; by 1880 the number had fallen only slightly to 170.[68] Not only were there close links between Lords and Commons, but the landowners active in parliament were drawn heavily from those who had diversified into other economic activities. In the period 1841–7 the total of 815 MPs in seats at some time during the period included 234 non-peerage landowners. This total included 81 baronets and 48 sons of baronets. The 166 heads of landowning families in parliament included 26 who had active business interests and many more who held directorships in railways, insurance companies and joint-stock banks. Most of the 26 with active business interests were private bankers or merchant bankers, and only 6 were manufacturers: 3 from textiles, 2 from iron and 1 from the copper industry. Taking account of all business directorships, the 166 heads of gentry families held 29 railway directorships, 21 insurance directorships, 9 directorships in joint-stock banks, 5 East and West India proprietorships, 7 mining directorships and 7 dock and canal directorships.[69]

This elitist pattern of representation was not confined to the Houses of Parliament and the central government. Not only did it permeate local administration, it also structured such an important aspect of the state apparatus as the military. The pattern of recruitment to the officer corps meant that the structure of authority in the army reflected that in the wider society and that the army constituted a pool of suitable recruits for political careers. For example, in 1808 there were 27 general officers who were members of the Commons, and in 1833 there were 16 such officer MPs. In each of these years a half of the generals serving in the Commons were from peerage families.[70] Table 5.3 shows the involvement of the peerage and baronetage in the officer corps of 1838: of the 1,398 members of these hereditary titled groups, 128 had themselves served as officers and another 601 had close kin who had served as officers. Military participation, therefore, was

TABLE 5.3 *Military participation of peerage and baronetage (1838)*

	Total no. of titled people	No. serving as officers	No. of close kin as officers	Total
Dukes	30	5	41	46
Marquesses	36	4	37	41
Earls	213	18	178	196
Viscounts	65	9	36	45
Barons	204	22	112	134
Baronets	850	70	197	267
Totals	1 398	128	601	729

Note: the second column of figures gives the number of titled people who had served as officers; the third column gives the number of close relatives of each category who had served as officers.

Source: adapted from Harries-Jenkins (1977) tables 2 and 3, pp. 39 and 42.

an important part of the experience of a large proportion of the landed class, with military participation being proportionately more important for the higher ranks of the peerage. Looked at from the standpoint of the officer corps itself, 462 of the 6,173 active officers in 1838 were from peerage families and a further 267 were from the families of baronets. The 729 men from titled families accounted for a total of 12 per cent of the total officer corps. If account is taken of other landed families and of the lesser branches of the titled families, 53 per cent of the officer corps could be said to come from landed families.[71] It is particularly significant that the landowners tended to monopolise the higher ranks of the officer corps: of the 507 officers in 1838 of rank major-general and above[72] 248 were from titled families, and the representation of titled families was greatest for the rank of full general (58 out of 91). Three-quarters of full generals were landed, as were 89 per cent of lieutenant-generals and major-generals.[73] This fact is particularly significant, because the purchase of commissions was not, officially, possible above the rank of colonel – one could not buy a brevet rank.

Within this elitist format of political presentation the rival party groups of Conservatives and Whigs competed with one another for the support of the privileged classes. The Conservatives depended upon most landowners and farmers, together with support from the colonial and shipping interests and those attached to the established church. They were, in Marx's words, the guardians of Old England. In short, the Conservatives were supported by 'all those elements which consider it necessary to safeguard their interests against the necessary results of modern manufacturing industry'.[74] The Whigs, increasingly adopting the name of 'Liberals' in the 1850s, were also drawn from the landed class, but attempted to articulate the interests of the manufacturing and commercial classes. The main focus for the manufacturers and merchants of the large towns were the Manchester Liberals, who opposed government interference in the economy and simply wanted the government to facilitate the pursuit of individual capitalist interests. Partly allied with the Manchester group were the Benthamites, who advocated a measure of state provision in areas such as education and health. The Liberals, therefore, consisted of the old Whigs, the manufacturers and the City fraction.[75] During the 1840s the Conservatives began to broaden the base of their support in the commercial and manufacturing classes, and the eventual repeal of the Corn Law led to the Peelite group splitting-off from the rest of the party. From 1846 to 1867 the Liberals were normally able to form governments with the parliamentary support of the Peelites,[76] and in this way the landed class adapted to the changing balance of class forces by adopting a politics of compromise and concession. The growth of the 'free trade' movement within parliament was contained within the existing elitist pattern of political representation because the leaders of the movement were unwilling to push their demands to the point where their radicalism would strengthen the political position of the working class. The free traders allied themselves with the landed class, although Thompson has rightly pointed out that 'rule by the landed interest did not mean rule for the landed interest'.[77]

The move towards electoralism got under way in earnest in the early 1860s when both the Conservative and the Liberal parties set up national Registration Associations to take over the headquarters services provided by the political clubs. The nascent national parties, however, were not yet in a position to effectively determine parliamentary politics. The reforms of the 1830s had finally freed MPs from the webs of patronage and corruption through which the government had managed them. The absence of party control over parliament made it difficult for government policy to pursue any particular direction:

> The chief characteristic of party organisation in the nineteenth century was its impotence. Shorn of the patronage of the eighteenth century, and not yet fortified by the financial strength and undeviating party vote of the twentieth, the whips and party managers found their influence drastically circumscribed.[78]

The emergence of a national party system strengthened government in relation to parliament and began to integrate parliament into a formal system of electoral representation.[79] The creation in Birmingham in 1877 of a National Liberal Federation by the caucus of local activists was an important step in furthering the process by which parties, as vote-getting machines, became the dominant feature of political representation. This gradual build-up of electoral organisations broke up the old elitist system of representation, and the period from the second Reform Act of 1867 up to 1885 was essentially a period of alternating party governments under Disraeli and Gladstone. Both parties espoused what were essentially 'liberal' ideas, though in the case of the Conservatives these ideas were subordinated to Disraeli's Tory notion of 'One Nation'. It was in the Liberal party, however, that the new electoral principle was to be seen at its clearest. Epitomising the new axis between the parliamentary leadership and the local activists, Gladstone was able to mobilise a bloc of political support from the reformist followers of Cobden, Bright, and Mill, the Nonconformists and the new trades unionists. Under Gladstone's leadership the old guard of Palmerstonian Whigs were finally subordinated to the Cobdenite 'Manchester School'. The Liberal party became far more responsive to the manufacturing and commercial interests which were actively represented in its local and national organisations. In Gladstone's Liberal party 'a mass of industrial and commercial wealth had come together at a central point in the social pyramid',[80] and were able to stamp their character on the party and its policies. As Vincent has argued: 'The party was a coalition of convenience, not an instrument of a creed, and the popular enthusiasm that sustained it, arose reasonably enough from the novelty of participation in politics rather than attachment to programme or doctrine.'[81]

The emergence of electoralism involved an important transformation of the political system as the mode of political representation gradually came to reflect the changing balance of power among the privileged classes. But the old elitist pattern was modified rather than destroyed. The landed class remained an important social force and endeavoured to continue its strategy of compromise with the manufacturing class. The patrician oligarchy adapted to the party system by containing it within the shell of the elitist mode of representation. As a result, the last third of the nineteenth century saw the emergence of the 'establishment' as the newly prominent manufacturers and their party machines were admitted to the sphere of informality and personal connections which characterised the landed class.[82] In return for accepting the hegemony of the values and life-style of the landed class, the most prominent manufacturers were to be admitted as full members of the status group of 'gentlemen'. As the privileged classes moved closer together, so the patterns of representation and recruitment in the state and its allied institutions came to reflect this fact. The public schools, the professions and the church became essential supports of the establishment which now dominated British public life.

The period from the 1880s to 1914 saw a fundamental restructuring of party politics, as the Conservatives became the true party of the establishment. As the Liberals became more and more identified with intervention and reform, the Conservative party regrouped itself as a safe haven for all those who feared the idea of increasing the political power of the working class. Disraeli constructed a policy which would appeal to businessmen as well as the more affluent workers. In 1886 the old Whigs and the Liberal Unionists split from the official Liberals and made an electoral pact with the Conservatives; and in 1912 the Unionists entered into a full merger with the Conservative party.[83] The Conservatives became the Imperial party – the party of Queen and Empire, 'social justice' and 'social reform'. The traditional landed and agrarian groups gravitated towards the Conservatives, as did the commercial and financial interests and subsequently many manufacturers. The establishment party successfully balanced the principles of elitism and electoralism, drawing support not only from the privileged classes, but also from the middle stratum of clerks, shopkeepers and so on. 'Liberal Conservatism',[84] as the official doctrine of the party, expressed this alliance of class interests within the framework of the establishment party.

The establishment, then, was an all-pervasive social and political force, dominating all parts of the state apparatus. In the period after 1868 there was a greater representation of new wealth in parliament. In 1885 16 per cent of MPs were landowners, 12 per cent were from the military, 32 per cent were from the law and other professions, and 38 per cent were from industry and commerce.[85] In the period 1868 to 1886 27 of the 49 men holding Cabinet office were landowners, but in the period 1886 to 1916 the proportion fell to 49 out of 101.[86] This fall in the representation of landowners is brought out in Table 5.4, which shows that between 1868 and 1880 there was not simply a fall in the *number* of landowning MPs, but also a fall in the average *size* of their estates.

The gradual transformation in the social background of MPs is also apparent in Table 5.5, which shows the titles and professions held by members over the period 1832–1918. There was a fall in the number of hereditary titles represented in parliament, but there was

TABLE 5.4   *MPs from landowning families (1868 and 1880)*

	Number of MPs	
Size of estate	1868	1880
50 000 acres or more	59	40
20–50 000 acres	70	49
10–20 000 acres	88	62
5–10 000 acres	104	86
2– 5 000 acres	86	85
Total	407	322

Source: Hanham (1959) p. xv, n. 2.

TABLE 5.5   *Titles and professions of MPs (1832–1918)*

	Number of people				
	1832	1868	1885	1900	1918
Hereditary titles	158	137	109	107	93
Knights	44	28	55	41	82
Military	63	45	42	49	122
Lawyers	5	22	34	39	26

Note: the category 'lawyers' does not include solicitors. Some military and legal MPs are also counted as titled.

Source: adapted from Cole (1955) pp. 134–5.

a constant number of knights until 1918 when the number increased. Interestingly, if the composition of the 'hereditary titles' category is examined the fall is in those from the peerage: the number of baronets actually increased. These figures for knights and baronets seem to show the increasing importance of titled businessmen, who were receiving knighthoods and baronetcies rather than full peerages. Indeed, it is said that Queen Victoria regarded the baronetcy as appropriate to the 'middle classes', who might find difficulty in coping with the expense and responsibility of a peerage. Whilst the period showed a declining tendency for military MPs to be titled (except in the war year of 1918), the number of titled lawyers increased from 1 in 1832 and 1868 to 6 in 1900 and 1918 – though as a proportion of the total number of lawyers entering parliament this is not so significant. The character of the new men entering parliament is clear from Table 5.6, which shows that in 1895 there were 31 millionaire MPs and that in 1906 there were 22; and, as was shown in Table 5.2, land was a decreasingly important source of millionaires at the end of the nineteenth century.

TABLE 5.6   *Wealth in parliament (1895 and 1906)*

| Wealth | Number of MPs | | | | | |
| | 1895 | | | 1906 | | |
	Cons.	Lib Unionists	Lib.	Cons.	Lib Unionists	Lib.
Over £2m.	6	2	3	2	2	3
£1m.–£2m.	8	5	7	5	1	9

Source: Rubinstein (1974a) table VII, p. 167.

A particularly important characteristic of the establishment was their public school and Oxbridge background. During the eighteenth century access to top social positions depended upon access to a particular individual patron. This system was increasingly replaced by the public schools and Oxbridge colleges, both of which were self-recruiting and self-perpetuating institutions composed of men recruited from the establishment. Access to top positions of all kinds was through a system of sponsored mobility operated by the Oxbridge colleges.[87] The system of collective patronage operated by the colleges ensured that the Christian gentlemen produced by the public schools and the ancient universities were recruited to the highest positions of the state and the professions and were well-placed for entry into parliament. The social and economic assets available to people were no longer so important for influencing or contacting *particular* well-placed individuals, but were of crucial importance in ensuring entry to the 'right' school and college. The system ensured superior life chances to those who were able to gain sponsorship, and it ensured that those already in the establishment were replenished by a constant supply of new recruits who were endowed with the cultural assets required of a member of the establishment. Whilst attendance at any public school gave enhanced opportunities for sponsorship, the major public schools were of particular importance – and Eton and Harrow retained a crucial role for the whole of the Victorian period.[88]

The establishment, as a dominant status group which brought together the most important members of the privileged classes, monopolised both national and local political positions as well as recruitment to the military arm of the state and to the important professions of the church and the law. At the local level the landowners who exercised power in the counties as Lord-Lieutenants and Justices of the Peace were allied with the industrialists who dominated municipal government. The Victorian episcopacy was recruited less through individual wealthy patrons and more through the sponsorship system of Oxbridge and the public schools. By the end of the century there were 60 bishops (26 having a seat in the House of Lords), of whom between a quarter and a third were recruited from the landed class and a half were the sons of clergymen. One-half of all the bishops had wives who came from landed families, and 9 out of 10 bishops were educated at Oxford or Cambridge.[89] Similarly, just under three-quarters of all judges in the period 1876 to 1920 came from landed or business backgrounds.[90] In the army of 1883 (see Table 5.7), following the Cardwell reforms,[91] a total of 554 commissioned officers were from

TABLE 5.7   *Regimental participation of aristocracy (1883)*

	Life Guards	Cavalry	Guards	Other	Total
Peerage	43	25	47	22	137
Greater Gentry	52	132	71	162	417
Total	95	157	118	184	554

Note: 'Life Guards' = 1st and 2nd Life Guards, Royal Regiment of Horse Guards.
'Cavalry' = Dragoon Guards, Dragoons, Hussars and Lancers.
'Guards' = Grenadier, Coldstream, Scots Fusiliers

Source: adapted from Harries-Jenkins (1977) table 1, p. 30.

a landed background, most of the landed officers entering the Brigade of Guards or the Household Cavalry regiments. Whilst this number was only a small proportion of the total officer corps, many other officers were younger sons of landowners or were smaller landowners. By 1897 one-third of all general officers came from public schools, and by 1913 this figure had risen to more than a half.[92] This ensured the continuing influence of the landed values transmitted by the public schools: 'The officer thought of himself as a part of the landed interest fulfilling his obligations of public service within the military establishment, in the same way in which a brother or other relative served in the Church or in Parliament.'[93]

At the heart of the establishment was the peerage, which still functioned as a marker of relative social standing. No longer allocated through political patronage, peerages gradually came to be seen as indicators of achievement in politics and public service.[94] Thus, the accommodation between the landowners and the manufacturing and commercial classes was reflected in the awarding of peerages and other titles to non-landowners. Of the 463 people who were accorded peerages in the period 1837 to 1911, 125 people were neither magnates nor gentry. Such new men constituted 10 per cent of new peerage creations at the beginning of the period and 43 per cent at the end of the period. Table 5.8 shows that the annual rate of peerage creations increased rapidly from the 1860s, the main new entrants being the politically active elements of the commercial and manufacturing classes. The changing composition of the peerage reflected the changing composition of the Commons as those who had served their time as active MPs were ennobled. Only after 1885, when the brewers Allsopp, Guinness and Bass and the railway contractor Brassey entered the Lords, did businessmen enter the peerage in any numbers. Between 1880 and 1914 200 new peers were created: one-quarter from the land, one-third from industry and one-third from professions such as the law and the army.[95]

TABLE 5.8   *Peerage creations (1837–1911)*

Period	Mean no. created each year
1837–51	4.3
1852–66	4.1
1867–81	7.0
1882–96	8.3
1897–1911	9.5

Source: extracted from Pumphrey (1959) table 1, p. 4.

Other titles also grew in importance as the gentlemen of the establishment sought to distinguish themselves from one another. Whilst 162 new peerages and 300 new baronetcies were created in the period 1875 to 1904, 2,659 knighthoods were granted in this same period.[96] New orders of knighthood were introduced for the diplomatic and Indian services,[97] the Royal Victorian Order was initiated for special public services, and the grade of knight bachelor was expanded for miscellaneous activities. Table 5.9 shows that the number of knights had increased from 650 to 1,700 between 1830 and 1914. Knights bachelor declined in number in the first half of this period, but became much more important later on with the entry of the new manufacturers to the ranks of the knightage. Between the 1880s and the first world war the number of knighthoods awarded for specific government services doubled, whilst those awarded to men from business and the professions trebled. The mixture of 'old' and 'new' in the establishment is brought out in the fact that between 1880 and 1914 more than a half of all knights had fathers who were peers, baronets, knights or landowners.

TABLE 5.9   *The grades of knighthood (1830–1914)*

| | Numbers | | |
	Knights Bachelor	Knights in Orders	Total
1830s	450	200	650
1885	470	230	700
1914	1 000	700	1 700

Source: Thompson (1977) p. 40.

The 'establishment' was a tightly knit group of intermarried families which formed the political rulers of Britain and which monopolised recruitment to all the major social positions. The new party organisations were a part of this establishment, with the party headquarters and parliamentary leadership being drawn into the pattern of exclusivity and informality of the London gentlemen's clubs where the ethos and values of the public schools were carried forward into adult life. In economic terms, however, the privileged classes remained relatively distinct; the drive towards a unified propertied class had not been completed.

Notes to Chapter 5

1. This has, of course, been widely discussed. Two fairly recent overviews are Amin (1975) and Wallerstein (1974b).
2. The Bank of Scotland and the Royal Bank of Scotland, rivals in Edinburgh, played a similar role in relation to the merchants and private banks of Edinburgh as the Bank of England did in relation to the London merchants and bankers. The Scottish financial system was somewhat distinct in that the British Linen Company Bank was specifically concerned with financing the linen industry as well as carrying on general banking. See Checkland (1975).
3. With limited liability those who subscribed the capital to a firm were legally liable only to the extent of their investment. With joint-stock capital a firm raises finance through the sale of shares rather than through a specific partnership agreement.
4. Checkland (1964) p. 191.
5. Bermant (1970).
6. E. P. Thompson (1963).
7. Mingay (1976b) p. 31.
8. Pollard (1965) p. 26.
9. Spring (1963).
10. On the concept of strategic control see Scott (1979) ch. 2.
11. F. M. L. Thompson (1963) p. 53.
12. Cannadine (1980); Checkland (1964) p. 282; Sutherland (1968) pp. 33–4.
13. See Spring (1971) p. 45.
14. See Gourvish (1980).
15. Mathias (1969) pp. 37–8; Neale (1975a) pp. 99–101.
16. See Clapham (1938) p. 209.
17. Hannah (1976) p. 13.
18. See Mathias (1969) pp. 385–6. The main voting capital in joint-stock companies is the 'ordinary' share capital. Preference shares generally take priority in dividends, but carry no voting rights. Debentures are not shares in the strict sense, but form part of the loan capital.
19. Payne (1967) p. 528; Payne (1978) pp. 206–7.
20. This distinction between gentlemen and players will be discussed further in the following section.
21. See Newby (1979) pp. 37–8; Mingay (1976b) pp. 46, 53.
22. Bateman (1883); Newby (1979) p. 33; Spring (1977). The original sources are Return (1874a), (1874b) and (1876).
23. Mingay (1976a) p. 59.
24. Newby *et al.* (1978) p. 95.
25. Earlier Scottish figures, for 1814, can be found in Halévy (1913) pp. 220–1, based on a survey by Sir John Sinclair.
26. Perkin (1969) p. 431.
27. Sutherland (1968) pp. 41, 169.
28. Perrot (1968) p. 160.

29.   Marx (1867) p. 804. Note that Marx's figures differ from those in Table 5.2 because different sources were used.
30.   Perkin (1969) p. 431.
31.   Bédarida (1976) p. 214.
32.   See Perkin (1969) pp. 254–5.
33.   Foster (1974) p. 163; Fraser (1976) p. 15.
34.   Clark (1962) pp. 118ff; Neale (1972); Payne (1978) p. 205.
35.   Cole (1955) p. 87.
36.   Thompson (1977) p. 29.
37.   Erickson (1959) table 15 on p. 45, and table 2 on p. 12. On the role of kinship see Crozier (1965).
38.   See Best (1971) pp. 245ff.
39.   Davidoff (1973) p. 15; Harrison (1971) pp. 93ff.
40.   Thompson (1977) p. 30.
41.   It should be noted that Burke's publications were not intended to be social registers, though this is undoubtedly how they were used. A full bibliography of the Burke publications can be found in Montgomery-Massingberd (1976).
42.   Davidoff (1973) pp. 24–5.
43.   Barnett (1972) pp. 21–4.
44.   Charterhouse, Eton, Harrow, Rugby, Shrewsbury, Westminster and Winchester. On the public schools in general see Gathorne-Hardy (1973).
45.   Wilkinson (1964) p. 4.
46.   See F. M. L. Thompson (1963) p. 184; Newby (1975); Harrison (1971) p. 89.
47.   Wilkinson (1964) pp. 22–3.
48.   Best (1971) p. 255.
49.   See in particular Aldcroft (1964) and Landes (1969). A review of the debate is contained in Wilson (1965b).
50.   Hobsbawm (1968) p. 82.
51.   Coleman (1973) pp. 10–11. See also Payne (1974) p. 26.
52.   McCloskey (1973).
53.   Payne (1974) pp. 38, 45, 56.
54.   Habsbawm (1968) pp. 187–8.
55.   Bendix (1956) p. 440. See also Checkland (1964) p. 299.
56.   See Wilkinson (1964) pp. 43, 45–6.
57.   Halévy (1913) pp. 14, 20.
58.   See Checkland (1964) pp. 339–40.
59.   See Fraser (1976).
60.   Foster (1974) pp. 177ff.
61.   I do not use the word 'elite' in the way in which it has been employed in recent sociology. In my opinion the word has generally been used to cover up ignorance of the real nature of the group to which reference is made. The only valid usage of the word 'elite' is in its original meaning of a dominant patrician status group.
62.   See Fraser (1976) pp. 17, 186ff.
63.   Bagehot (1867) p. 61.

64. Ibid. pp. 63–5. See also Habermas (1973) p. 48.
65. Bagehot (1867) pp. 86, 90ff.
66. Moore (1976) p. 414.
67. Guttsman (1963) pp. 33ff.
68. Thomson (1950) pp. 122–3.
69. Aydelotte (1962).
70. Harries-Jenkins (1977) p. 221.
71. Razzell (1963).
72. Major-general, lieutenant-general and general.
73. Harries-Jenkins (1977) pp. 50–1.
74. Marx (1852a) p. 200. See also Bulmer-Thomas (1965).
75. Marx (1852a) p. 201; idem (1852b) p. 204; Richards (1980) pp. 57ff.
76. Peel was the son of a wealthy textile capitalist from the first phase of the industrial revolution.
77. F. M. L. Thompson (1963) p. 279. See also Marx (1852b) p. 206.
78. Hanham (1959) p. 347; Clark (1962) p. 47.
79. See Vincent (1966) p. xlvii.
80. Clark (1962) p. 241.
81. Vincent (1966) p. 258.
82. The word 'establishment' dates from political commentaries of the 1950s and 1960s, by which time the social reality which it described had already crumbled. It seems appropriate to date its beginnings from the last third of the nineteenth century.
83. Dangerfield (1936).
84. Harris (1972).
85. Guttsman (1963) p. 82. There were 2 per cent in other occupations.
86. Ibid. p. 95.
87. I am grateful to Joe Banks for clarifying this point for me.
88. Guttsman (1963) pp. 95, 98.
89. Thompson (1977); K. Thompson (1974).
90. Giddens and Stanworth (1978).
91. Barnett (1969) and (1970).
92. Otley (1966) p. 242.
93. Harries-Jenkins (1977) p. 23.
94. See McCahill (1980).
95. Pumphrey (1959); Guttsman (1963) p. 121; Bédarida (1976) p. 129; F. M. L. Thompson (1963) p. 299.
96. Hanham (1960) p. 279.
97. The Order of St Michael and St George, the Order of the Star of India and the Order of the Indian Empire.

6

Capital, Wealth and Control

The predominant trend of the later nineteenth century had been towards the creation of a unified propertied class, and by the first world war this process was well under way. The landed, commercial and manufacturing classes were rapidly becoming assimilated to one another in terms of market situation, social standing and life-style. Although the provincial manufacturers were perhaps the least assimilated, the tendency towards class unification was clear. The inter-war years saw the completion of this process, but the emergent propertied class was subtly transformed into what might most appropriately be termed 'a business class'. The trend towards the joint-stock company as the predominant form of business seemed to suggest that the market situation of the propertied rentier would predominate in land, commerce and industry. However, property in all these sectors underwent a series of transformations, which meant that the actual outcome was rather different. These fundamental economic changes meant that the class as a whole could not adopt the stance of the rentier. Active participation by the propertied in the use of capital became central to the perpetuation of this privileged social class. This class is, indeed, a propertied class: its members both monopolise privately owned wealth and depend upon the uses to which property is put. But the core of the class consists of those who are actively involved in the strategic control of the major units of capital of which the modern economy is formed. This is perhaps the most important facet of the process which C. Wright Mills has described as the 'managerial reorganization of the propertied class'. The class of property-owners is transformed into a business class.[1] The economic basis of this transformation involved an increase in the level of concentration in business activities and an associated alteration in the whole pattern of capital ownership and other economic inequalities. Later parts of this chapter will show how these distributive features are related to the control of units of capital in the monopoly sector of the economy and will outline the major groupings within the business class.

Wealth and the wealthy

A long tradition of research into the distribution of income and wealth has been punctuated by a series of heated debates and has culminated in the reports of a Royal Commission and in numerous textbooks and monographs.[2] Although the 'facts' of economic inequality have been frequently disputed, the broad pattern of inequality is fairly clear and it is possible to build up an accurate picture of the size and significance of the groups which are most privileged in relation to income and wealth.

One of the most influential of the early reports was that carried out by Wedgwood, who drew upon earlier studies by Bowley and Stamp as well as carrying out his own investigations. Like most of the studies in this area, Wedgwood presents his results in terms of the proportion of income and wealth held by successive percentage 'slices' of the population. Examining income before tax, Wedgwood's estimates for 1910 showed the top 1 per cent of income recipients as having 30.2 per cent of total income. Among this small group there were 327 people with annual incomes of more than £45,000. By 1920, argued Wedgwood, the share of the top 1 per cent had fallen to 20.47 per cent; and the people with the highest annual incomes were the 165 with incomes of £100,000 or more. It also emerged as a particularly important finding from

TABLE 6.1   *Income distribution in the UK (1929–70)*

	1929	1938	1949	1970
% of families	0.6	0.4	0.3	0.5
% of income	16.2	11.9	5.9	4.3

Note: the categories are not strictly top income groups, but are variously defined 'aristocratic' and 'upper-middle-class' categories.

Source: adapted from Bédarida (1976) tables 5 and 6, pp. 214–17.

Wedgwood's investigations that unearned income was distributed on an even more unequal basis than was earned income: the top 1 per cent of 1920 received 67.8 per cent of all unearned income.[3] It is possible to put these figures in the context of longer-term trends by examining Table 6.1, which is drawn from Bédarida's rather more impressionistic investigations. It is apparent that there has been a continuous and steady decline in the share of the upper income groups. This reduction in the degree of income inequality occurred mainly in the post-war period until about 1957, the share of the top income groups having levelled off since that time.[4]

Wedgwood's findings on wealth distribution suggest a level of inequality very similar to that found for unearned income. In both 1912 and 1924 the top 1 per cent of wealth-holders had about two-thirds of wealth, though the absolute number of people holding more than £250,000 had increased from 1,305 to 2,198 over this period. Since the time of Wedgwood's survey there has been considerable debate and discussion about the facts of wealth distribution, each successive study revising the figures produced by its predecessor. Perhaps the most comprehensive overview of some of the results of these studies has been published by Atkinson and Harrison, and Table 6.2 gives a summary of some of their conclusions. It can be seen that the share of the top 1 per cent of individuals stood at about two-thirds of personal wealth between 1911 and 1930. Since that time the share of the top 1 per cent has fallen from that level. This fall took place at a relatively steady rate until the share of the top 1 per cent reached about one-third of personal wealth during the 1960s. Throughout the 1970s the proportion of wealth held by the top 1 per cent fluctuated around this same level, as can be seen from the short-term comparisons which are given in Table 6.3. It can be concluded that both income and wealth have been unequally distributed, with the top 1 per cent of the population continuing to hold a particularly high proportion of national wealth and to monopolise the unearned income derived from income-generating assets. Although the degree of inequality seems to have declined over the course of the century, it remains at a high level. The meaning of this apparent diminution in inequality is a topic that it will be necessary to return to at a later stage.

In a major study of poverty Townsend has estimated the inequality of income and wealth on a slightly different basis.[5] Using a national sample survey Townsend found that the top 1 per cent of

TABLE 6.2 *Estimates of top wealth-holding (1911–70)*

Study	Percentage share of top 1 per cent of wealth-holders						
	1911–13	1924–30	1936	1951–4	1960	1965	1970
Polanyi and Wood	66	60	56	42	39	34	31
Royal Commission	69	62	56	43	38	33	29
Atkinson and Harrison	n/a	58	54	44	34	33	30

Note: the studies referred to by Atkinson and Harrison are Polanyi and Wood (1974) and the Diamond Commission (1975).

Source: Atkinson and Harrison (1978) tables 6.1, 6.2 and 6.7 from pp. 139, 141 and 165.

TABLE 6.3 *The share of top wealth-holders (1966–72)*

	Percentage share of top 1 per cent of wealth-holders						
	1966	1967	1968	1969	1970	1971	1972
'Realisation' basis	34.8	35.1	36.9	34.2	33.3	31.6	34.7
'Going concern' basis	31.1	31.3	32.9	30.2	29.4	28.1	31.4

Note: the figures are corrected from figures produced by the Diamond Commission (1975). 'Realisation' and 'Going concern' bases are alternative valuations of wealth according to whether or not the marketability of the assets are taken into account. See Atkinson and Harrison (1978) pp. 5–6.

Source: adapted from Atkinson and Harrison (1978) table 5.4, p. 123.

his respondents received 6.2 per cent of total net disposable income in 1968–9.[6] In the same year the top 1 per cent of respondents in terms of wealth held 26 per cent of the net assets of households. It is important to point out that although there is, of course, a high correlation between income and wealth, it is not necessarily the case that all top wealth-holders are also top income-recipients – and vice versa. Each of the 'top 1 per cent' categories is a 'slice' from different distributions and they may not include precisely the same people. The main reason for the slight mis-match between income and wealth-holding, argues Townsend, is that a high household income in a household with relatively low wealth may be due to the presence of three or more income-earners in the same household, none of whom possess a large amount of wealth. In order to try to take account of this and so arrive at a comprehensive assessment of economic life chances, Townsend attempted to build household structure into his assessments and to combine income and wealth into one measure. Townsend's measure combined income with the income equivalent of assets in order to measure what he called 'income net worth', and the results of this attempt are given in Table 6.4.

TABLE 6.4   *Distribution of income net worth (1968–9)*

% of households	% of income net worth
Top 1%	7.5
Next 4%	11.1
Next 5%	8.9
Top 10%	27.5

Source: Townsend (1979) p. 348.

A number of factors have been adduced to explain these facts of income and wealth distribution. Long-term factors in operation have been the general growth in national wealth and changes in estate duty arrangements. Over the short-term, factors such as changes in stock exchange prices have had a considerable impact. Arrangements for the distribution of wealth among the members of a family have perhaps had the most marked, and least understood, influence on economic inequality. Although Atkinson and Harrison found in their investigations that the share of the top 1 per cent of wealth-holders was hardly affected if nuclear families rather than individuals were taken as the unit of account, they do suggest that changes in marriage and inheritance patterns within the extended family may have led to the appearance of a greater degree of equality than is in fact the case. Wealthy individuals have increasingly distributed their wealth to the members of their extended families during the course of their own lifetimes, and have tended to transfer family wealth-holdings to complex family trusts and settlements. Unfortunately, this is difficult to discover from most existing studies. Because wealth-holding is normally studied in terms of statistical aggregates rather than concrete families, the figures tend to give a false impression of the real situation. What appears to be a redistribution of wealth between the rich and the poor is in fact a redistribution of wealth among the wealthy. Seen in these terms the facts of income and wealth-holding at the upper levels tell us a great deal about the internal structuration of the business class; but the statistics are apt to overstate the significance of the changing structure of inequality between the business class and other social strata.[7].

What is brought out by this discussion is the continuing importance of the family in the perpetuation of economic privilege. Inheritance remains the major determinant of wealth inequality as well as the other life chances which depend on this. As Townsend has argued:

> Inheritance of wealth must not be interpreted just as a 'passive' factor in life chances. It provides advantages in securing admission to top private schools, supplementing education, offering the surroundings and leisure to meet well-endowed individuals of the opposite sex, secure credit and launch new businesses, offset risks and secure disproportionate representation in political bodies.[8]

In the face of continual threats to wealth-inheritance, wealthy families have had to engage in deliberate actions to defend and extend their wealth. Definite practices and strategies aimed at the reproduction of the family patrimony intact have had to be evolved, and family strategies of tax minimisation, occupational placement and capital mobilisation are all central aspects of those strategies of conversion and reconversion which ensure that privileged families maintain their cumulative command over resources.[9]

Some of the economic consequences of these family strategies have been studied by Harbury and Hitchens. It can be seen from Table 6.5 that between one-half and one-third of top wealth-leavers had fathers who had left a similar-sized estate.[10] There is a clear association between the wealth of the two generations. Indeed, if the figure for a 'substantial' inheritance is lowered to £25,000 then the proportion of top wealth-leavers over the whole period 1956–73 who received such an inheritance was 67 per cent. That is to say, two-thirds of top wealth-leavers started out in life with a substantial inheritance. These estimates are based solely on inheritance by a man from his father, and a real understanding of the importance of inheritance would have to go beyond this direct

TABLE 6.5   *Size of fathers' estates of top wealth-leavers (1956–73)*

Size of father's estate (£)	% of top wealth-leavers in			
	1956–7	1965	1973	1956–73
Over 1m.	9	4	7	8
500 001–1m.	10	8	6	9
250 001–500 000	14	12	8	13
100 001–250 000	18	21	15	18
100 000 or less	49	55	64	51
	100%	100%	100%	100%
	(532)	(94)	(108)	(734)

Note: 'top wealth-leavers' are those who died in the relevant period with an estate of £100,000 or more. The columns show the proportion of top wealth-leavers having fathers who were also top wealth-leavers. Figures in parentheses are the actual number of estates.

Source: adapted from Harbury and Hitchens (1979) table 3.3, p. 45.

father to son transmission of property and examine inheritance from mothers, fathers-in-law, grandfathers and other relatives.

So far, my discussion of the wealthy in Britain has concentrated on the various statistically defined categories and has made little reference to the social composition of the category of wealthy people. It is, therefore, necessary to ask 'who are the rich?'. On the basis of a larger selection of rich individuals dying in 1924–5

TABLE 6.6   *Occupation of fathers of large wealth-holders (1924–5)*

Occupation of father	Average estate(£) of wealth-holder	No. of estates
Peerage and gentry	580 000	15
Financiers, manufacturers and merchants	385 000	34
Other 'gentlemen of means'	65 000	5
Professions	–	6
Small business	8 000	18
Farmers	–	2
Clerks and officials	–	3
Manual workers	–	4
		87

Note: 87 estates of £200,000 or more were investigated and the occupations of fathers were traced.

Source: Wedgwood (1929) pp. 166–7.

Wedgwood discovered the results presented in Table 6.6. The largest fortunes were to be found amongst those from landed and business backgrounds. Fully 34 of the 87 estates investigated were left by people whose fathers had been engaged in finance, commerce or manufacturing. Although the number of large estates left by the sons of small businessmen was fairly high, the average size of their estates was considerably smaller than the estates of those drawn from the big-business sector.[11] Rubinstein's data on large wealth-leavers, which are presented in Table 6.7, confirm this fact. The apparent decline in the number of millionaires over the course of the century is, in large part, to be explained away by the

TABLE 6.7   *Landed and non-landed millionaires (1900–69)*

	1900–19	1910–19	1920–9	1930–9	1940–9	1950–9	1960–9
No. of millionaires dying	66	81	102	78	73	46	55

Note: the number of landed millionaires is seriously underestimated after the 1930s.

Source: calculated from Rubinstein (1974) table 1, pp. 149–51.

absence of any reliable national records of landownership after the official investigation of 1873. Thus, the 66 millionaires dying in 1900–19 included 24 large landowners, whilst the 55 millionaires dying in 1960–9 included only the 6 large landowners on whom Rubinstein was able to trace firm evidence. Up to the end of the second world war most millionaires were the sons of very wealthy men, but during the 1950s and 1960s the number of 'self-made' millionaires increased. By the 1960s one-third of all deceased millionaires were self-made, often making their fortunes in the retail and commercial property sectors.[12]

It can be seen from Table 6.8 that the great inheritors of wealth who died in the period 1956–73 were from the higher status groups. Thirty per cent of peers and baronets with estates in excess of £100,000 had fathers who left more than £1m. Between one-half and two-thirds of all the top wealth-leavers in the three status categories considered had fathers who left more than a quarter of a million pounds. One-third of the top wealth-leavers studied by Harbury and Hitchens were included in reference books such as *Who's Who* and *Kelly's Handbook*,[13] and a half of these people

TABLE 6.8   *Social background and inheritance (1956–73)*

Size of father's estate (£)	Social background of top wealth-holder (%)		
	Peers and baronets	Knights	County families
Over 1m.	30	13	23
500 000–1m.	15	15	25
250 000–500 000	19	19	12
100 001–250 000	20	18	20
25 001–100 000	17	19	10
25 000 or less	8	26	10
	100%	100%	100%
	(56)	(38)	(88)

Note: the column headed 'knights' includes both knights bachelor and knights in orders. The column headed 'county families' refers to families included in *Burke's Landed Gentry*. I am grateful to Professor Harbury for clarifying the meaning of some of the entries in this table.

Source: adapted from Harbury and Hitchens (1979) table 6.3, p. 102.

TABLE 6.9   *Britain's wealthiest families*

Family	No. of half-millionaires in last 150 years	Origins of family fortune
Rothschild	21	finance
Wills	21	tobacco
Coats	16	textiles
Colman	10	food
Palmer	10	food
Morrison	9	commerce
Ralli	9	commerce
Gosling	7	banking
Baird	6	iron
Courtauld	6	textiles
Garton	6	sugar
Guinness	6	brewing
Joicey	6	coal
Pilkington	6	glass
Ratcliff	6	brewing
Reckitt	6	starch
Tate	6	sugar
Watney	6	brewing
Wilson	6	shipping
Sebag-Montefiore	6	finance
Dukes of Northumberland	6	coal/land

Note: the importance of landed wealth is not apparent from this table.

Source: Rubinstein (1974) pp. 146–7.

had fathers who left more than a quarter of a million pounds. Thus, inheritance and entry into high-status positions continued to be important concomitants of wealth. Table 6.9 gives further information on this feature of the wealthy by listing the wealthiest families in Britain over the last 150 years. It can be seen that 21 families contained six or more members leaving over half a million pounds each. A further 21 families had five members leaving this amount, and 25 families had three half-millionaires each. It can be seen from the list that great manufacturing fortunes ranked alongside the wealthy financiers of the City of London, a fact that is also apparent from listings of the largest estates of particular years: in 1924–5 the millionaire estates included Hambro (merchant banking), Hulton (newspapers), Cain (brewing) and Leverhulme (soap and groceries);[14] and in 1980 the millionaire estates included Earl Fitzwilliam (land), Cohen (retail stores), Lewis (electrical) and Adeane (finance).[15] Within the business class it is increasingly difficult to distinguish 'land', 'finance' and 'manufacturing'. All such distinctions are relative, and business families have increasingly diversified their wealth-holdings. The wealthy business families tend not to be tied to particular enterprises, but to have a wide spread of interests throughout the economy. This tendency reinforces the community of interest among the members of the business class.[16]

The struggle for control

The core of the business class consists of those who participate in the strategic control of the enterprises which form the monopoly sector of the British economy. The monopoly, or oligopoly, sector of 'big business' consists of the one thousand largest firms in the economy, these firms dominating the various markets in which they operate. The non-monopoly sector, the structural basis of the petite bourgeoisie, is distinct from but dependent on the monopoly sector. The non-monopolised sector of small- and medium-sized firms is based, in part, on the conditions of competitive capitalism, but these conditions are transformed by the dependence of the firms on the monopoly sector. The basic constraints upon the business decisions of firms in the non-monopoly sector are the activities of the large enterprises which supply raw materials, buy finished goods or offer credit. Within a typical industry the large firms which assemble final consumer goods, such as motor cars, may dominate the smaller component manufacturers and retail outlets; or the large multiple retailers may dominate the activities of the smaller firms which produce the goods that are sold. This dependence of the non-monopoly sector on the monopoly sector is the basis of the inequality of life chances between the petite bourgeoisie and the business class. It is the structure and operations of the monopoly sector which generate the privileges enjoyed by the business class.

The business class is not the 'top 1 per cent' that appears in the various studies reported in the previous section. It is, in fact, a much smaller group than this and its core is extremely small. If the outer limits of the monopoly sector in the 1980s are taken to include the one thousand largest companies and their associates, then the number of directors, top executives and principal shareholders would, together with their immediate families, number between 25,000 and 50,000 people. This is, of course, only a rough estimate, but it is clear that the core of the business class consists of less than 0.1 per cent of the population. For this reason this group tends to 'disappear' in many studies of social stratification: it is simply too small to appear in a national random sample. On the basis of its size it is likely that a maximum of only five members of the class core would appear in a national sample of, say, 5,000.[17] Around this core, and linked to it through kinship, education and culture, are those people of property who have retired from business or who follow careers outside the business world. Many such people are to be found in the civil service, the law, the church, the army, the universities, medicine and other similar occupations. These are people who have a great deal of wealth, whose families have enduring links with active business families, and whose children are as likely to enter business as they are to follow their parents' careers. It is in these ways that the more peripheral members of the business class are distinguished from the other members of the same occupations. On this basis the business class as a whole cannot embrace much more than about 0.2 per cent of the population, though its extreme outer fringes reach out into the rest of the top 1 per cent of wealth-holders and income-recipients. Included within this class are those engaged in large-scale landownership and farming, who have increasingly been assimilated with the other businesses of the monopoly sector. As will be shown later in this chapter, the growth of 'agribusiness' and institutional landownership has finally transformed farming into simply another branch of industry.[18]

This small but extremely wealthy social class depends upon the operations of the monopoly sector of the economy for its various privileges. The life chances of the whole class are dependent upon the activities of the core of people who participate, more or less directly, in the strategic control of the enterprises in the monopoly sector. The economically active members of the core of the business class do not form a unitary category of people. The three main elements in the core are the entrepreneurial capitalists, the internal capitalists and the finance capitalists. The *entrepreneurial capitalist* has a substantial ownership stake in the enterprise with which he or she is associated. The enterprise has generally been founded by the entrepreneur or his family, and the success of the particular company is the main concern of the entrepreneur. The *internal capitalist*, too, has a primary business interest within one particular company, though his or her personal wealth does not include a large percentage shareholding in this company. The internal capitalists are executives who head the immense managerial bureaucracies through which large enterprises are administered, and they are perhaps the most numerous category among company directors. Finally, the core of the business class includes a smaller but important group of *finance capitalists*. Whilst a finance capitalist may have a primary business interest in a particular company, he or she has additional interests in a number of major enterprises and plays a crucial role in relation to the monopoly sector as a whole rather than simply in relation to its constituent enterprises. The interplay between entrepreneurial capitalists, internal capitalists and finance capitalists determines the shape of the monopoly sector, and thereby structures the whole pattern of privileges enjoyed by the business class. It is for this reason that it is necessary to understand some of the mechanisms through which their business activities are shaped in the enterprises and groups of enterprises which constitute the monopoly sector of the economy.

The members of the core of the business class are involved in the process of business leadership in relation to those units of capital whose operations are central to the British economy. Business leadership involves participation in the formulation of the corporate strategy followed by the large enterprises. This 'strategic control' of business enterprises involves setting or altering the basic parameters within which the enterprise is to act.[19] But the business leaders exercise their power only within a framework of constraints set by subordinate managers, other workers, trades unions and the state. Perhaps the most important constraints are those inherent in the market situation of the firm. The market situation determines the strength of competitive pressures and the availability of capital, and so sets the limits within which business leaders can attempt to formulate a corporate strategy. These various constraints have their focus in the board of directors of the large enterprise. The company board is the institutional locus of strategic control. This is not to say that each board should be taken as a unified *agency* of control – far from it. The boardroom should be seen as the *arena* within which the struggle for control is located. It is extremely implausible to suggest that all board members have equal power, but it is reasonable to assume that all those who participate in the strategic control of an enterprise will have an interest in the composition of its board of directors. The board is the arena within which the business leaders are to be found.

Those with an interest in the corporate strategy of an enterprise may be either persons or other enterprises and can be classified in terms of the roles of 'executive', 'shareholder' and 'financier'. Executives are those who have a full-time responsibility at the higher levels of operational management.[20] Many such executives will be internal capitalists, but finance capitalists and entrepreneurial capitalists may also have executive responsibilities. As a role occupant the executive has a distinct interest in relation to corporate activities: the interest of the executive concerns such things as remuneration, security of employment and enhancing personal and corporate reputations. The role of 'shareholder', whether individual or corporate, embraces interests relating to dividend level stock-market valuation and future earnings prospects. The final role, that of 'financier', involves those who allow credit to the enterprise, whether this be as an overdraft, as a long-term loan or as a holding of loan stock. The interest of the financier differs from the interests of the executive and the shareholder, and concerns loan security and the ability of the firm to cover both its interest and dividend payments without endangering continued capital accumulation.[21]

Any particular participant in the strategic control of an enterprise may fulfil one or more of these three roles. Whilst there is a latent conflict of interests involved, the actual pattern of conflict will depend upon how these various roles are combined in the concrete participants in the struggle for control. Any particular participant may fill one or more of the roles, and the agent's orientation towards strategic control will vary with the combination of roles that it takes on. Each agent acts in terms of what it sees as being in its own interest and will, therefore, attempt to counter those actions of other participants which threaten its interests. It is for this reason that I have used the phrase 'struggle for control'. Whether or not there is an overt struggle between participants – and such struggles are, in fact, exceptional – struggle is always present as a potential feature of the exercise of strategic control. For example, a company having a shareholding or credit interest in another enterprise may seek to ensure that its interests are represented on the board, and in doing so may find its path blocked by executives seeking to hold sway themselves. The various participants are, potentially, in a state of conflict, and the composition of the board of directors will reflect the balance of power amongst them and the extent to which the potential for conflict has been realised and acted upon. The board-level relationships between finance capitalists, internal capitalists and entrepreneurial capitalists are the outcome of the underlying relationships between shareholders, financiers and executives.

The struggle for control does not take place in a vacuum. The struggle takes place within the limits set by the control type of the enterprise, and it is in this context that the much debated notions of 'ownership and control' have their relevance. That is to say, the distribution of the share and loan capital of an enterprise sets conditions on the possibilities of action for shareholders, financiers and executives in the struggle for control. The conventional categories of majority control, minority control and management control do not point directly to the dominance of *specific* leadership groups – though this is the way in which they have generally been taken. The categories point to possible variations in the internal structure of the group of business leaders.[22] Where a family holds the majority of the shares in a company, for example, it will be relatively difficult for non-family executives to participate in strategic control if family members seek to monopolise top executive positions for themselves. If that same firm has a high level of loan capital in relation to its share capital then any difficulties which it experiences may lead the financial interests to seek to replace family members with their own appointees or with career executives. Where the largest shareholder has minority control – i.e. the shareholding stake is substantial but less than a majority of the issued shares – the possibilities for financier and/or executive influence are much enhanced. This is not the place to attempt to construct a typology of the many possible outcomes associated with each control type. It is simply necessary to realise that the control type of the enterprise is the basic constraint on the composition of the board of directors and, thereby, on the determination of the business leaders. The leadership group which results from this process then formulates the corporate strategy within the constraints of the market and the other factors discussed above.

The business leaders undertake the strategic control of large enterprises, but they are not necessarily involved in day-to-day control over the detailed operations of the enterprise. This operational administration is delegated to a bureaucratic hierarchy which functions within a framework of financial targets set by those who exercise strategic control. The operational administrators are those who Burnham referred to as 'managers' in his statement of the theory of the 'managerial revolution'. Although his claim that these managers would form a new dominant class has now been refuted, he was certainly correct to point to the enhanced power of those who carry out the 'technical direction and coordination of the process of production'.[23] It is this power in the process of production which gave credence to the notion of 'management control' in the large enterprise. It has been widely held that the dispersal of share ownership reduced the power base of family shareholders and created a power vacuum into which the managerial executives could enter.[24] Although this is undoubtedly a possible outcome of corporate development, it is important to note that a gulf exists between those executives who do participate in the exercise of strategic control and those mere managers who are concerned exclusively with operational decisions. Business leaders retain control over the flow of investment funds, and therefore over alternative strategies of capital accumulation. The managers have delegated to them the 'administrative labour' involved in guiding and organising both labour and the physical means of production. Management involves a complex hierarchy of social control through which the practices of labour surveillance and discipline are carried out. Managerial control over methods of work and methods of payment is aimed at ensuring that labour can be treated as simply another 'factor of production'.[25]

Although they are structurally distinct from the top executives, the subordinate managers do not differ from them in their orientation towards business. The managerial hierarchy is an important mechanism for the implementation of capitalist values. By virtue of their structural location in the large enterprise the operational managers are committed to the forms of calculation and monetary accounting, criteria of profitability and growth, and so on which are required by modern capitalist production. The actions of managers are constrained by their social position independently of whatever individual commitments they may have to the achievement principle of work motivation and the pattern of distribution which it legitimates.[26] This is important in view of the frequent claim that the enhanced power of managers is a sign of the transcendence of capitalism. Sombart, for example, claimed that the capitalist spirit dies as enterprises become more bureaucratic: 'in a huge business run on a bureaucratic basis, where economic rationalism no less than the spirit of enterprise is a mechanical process, there is no room for the capitalist spirit'.[27] Sombart saw this as a prelude to the decay of capitalism, but Weber recognised that the bureaucratisation of capitalist management could actually reinforce the hegemony of capitalist practices. The disappearance of the capitalist spirit is of little importance when the enterprise is hemmed in by the objective constraints of the market which serve to maintain the enterprise on the lines of capitalist rationality. Indeed, the formal 'mechanical' hierarchy of managers may even respond to these constraints in a more rational way than entrepreneurs imbued with the capitalist spirit.[28] The position of managers as cogs in a machine, as prisoners in an 'iron-hard cage', determines their fulfilment of the function of control and surveillance over the labour process.

The structural location of the managers in the large enterprise is the determinant of a class situation distinct from that of the business leaders. As workers who perform a technically necessary role in the labour process they occupy a contradictory class location 'between' labour and capital.[29] The operational managers are members of a distinct social class, the 'service' or 'lieutenant' class. The service class, those who exercise power on behalf of the corporate authorities, encompasses higher and lower grade professional, administrative and managerial workers, and it has been estimated that the service class as a whole includes between 10 and 12 per cent of the economically active male population.[30] Corporate strategy is formulated by those members of the business class who predominate in the struggle for control, and this strategy is implemented by the managerial cadres of the service class. The broader class relations of British society, therefore, have their focus in the structure of the large enterprise. The struggle for control, as I have argued, is conditioned by the pattern of ownership in which the enterprise is embedded, and the following section will examine the impact which recent changes in the pattern of ownership have had on the structure of the business class.

Institutional holdings and finance capitalists

The various features of the business class which have been discussed have to be seen as consequences of certain changes in the structure of the economy; and the activities of the members of this class have been causal influences on these same economic transformations. In particular, the progress towards ever higher levels of concentration in economic activity and the growth of 'institutional' shareholdings have fundamentally altered the basis of the business class. The increase in the level of concentration has resulted in the rise to dominance of a relatively small number of large enterprises. The influence which these processes exert on the structuration of the privileged class is such as to transform the pattern of recruitment into positions of business leadership from a personal to an impersonal basis. As families diversify their wealth into a larger number of relatively small holdings in the largest enterprises, so the mechanisms of direct inheritance become less and less important for business recruitment. Where there is no single dominant shareholder, recruitment to positions of strategic control must take place on some basis other than personal shareholdings. The managerial reorganisation of the propertied class – its structuration as a business class – involves a depersonalised structure of property holding within which the shareholdings of 'institutions' in the large enterprises buttress the continuity of class privilege. The remainder of this chapter will discuss these changes in the structure of ownership and the patterns of business leadership associated with them; the changing patterns of recruitment will be one of the topics of the following chapter.

The overall level of concentration in the British economy increased at a relatively slow rate during the first thirty or forty years of the twentieth century. Prior to the first world war the railway companies continued to dominate the capital market, but a number of large industrial oligopolies had begun to emerge. The ten largest manufacturing enterprises in 1904 (see Table 6.10) include a number of companies which are still prominent today, and their importance in the generation of private privilege is evident from the fact that four of the ten companies were associated with families listed in Table 6.9.[31] In 1909 the 100 largest manufacturing companies in Britain accounted for 15 per cent of the total output of the manufacturing sector. By 1930 the share of the top 100 companies in total output had risen to 26 per cent, but by 1948 this figure had fallen back slightly to 23 per cent.[32]

TABLE 6.10 *The ten largest manufacturing companies (1904)*

Company	Capital (£m.)
1. Imperial Tobacco	15.5
2. J. & P. Coats	10.0
3. Watney, Combe, Reid	8.7
4. United Alkali	5.7
5. Vickers Sons & Maxim	5.2
6. Calico Printers	5.0
7. Bleachers Association	4.6
8. Fine Cotton Spinners	4.5
9. Arthur Guinness	4.5
10. Associated Portland Cement	4.1

Note: companies are ranked by issued share capital.

Source: see note 31.

From the end of the second world war the level of industrial concentration increased rapidly. From a level of 23 per cent in 1948 the share of the 100 largest manufacturing companies in industrial output increased to 33 per cent in 1958, 38 per cent in 1963 and 45 per cent in 1970.[33] This increase in concentration led to the creation of an oligopolistic sector of big business. In the 1960s the 2,000 largest quoted companies accounted for virtually all the assets of publicly quoted companies. Of these the 200 largest accounted for 50 per cent and the top 15 accounted for 25 per cent. In the middle of the 1970s the 1,000 largest quoted companies had a total turnover of £95,000 million, of which the 100 largest accounted for 62 per cent, the 50 largest accounted for 49 per cent and the top 10 accounted for 24 per cent.[34]

At the same time as industry and commerce were becoming more concentrated, so the financial sector was also changing. The banking sector at the turn of the century showed a relatively low level of monopolisation, with numerous London banks, northern banks and Scottish banks. By 1917 a series of bank mergers had led to the emergence of the 'big five' banks in England and to close links between the English and Scottish banks. During the inter-war years the financial difficulties of many large industrial companies forced the clearing banks to intervene in order to protect the immense overdrafts which they had granted. In this same period the declining opportunities for profit-making overseas led the merchant banks to develop their industrial financing activities on a greater scale than before. The net result of these trends was to end the separation which had previously existed between the City and industry, an essential precondition for the formation of a unified business class. From the end of the second world war the relations between the industrial and financial sectors rapidly became more closely integrated.

The monopoly sector which emerged from these economic trends is, as has been argued, the basis of the privileges of the business class. The monopoly sector does not consist exclusively of monopolistic one-firm markets: most markets are, in fact, oligopolistic in structure. Rather is it the case that the large enterprises within this sector are able to successfully monopolise the major business opportunities. Any large enterprise depends upon the availability of bank loans and marketable securities, and its business decisions will be constrained by the movement of capital within the financial credit system. The largest of the large enterprises today have a diversified spread of activities and have moved away from their original areas of specialisation to embrace activities in finance, commerce and manufacturing. These various characteristics of the monopoly sector have led writers such as Hilferding to define the sector as involving a 'merger' or 'fusion' of banking and industrial capital.[35] This fusion involves the greater dependence of production on the availability of money capital through the credit system and the gradual creation of unified enterprises which straddle the boundaries between finance and industry.

The large landowners and the financial interests of the City of London had already moved closer together towards the end of the nineteenth century. The transformation of landownership during the twentieth century contributed further to the making of a unified business class. The agricultural depression of the late nineteenth century was far from being a short-lived phenomenon and lasted well into the twentieth century. Tenant farmers found it extremely difficult to farm at a profit, and many landlords were forced to take back the land themselves. But since the landlords faced their own problems of declining revenue, they came under considerable pressure to sell off parcels of land. The long-drawn-out nature of the agricultural depression forced the break-up of the large estates, a process which was hastened by a number of fiscal changes introduced by Lloyd George. It has been estimated that between six and eight million acres of land changed hands between 1918 and 1926, much of this land passing to smaller owner-occupier farmers.[36] Although the large landowners were left with much-diminished estates, their skilful management of the sale of their lands ensured that their total wealth was hardly affected. Wealth released from the land in this way was reinvested in trade, industry or overseas property. By the end of the second world war the owner-occupying farmers were becoming predominant in land-ownership; and in the lowland arable areas the big landlords had become less and less significant. Much of the land sold by the big landowners during the 1950s and 1960s passed to the smaller owner-occupiers, often tenants who bought the land which they rented. Land was also bought by those who had their primary interests in finance or industry – landownership remained an attractive idea for those with their main interests in other fields of business.[37]

The large landowners have not, of course, disappeared. There are still a considerable number of major landowners, and in many parts of the country they remain an important social force. Perrott has estimated that there were approximately 900 owners of large estates in 1967. Although only one-third of the peerage were among these large landowners, about 200 peerage families holding estates of 5,000 acres or more owned about one-third of the British land area. The largest of these large landowners were the Queen and the Dukes of Westminster, Beaufort and Northumberland, with numerous other peers and commoners holding estates of 1,500 acres or so. Although the large landowners were sharply distinguished from the smaller landowners and owner-occupiers,[38] the distinction between peers and 'gentry' had become largely artificial. Only the 30 or 40 really big landowners (especially the dukes) stood out above the others. Large landowners, then, are still an important feature of the English counties. A typical county might consist of between 6 and 12 large landowning families with historic attachments to the area. These families will be intermarried with one another and are likely to be involved in the territorial army, the county regiment, the magistrate's bench, the county council and the local Conservative Association.[39]

Although there are no reliable statistics for landownership in England or Wales, McEwan has carried out painstaking research to produce accurate figures for Scottish landownership. Table 6.11 shows the extremely high concentration of landownership in

TABLE 6.11 *Landownership in Scotland (1970)*

Size of estate	No.	Total acreage	% of acreage
more than 100 000 acres	6		
75 000–100 000	6	2 592 000	13.59
50 000– 75 000	22		
20 000– 50 000	87	2 598 900	13.63
5 000– 20 000	425	4 167 200	21.85
1 000– 5 000	1 193	2 672 200	14.01
less than 1 000	n/a	4 500 000	23.60
publicly owned		2 500 000	13.11
Total acreage		19 030 300	

Note: the figures for the smallest estates and publicly owned land were rounded by McEwan and therefore percentage figures do not add to 100 per cent. The actual figure for total acreage in Scotland is 19,068,807.

Source: McEwan (1977) p. 88.

Scotland, with just 34 estates accounting for 13.59 per cent of the Scottish land area. The fact that some landowners hold more than one estate means that concentration is slightly higher than even these figures would suggest. The large landowners in Scotland included a mixture of the old and the new landlords. The largest landowner was the Duke of Buccleuch, with more than one-quarter of a million acres spread over three counties. Other 'traditional' landowners with substantial property included the Countess of Sutherland, the Duke of Atholl, the Duke of Roxburgh and such 'southerners' as the Duke of Westminster. Newcomers who have bought large estates include the Wills family, E. H. Vestey and Lord Cowdray. In both Scotland and England the traditional landowners, as the direct 'spiritual' descendants of the old landed class, regard their land as more than simply a capital investment. But even these traditional landlords are forced to ensure a satisfactory rate of return and have diversified their landed interests. The well-established avenues of diversification have been supplemented by newer ventures such as country parks, zoos, museums and, of course, 'stately homes'. As businessmen based on the land, the large individual landowners have been joined by large industrial enter............................ e the productive use o....................................... y own the land. Mark.. th fertiliser and seed .... e many owner- occup.. y small- and mediu.. ore dependent upon .... are integrated fully w..........

Alth............................ ownership of landed............................ ate nineteenth century............................ contemporary scene.............................. asing level of econom.. of individual and fam.. capitalists still play an.. is necessary to understa..................................... al capitalists. The arc.. is the family business....................................... dynasty. Such people h...................................... owned by the family, t..................................... nks, and they

COUNTRY *Brazil*
HEARTTHROB
Antonio Fagundes
DISTINGUISHING
FEATURES
Mature, with a gentle paunch

Plump and past 50, Fagundes was voted the most desirable man in Brazil by a popular magazine. A former stage actor, he won the hearts of millions as star of the country's biggest soap *O Rei Do Gado* (The King Of Cattle). Apparently, women love him for his character as well as his off-screen reputation as an honest man – he's married and relatively scandal-free. He's also known to wear red underwear as a source of sexual energy.

have relatively few formal positions outside the economic field. In the family enterprise the strategy of developing the firm is inseparable from the strategy of reproducing itself. All aspects of economic and family activity are subordinated to strategies aimed at maintaining the integrity of the family enterprise as a unit of capital.[41] This old type of family control has come under increasing pressure as take-overs and the diffusion of share ownership has forced many companies out of the grasp of the family entrepreneurs. Between 1890 and the first world war many family firms experienced a transition from a situation of majority control to one of minority control. Shares not held by the controlling families passed to numerous small shareholders who were generally uninvolved in business leadership. As a result of the existence of a large number of relatively powerless small shareholders, entrepreneurial families could hold sway with a minority of the shares. For example, whilst the annual return of Imperial Tobacco in 1914 showed that the share register listed 107,000 separate holdings of shares, the Wills family had firm control of the firm.[42] During the inter-war period the movement towards minority control progressed further, though many families were able to buttress their positions through the issue of non-voting shares which gave them a majority of the votes on the basis of a minority capital holding. Similarly, the use of family trusts and holding companies to co-ordinate the shareholdings of a large number of family members enabled control to be centralised even where many of the family members had withdrawn from the business.

Until the 1930s it was still possible, in many cases, to find successors to executive positions from within the large families born in Victorian times. After 1940 there was a smaller base of recruitment because of the general decrease in family size and the massive losses of men in two wars.[43] When a company was faced with a failure of succession it was more likely to succumb to a take-over bid. Those companies which attempted to carry on with inadequate family management only succeeded in making themselves prime targets in the take-over boom of the 1950s and 1960s. Erickson's study shows that family continuity for more than two generations was, in the steel industry, relatively uncommon – though 19 of the 80 companies studied did have family executives for three or more generations.[44] Increasingly, members of the founding families have been forced to appoint executives from outside the family circle, to take on non-executive positions for themselves or to withdraw from the business altogether.

Entrepreneurial capitalists have fared rather better in some industries than in others: in retailing and in merchant banking, for example, the family principle remains strong. In the retail sector and in property new entrepreneurial capitalists have emerged alongside the old and have followed the tendency of the family capitalists to remain relatively isolated from the wider business community.[45] The new entrepreneurial capitalists, even those who adopt a 'family' style, are operating in a fundamentally different economic environment from their nineteenth-century and early twentieth-century predecessors: entrepreneurs such as Charles Clore arose precisely because the older firms were in difficulties during the 1950s and were unable to fight off the aggressive take-over bids which they received.

As a family's holding in the family company becomes more and more diluted and family members diversify their investment portfolios, so their particular interest in their company becomes less all-pervasive in relation to their other interests. The historic attachments of such families to their base companies become loosened and their broader interests in the wider corporate system lead many such entrepreneurial capitalists to adopt a business style similar to that of the finance capitalist. The rise of the finance capitalist has been brought about by those very changes in the structure of capital ownership which have undermined the old entrepreneurial capitalists. Although the precursors of the finance capitalists – the City financiers – took on many business interests in finance and commerce, the full integration of the City and industry only got under way in earnest during the 1930s with the upsurge in 'institutional' shareholdings. Insurance companies traditionally held their assets in the form of government securities and company debentures, but this policy changed as a result of the high level of inflation generated during the first world war. The higher yield which could be earned on ordinary shares encouraged insurance companies to shift the balance of their investments towards such equity holdings. The proportion of insurance company assets held in ordinary shares increased from 3 per cent in 1914 to 10 per cent in 1938 and 23 per cent in 1957. By 1973 this figure had reached 42 per cent.[46]

Insurance companies were soon taking large proportions of new share issues and dominated the market in corporate securities. As a result the proportion of the population which holds shares has become progressively smaller. In 1970 only 6.6 per cent of adults owned any shares, and the top 5 per cent of wealthy individuals held over 96 per cent of all personally owned shares.[47] Company directors form the single most important category of personal shareholders. Even if directors do not hold a large proportion of the shares in the companies which they direct, the shares they hold are an important determinant of their life chances. Their market situation includes the wealth and dividend income derived from their shareholdings as well as their earned income. It is their ownership of shares and their ability, within limits, to determine their own incomes which distinguishes the market situation of top company directors from mere salaried managers. A study of directors of the top 100 largest companies in 1965 found the average salary before tax to be £13,000, about £4,000 to £5,000 higher than the pay of top civil servants. The salaries of the chief executives of the biggest companies rise well above this level: in 1975 there were 25 directors earning £50,000 or more.[48]

This squeezing-out of individual shareholders is the result of the increased buying by the various institutional shareholders. Initially the insurance companies bought into the largest companies, and by 1942 they held about a half of the issued shares of the 30 largest companies. The growth of the unit-trust movement and the pensions industry massively increased the institutional funds available, and this led to the total level of institutional shareholdings in British companies rising to 50 per cent by 1975.[49]

This trend towards institutional ownership is also apparent on the land. In the 1950s over a half of the land in Britain was held by private individuals and just under one-fifth was held by central and local government and public bodies. A mere 6 per cent of the land was held by companies, and most of these companies were, in fact, private family companies set up for tax reasons.[50] The major 'institutional' holders of land at this time were the universities and the Church of England, which owned agricultural, commercial and housing land as well as company shares. By 1971 City institutions owned more land than the church, and almost as much as the ancient universities.[51] This growth in landownership by financial enterprises continued through the 1970s, and became a particularly important aspect of large-scale landownership. This created a move away from owner-occupation and towards a modernised version of the traditional landlord/tenant relationship. An increasingly popular pattern is for a financial company to buy land and then to sell bonds and shares in the land to insurance companies and pensions funds which stand in the same relation to farming as they do to other businesses. Within these 'agribusiness' enterprises the actual farming is delegated to subordinate executives whose managerial style has more in common with manufacturing executives than it has with the old-style farmers.[52]

Those who hold substantial numbers of company shares and those who own the larger landed estates have been brought together into a closer unity by the growth of institutional ownership. These *individual* property-owners are the major beneficiaries of *institutional* property-ownership, since these institutions operate in such a way as to generate and reproduce the privileges and advantages of the members of the business class. More than this, the core of the business class comprises those who actively participate in the control of these institutions and the units of capital subject to institutional ownership.[53] The monopoly sector of the economy is such that individual enterprises tend to become increasingly independent from particular ownership interests and to become simply units in a class-controlled system of private appropriation. This structure of relationships creates a sharp separation between those who control and benefit from the use of capital and those who do not. Whatever internal divisions there may be within the business class are secondary in importance to their common interest in the continuing success of the system of big business as a whole. But the business system is not a seamless web; in order to operate as an efficient system of production and an efficient mechanism of class structuration it must possess a definite internal structure. In particular, the concepts of 'constellations of interests' and 'spheres of influence' constitute the keys to understanding the role played by finance capitalists in the structure of controls to which the economy is subjected.

It can be seen from Table 6.12 that just over one-third of all the 200 largest non-financial companies in 1976 were majority-controlled. That is to say, entrepreneurial capitalists, the state or foreign corporations held a majority of the outstanding shares in these companies.[54] The proportion of large companies with families as the majority shareholders has fallen considerably over the course

TABLE 6.12   *Mode of control in top British companies (1976)*

Mode of control	No. of companies	%
State enterprise	13	6.5
Exclusive majority	59	29.5
Shared majority	5	2.5
Exclusive minority	30	15.0
Shared minority	12	6.0
Limited minority	8	4.0
Constellation of interests	73	36.5
Totals	200	100.0

Note: the definitions are based on holdings by directors and by known interests with stakes of 5 per cent or more of the share capital.

Source: see note 31.

of the century. Many firms had become minority-controlled,[55] and, in a significant number of cases, families depended upon the tacit support of large institutional shareholders (shared minority control). Yet other family enterprises had passed into a situation of limited minority control, where the family had board representation but slightly less than 10 per cent of the shares. The category which has increased most in importance in the last fifty years, and now accounts for over one-third of all top companies, is that which has been designated as 'control through a constellation of interests'.[56] In these companies the twenty largest shareholders collectively have majority or minority control, but these dominant shareholders constitute too diverse a group to speak with one voice. These shareholders are generally the insurance companies, pension funds and unit trusts, but they include some residual family shareholders who now have to justify their board positions to the institutional shareholders and creditors. The boards of directors of these companies reflect the balance of power among these large shareholders, and any substantial change in shareholdings or in the fortunes of the companies are likely to be translated into a board reshuffle. It is the growth of this mode of control which has been the basis for the predominance of the finance capitalists who sit on their boards. Although the boards include many executives without other business interests (the internal capitalists) and a number of representatives of founding families, an increasingly significant role is played by the finance capitalists. This group includes those executives who take on outside directorships[57] as well as those who have no specific base company. More specifically, it corresponds closely to those normally designated as 'multiple directors' in studies of interlocking directorships, though it includes also those with substantial capital interests or kinship links in two or more large enterprises.

Finance capitalists, then, have interests in two or more otherwise independent companies, and this gives them an important additional role in the monopoly sector: in addition to their particular interests they have a role in relation to the system as a whole. The increase in the overall level of economic concentration and the growth of interfirm share-ownership have led to the dominance of a small number of firms and to closer relationships between these firms. Directorships, shareholdings and loans between companies link enterprises together into chains of connections. The resulting network of intercorporate relations is both inclusive and diffuse: it includes most of the large companies and it ties them into a unending series of overlapping chains. An inclusive and diffuse network of this kind enhances the structural capacities of action enjoyed by the business class.[58] As a result of the various changes in the structure of the economy which have been discussed in this chapter there has emerged a group within the class which is able to act on behalf of the class. This is not to say that these 'finance capitalists' act in some impartial way as the spokesmen of the general interests of capital. The point is that the finance capitalists are well-placed to overcome the division of the monopoly sector into competing interests and to promote some degree of economic co-ordination in terms of more generalised corporate interests.[59]

Although finance capitalists may exercise considerable power within the particular companies with which they are associated, especially if they are chairmen or members of the executive, this is not necessarily the case. Equally, non-executive directors may be marginal to the exercise of strategic control in particular enterprises, though their lack of power should not be assumed *a priori*. Whatever their power position within particular enterprises, finance capitalists play a particularly important role in connection with the corporate system as a whole. Their system role is, however, likely to give them an added importance in the deliberations of the particular enterprises with which they are associated. Those who are directors of more than one enterprise are able to bring to policy deliberations the knowledge and background information which they have acquired in their business activities. This knowledge and information is useful in monitoring the environments of firms, and many chief executives find it useful not only to recruit such people to their boards, but also to take on outside directorships themselves. In the policy deliberations of a particular enterprise even those without executive positions in the company will be regarded as people whose views must be taken into account, and such people are likely to be influential in corporate decision-making. The finance capitalists play a particular role in the corporate system as a whole, a role that is distinct from any relations of control which may exist between particular enterprises.

The role of the finance capitalists in system co-ordination makes them the main means through which the interests of the monopoly sector can be aggregated. This is reinforced through their common culture and education, club memberships and other informal personal links which create a high degree of social cohesion. The finance capitalists meet together also on formal committees and agencies where the interests of the business class can be further articulated. In this way the finance capitalists undertake a liaison role between the monopoly sector and the state, this role as political 'brokers' making them the 'political leading edge for the capitalist class as a whole'.[60] These aspects of the structuration of the business class will be discussed in more detail in the next chapter.

The process of interest aggregation which the finance capitalists undertake is not possible in an unstructured, seamless web of intercorporate linkages. For this process to occur the monopoly sector must be focused on certain central enterprises which function as the organisational means for the co-ordination of the corporate system. The corporate system is structured in such a way that the clearing banks[61] are thrust into central positions, and the finance capitalists are particularly likely to hold a bank directorship. The banks are the hubs of spheres of interconnected enterprises – 'spheres of influence' – and it is through these spheres that capital, information and personnel can be co-ordinated on a system-wide basis.[62] Over and above whatever control they have over the flow of capital, the banking hubs are important as collators of information; they are, literally, information banks. The clearing banks and the finance capitalists who sit on their boards are formed into a vast network for the collection and

communication of information. The information available to each
director can be collated and mobilised for transmission via the
banks which lie at the centre of this network. It is important to
emphasise that this does not occur in a deliberate and
conspiratorial manner. It is an unintended, but very important,
consequence of the increase in the level of concentration and of the
growth of institutional shareholdings. Finance capitalists meet one
another in various capacities in a number of formal and informal
settings. They exchange corporate intelligence and discuss general
business affairs with one another and, as a result, the information
which they generate flows from one enterprise to another through
this network of personal connections.

It is because of the central position of the clearing banks in this
process that many writers have lent their support to theories of
'bank control' over industry. But this notion is more than a little
misleading. Clearing banks are the *means* through which finance
capitalists can influence decisions which are made in all parts of the
monopoly sector, and thereby exert a considerable influence over
the dependent non-monopoly sector. This does not mean that they
are *agencies* for control over industry by bankers. Finance
capitalists, many of whom sit on bank boards, are recruited from
banking, manufacturing and commerce, not solely from banking.
In fact, full-time bankers are normally outweighed in numbers by
the many outside directors who sit on the bank boards. The banks
are the means through which the major capitalist interests coalesce
in order to co-ordinate the behaviour of the system as a whole.
Each of the banks brings together a relatively distinct group of
interests to form a bank-centred sphere of influence.[63] These
spheres – currently centred on Barclays Bank, Lloyds Bank,
Midland Bank and National Westminster Bank – overlap with one
another and their membership shifts over time, but at any
particular moment they have a great significance in relation to the
allocation of capital, the recruitment of business leaders and the
flow of information. Share and loan capital comes from the
insurance companies, pensions funds, unit trusts and investment
trusts, and capital is generally mobilised and syndicated by the
merchant banks with whom these 'institutions' are associated. The
clearing banks, aided by the merchant banks, oversee the allocation
of this capital and help in the provision of personnel for the
institutions and the enterprises in which the institutions are

involved. The clearing banks co-ordinate the constellations of interests which are involved in the control of the majority of the largest enterprises, and the smaller merchant banks act as brokers between the institutions and the various spheres of influence.

The network of communication in which the banks are embedded is the framework within which the corporate strategies of particular enterprises are formulated. The main companies isolated from this network are the subsidiaries of multinational enterprises and the companies controlled by entrepreneurial capitalists. Whilst the entrepreneurially controlled companies may be autonomous centres of decision, the multinational subsidiaries are run by operational managers who act within the constraints of the financial targets set by their masters in New York, Düsseldorf and Tokyo. In the companies which are part of the network of communication, decisions are influenced by the structural position of the enterprise within the network. Even if non-executive directors do not actively intervene in an attempt to influence the decision-making process, the structuring of information which is inherent in the pattern of interlocking directorships will affect those decisions which are made. This structuring of information can ensure that the specific requirements of the monopoly sector at a particular time are translated into corporate decisions. The finance capitalists, as the embodiments of the power of capital, are able to ensure that these requirements make themselves felt in corporate decision-making. As in the political arena, the processes of non-decision-making are of crucial importance in the formulation of corporate strategy. The decisions made within particular enterprises are co-ordinated by the finance capitalists in such a way that, without deliberate intent or intervention, potentially disrupting tensions are damped down in the wider interests of the monopoly sector as a whole.

Through the mechanisms described in this chapter the business class is reproduced over time. The core member of the class are those who undertake the strategic control of the major enterprises of the monopoly sector. It is the activities of these enterprises which generate the privileges enjoyed by the business class as a whole. The class is not divided into clearly delineated fractions, although there are a number of lines of division within the class. One such line of division is between those who participate in strategic control and those who do not, whilst another line separates the old-style landowners from other members of the class. But the divisions which have been focused on in this chapter are those between internal capitalists, entrepreneurial capitalists and finance capitalists. Of these three groups the finance capitalists are, in many respects, the most important. This small group undertakes crucial responsibilities for the class as a whole. There is a surprising agreement about the size of the finance capitalist fraction of the business class. All commentators are agreed that it consists of a very small number of people. Writing in the 1930s two writers of the Left estimated the number at between 200 and 300 families. For the 1950s Sandelson writes of the 400 dominant people, and Aaronovitch focuses his attention on 253 central directors.[64] Recent research on the 250 largest financial and non-financial companies in 1976 has studied the 282 directors who sit on two or more of these companies.[65] Imprecise as they are, these figures point clearly to the order of magnitude involved: the finance capitalists are an extremely small group in relation to the business class as a whole. It is this fact which gives some credence to the notion of the existence of a 'financial oligarchy'.[66] Whilst it is a gross exaggeration to depict finance capitalists as a ruthless and powerful group of cigar-smoking conspirators, it is nevertheless the case that they occupy an important position within the structure of the business class. As a dominant group within the class they play a key role in the affairs of individual enterprises and in the co-ordination of the business system as a whole.

The line which divides finance capitalists from the rest of the class is not a sharp division between distinct class fractions. Many finance capitalists are recruited from the ranks of the internal capitalists, the finance capitalist role often being one which is taken on by top executives in the middle and late phases of their careers. Entrepreneurial capitalists have remained relatively more distinct, though the continuing decline in the number of family enterprises has reduced their numbers and has drawn them closer to the finance capitalists. Entrepreneurial capitalists, especially where they control their firms through minority holdings, are more than ever likely to take on outside directorships and so to become assimilated to the finance capitalists. The interplay between these groups is based upon the changing structure of the economy, and their actions contribute to its reproduction and transformation. They are the active business leaders in a system of class-controlled large enterprises, and it is their actions in this respect which are the source not only of their own income and wealth, but also of the privileges of the wider business class.

Notes to Chapter 6

1. Mills (1956) p. 147.
2. See Diamond Commission (1975) and Atkinson (1975). A useful overview of sources can be found in Rubinstein (1980).
3. Wedgwood (1929) pp. 63, 65.
4. See Westergaard and Resler (1975) pp. 40–2; Scott (1979) pp. 113–14.
5. Townsend (1979) p. 342. See also Westergaard and Resler (1975) p. 112.
6. Net disposable income is defined as income after tax and after allowing for work expenses and travel to work.
7. See Atkinson and Harrison (1978) pp. 239–40; Goldthorpe and Bevan (1977) p. 285.
8. Townsend (1979) p. 363; Westergaard and Resler (1975) p. 376.
9. Townsend (1979) pp. 389–90; Bourdieu (1971).
10. It is important to note here that the term 'estate' as used here refers not to a landed estate, but to a quantity of wealth left at death.
11. See Wedgwood (1929).
12. Rubinstein (1974) pp. 151, 165. A list of people making fortunes in commercial property in the post-war period can be found in Marriott (1967). Rubinstein (1981) has brought together much useful work on wealth.
13. This group were designated 'VIPs' in Harbury and Hitchens (1979).
14. Wedgwood (1929) p. 183.
15. Jenkins (1980) pp. 121–3. A full list of millionaire estates between 1809 and 1949 can be found in Rubinstein (1974b).
16. See Scott (1979) pp. 119–20.
17. The Scottish Mobility Study, for example, found only two or three people of this kind in a sample of 4,887 men (personal communication from G. Payne).
18. Those 'gentlemen farmers' who are not solely dependent on farming for their income may, of course, be counted as members of the business class. Family farmers who are totally dependent on farming for their living are perhaps best seen as petit bourgeois. See Newby *et al.* (1978).
19. See Scott (1979) pp. 36–7. The arguments of this section are elaborated in Scott (1981).
20. Although executives are normally people, this role can also be taken

by corporate bodies. For example, ICI for some time operated its main subsidiaries by making the holding company itself legally responsible as the 'sole director and manager' of each subsidiary.

21. This is not intended as a full delineation of the interests latent in each of the roles. My aim is simply to point out some of the similarities and differences.

22. This point was not, perhaps, made sufficiently clear in Scott (1979) ch. 2, where the various control types are defined.

23. Burnham (1941) p. 70.

24. The classic statement of this, of course, is Berle and Means (1932).

25. The most recent statements of this view are: Wright (1978) pp. 70–1; Poulantzas (1974) pp. 180–1; Carchedi (1977) and (1975). See also Nicolaus (1967); Urry (1973); Becker (1971) and (1973).

26. On the achievement principle see Offe (1970).

27. Sombart (1913) p. 359.

28. See also Bendix (1956) p. 7.

29. See Wright (1978). The classic sources on the class situation of managers and clerks are Lederer (1912) and Lederer and Marschak (1926).
The service class comprises categories I and II of the sevenfold Hope–Goldthorpe categorisation. See Goldthorpe (1980) p. 40; Heath (1981); and Bechhofer *et al.* (1978). Relevant studies of industrial managers are Acton Society (1956) and Leggatt (1978).

31. The data presented in Table 6.10 and 6.12 are drawn from a project on the ownership and control of British companies which I am directing. This project is financed by the Social Science Research Council.

32. Hannah (1976) p. 216.

33. Ibid.

34. Scott (1979) p. 15. Hannah (1976) and Prais (1976) are excellent sources on these developments.

35. Hilferding (1910). See also Poulantzas (1974) p. 137. As will be apparent, there are many of the conclusions of these writers with which I disagree.

36. See Newby *et al.* (1978) p. 35; Perrott (1968) p. 161.

37. See Newby *et al.* (1978) pp. 37–8, and table 5 on p. 152.

38. At this time the value of agricultural land was about £100 per acre in England and Wales, and somewhat less in Scotland. See also Rose *et al.* (1977).

39. See Perrott (1968) and Sutherland (1968).

40. See Newby (1979) and Bell and Newby (1974).

41. See Bourdieu and Saint-Martin (1978) pp. 18–19.

42. On the general point see Payne (1978), Scott (1979), and Scott and Hughes (1980).

43. Wright (1979).

44. Erickson (1959) table 20, p. 53.

45. See Thomas (1978).

46. Wright (1979) p. 74.

47. Atkinson (1972) p. 30; Westergaard and Resler (1975) p. 158.
48. See Stanworth (1974); Nichols (1969); Westergaard and Resler (1975) pp. 53, 161–2; Merrett (1968); Thomas (1979) p. 139.
49. See Scott (1979) p. 66.
50. Massey and Catalano (1978) p. 61.
51. Newby (1979) table 2 on p. 43; Newby *et al.* (1978).
52. See Newby (1979) pp. 64–5.
53. See Minns (1980).
54. A number of the state enterprises were legally constituted as 'public corporations' rather than joint-stock companies.
55. Minority control is defined here as ownership of between 10 and 50 per cent of the shares.
56. Further research into shareholdings for the project described in note 31 will produce some reclassifications of particular companies, but the general proportions are likely to remain unchanged.
57. Unless these outside directorships are associated with the exercise of control by one company over another. In such cases the enterprises are formed into a group and the director who links them together still has an interest within a *particular* unit of capital. On groups see Berkowitz (1978).
58. On 'structural capacities' see Wright (1978) p. 101.
59. For an analysis of finance capitalists as an 'inner group' see Useem (1978), (1980) and (1981). For a slightly different view see Soref (1976) and (1980), and Zeitlin (1980).
60. Useem (1981) pp. 27, 54.
61. Clearing banks are the large high-street banks which operate a system of reciprocal credit exchanges through a central clearing house.
62. See Mintz and Schwartz (1980); Scott (1979) pp. 98ff; Whitley (1973).
63. On the nature of bank spheres of influence see Levine (1978), Mariolis (1978) and Mintz and Schwartz (1981).
64. See 'A Citizen' (1938), Schaffer (1939), Sandelson (1959) and Aaronovitch (1961).
65. This is the project described in note 31.
66. See, for example, Aaronovitch (1961).

7
Class, Status and Power

Discussions of the distribution of power in modern British society have tended to centre on such notions as the 'ruling class' and the 'political elite'.[1] Britain has been depicted as a society in which political power is concentrated in the hands of a dominant social class; a class which has carried into the present the traditional outlook and values of the landed class. In this chapter it will be shown that there is, indeed, a large element of truth in this view. The dominant status group – the establishment – accommodated itself to the creation of a business class, and continued to be a key mechanism in the articulation of the economy with the political system. The establishment has successfully monopolised the major positions within the state and the social institutions allied with the state, and it has exercised a pervasive influence over those outside its own ranks. The structuration of the business class as a whole has, to a considerable extent, been determined by the hegemony within it of the establishment families. As a result, the business class exhibits a high degree of integration and social cohesion, and it continues to be heavily influenced by the values of the establishment. But the establishment has come under increasing pressure as the various changes in the economy which were discussed in the previous chapter made themselves felt. The increased level of economic concentration, the growth of institutional shareholding and all the economic consequences of these processes have undermined the informal procedures upon which the establishment has relied. The need for more formal mechanisms of interest representation generated a transformation of the old pattern of political power in the second half of the twentieth century. The aim of this chapter is to document these changes and to show how they have not altered the fundamental pattern of class power.

Master symbols of legitimation

The establishment evolved around certain of the core ideas of the gentlemanly ethic of the landed class and it stood at the apex of the status hierarchy which these ideas define. Whilst this hierarchy is not so rigid and formalised as it had been in the seventeenth and eighteenth centuries, the peerage, the knightage and the various non-titular honours remain important as master symbols of legitimation. The pattern of privileges and the forms of state and economy with which they are associated continue to be justified in terms of these surviving elements of the traditional meaning system. Indeed, certain of the trends in the modern economy have actually enhanced the importance of such traditional ideas. The growth of state expenditure associated with the welfare state and Keynesian economic policies of state intervention have meant that the cyclical processes of the economy now have political repercussions within the state itself. As the sphere of action of the state increases, and as the state becomes an ever more positive force in economic activity, so economic tensions are translated into strains and tensions of the *political economy*. The growth of state intervention has not ended the separation of the 'political' and the 'economic', although the relationship between the two spheres has been transformed: 'The decline of *laissez faire*, and the rise of the modern welfare state, must be understood in terms of . . . mechanisms of mutual realignment of polity and economy.'[2]

In addition to the normal cyclical dislocations of the economy, the modern political economy experiences periodic and related political dislocations. The endemic fiscal problem of the state – the problem of matching expenditure to revenue – is given a new driving mechanism as the requirements of continued capital accumulation come into conflict with the need to maintain higher levels of state expenditure. The budgetary gap may be resolved on a temporary basis by allowing the inflationary tendencies of the economy to run on; but the further problems generated by inflation lead to the adoption of deflationary policies. As a result the pace of expansion and contraction in the economy becomes the outcome of two countervailing practices: the practices of capitalist enterprises concerned with maintaining profitability, and the practices of the state aimed at controlling the budget in the face of the many demands placed upon it.[3]

These problems are compounded by the fact that the internal structure of the state precludes it from responding to its fiscal problems in a fully rational and co-ordinated way. The modern state is a complex system of interrelated and partly autonomous departments, organisations and agencies, and the logic of action followed by each part of the state will result from the structure of its particular local environment. For this reason it is virtually impossible for one part of the state, such as the Cabinet, to impose its own logic of action on all other parts and to ensure that a coherent policy is carried through by all branches of the state. The fiscal problems of the state are, therefore, compounded by the 'rationality' problems which prevent it from pursuing a coherent fiscal policy.

It is in the light of these features of the modern British state that the continuing relevance of the traditional social hierarchy can be understood. The state stands in danger of delegitimation through its fiscal and rationality problems unless it can continue to trade on the decaying remnants of the traditional status criteria of the gentlemanly ethic.[4] The social meanings embodied in this ethic are important in containing the potentially disruptive tensions of the system. Without these social meanings to trade on, there is the ever-present possibility that the tensions of the political economy will overload the mechanisms of social and cultural integration and so produce a crisis of legitimation for the system as a whole. The status hierarchy evolved over a long period of time and had its high point in the eighteenth century, when the formal gradations and distinctions were employed to their full effect. To be a marquess rather than an earl was to be seen as a person with a very particular level of wealth and political involvement. In the twentieth century such fine distinctions have lost much of their meaning. Nevertheless, being a 'Lord' or a 'Sir' still tends to set a person apart from others in social interaction; and knowing the grade of a person's title enables one to make certain inferences about that person's background – though not with the certainty that might have been possible in the past.

Official honours are now awarded in regular Honours Lists, a practice which developed towards the end of the nineteenth century. Such lists of awards are issued regularly in the New Year and on the monarch's official birthday, with additional lists issued to mark prime-ministerial resignations and royal events such as coronations and jubilees. Although the monarch remains officially the 'fount of honour', status is actually attributed through more prosaic procedures. Honours are included in an Honours List after a formal process of referral through government departments and party organisations, with the Prime Minister's office putting together a list for scrutiny by the Political Honours Scrutiny Committee.[5] The final list is then forwarded to the monarch, who normally has to accept it as a *fait accompli*. Receipt of an honour, therefore, depends upon access or proximity to someone who is willing and able to put names forward to the appropriate authorities. In the case of the civil and the military services there are, inevitably, formal channels for nomination, and so honours tend to be awarded automatically in relation to promotion. Such formal channels are not found outside the public sector and the political parties and so fewer honours are awarded to occupational groups where there are no regularised channels for nomination.[6]

It can be seen that the parallel emergence of large formalised honours lists and of national party systems was no coincidence. The pressing financial requirements of the party machines and the need to exercise political control over backbench MPs created fertile conditions for the use of honours for political ends. Those who toed the party line and those who gave to party funds might expect, in due course, to receive an appropriate token of recognition. Clear-cut cases of the purchase of honours, however, were relatively infrequent, the first sign of public disquiet concerning the de Stern and Williamson peerages of 1895. The sale of honours did not become a widespread practice until after the first world war, when Lloyd George and his political henchmen engaged in regularised sales through semi-official touts and agents. Indeed, Lloyd George is said to have raised more than £3 million through the sale of honours.[7] Public concern over the cynical use of honours for political purposes was a relatively new phenomenon, since this was the accepted norm until well into the nineteenth century. What had changed was public opinion. In the wake of the political reforms of the nineteenth century an increasing number of people began to espouse the idea that an honour should accord with some kind of 'merit' or 'public service'. Whilst this idea was never institutionalised as the sole criterion for the giving of honours, it did become an important aspect of the conceptual vocabulary used in attributing and recognising social status. It was because the ideas of merit and service became such an important 'vocabulary of motive' that there were grounds for criticising practices which were little more than a continuation of the practices of earlier periods. Honours continued to be used for pragmatic reasons, but the scale of awards and the ends to which they were put had changed. At the same time, public opinion came to regard 'merit' or 'service' as the norm, with political expediency as a departure from this norm. Although not in accordance with the real mechanisms determining the allocation of honours, this vocabulary of motive has considerable importance in legitimating the social hierarchy. Those who have honours are normally presumed to deserve them, unless the party machines have excessively and obviously bartered honours. The periodic bursts of disquiet which have greeted certain Honours Lists show how fragile is the credibility of the modern system of social honours, and how easily its role in the legitimation of social inequality might be undermined.

Table 7.1 shows the number of various titles created in each of a number of years from 1898 to 1978. It can be seen that the number

TABLE 7.1   *Honours awarded (1898–1978)*

Title	1898	1908	1918	1928	1938	1948	1958	1968	1978
Earl and Viscount	1	0	3	0	3	1	0	0	0
Baron	4	4	7	6	7	7	4	10	11
Baronet	9	11	34	10	11	0	6	0	0
Knight (Br. Emp.)	–	–	169	13	17	17	15	28	22
Knight Bachelor	15	25	88	66	70	58	69	95	84
Totals	29	40	301	95	108	83	94	133	117

Note: the cateory 'Knight (Br. Emp.)' refers to knights and dames in the Order of the British Empire.

Source: figures for 1898–1958 from Richards (1963) p. 185; figures for 1968 and 1978 calculated from the *Daily Mail Year Books*.

of creations in the Lloyd George Honours Lists of 1918 were far greater than in the two previous periods, with the greatest increases occurring in the categories of knight bachelor and knight in the newly created Order of the British Empire.[8] In the four years 1921–5 1,026 knighthoods were awarded in total.[9] In the wake of the Lloyd George creations the number of annual awards fell back, especially in the Order of the British Empire, but the level remained higher than before the first world war. Labour and Conservative governments since the second world war have continued with creations at a similar level, except that the Labour governments virtually ceased creating baronets. In addition to these changes in the annual level of creations there have been changes in the composition of the various categories of title, and it is perhaps important to understand how the gradations of the social hierarchy have changed since they crystallised during the seventeenth and eighteenth centuries (see Figure 3.1).

The distinctions amongst dukes, marquesses, earls and viscounts still exist, but they are far less salient than was the case during the nineteenth century. Many of the remaining dukes are still to be found among the very largest of the private landowners, and a number are of ancient lineage. Only 5 of the 26 non-royal dukes have titles dating from the nineteenth century (Wellington, Sutherland, Abercorn, Westminster and Fife) and no new dukedoms have been created during the twentieth century. Marquesses are also a disappearing group, the last one having been created in 1937. The last five non-royal marquessates all went to retiring Indian viceroys (Lords Linlithgow, Aberdeen, Curzon, Reading and Willingdon). Slightly more resilient have been the earls and viscounts, who are shown in Table 7.2 as numbering 321 in 1980. An earldom has been the normal reward for retiring military commanders and Prime Ministers, and a total of just 13 have been created since 1945. Retiring MPs who have served in

TABLE 7.2   *Peerage, baronetage and knightage (1980)*

Title	Number	
Duke	26	
Marquess	37	
Earl	194	
Viscount	127	
Baron (hereditary)	476	
Baron (life)	346	
Total peerage		1 206
Baronet, Knight and Dame		4 546

Note: the total of baronets, etc., does not include peers who also have knighthoods. After allowing for minors and Irish peers, 1,148 peers have seats in the House of Lords.

Source: calculated from *Whitaker's Almanack.*

government have often been rewarded with a viscountcy and such titles continued to be created until the 1960s, with a total of 50 new creations since the second world war.

All the above 'higher' titles have long since been eclipsed in number by the growth of the baronage. A number of industrialists were made barons towards the end of the nineteenth century, with the main growth in industrial peerages occurring after 1905. Land ceased to be regarded as a necessary concomitant of a peerage after the turn of the century, and a majority of the industrial barons had little or no land at all. The majority of barons have been created during this century and a barony can now be regarded as the normal peerage title, with the increased significance of life peerages reinforcing this trend. Life peerages have been used since the 1850s for law lords, but were introduced in a modified form in 1958 as a way of bringing outsiders into parliament without running the risk of swamping future parliaments with the descendants of new hereditary peers. These various changes crystallised in the mid-1960s: in 1963 Scottish peers and hereditary peeresses were given the right to sit in the House of Lords,[10] in the same year hereditary peers were permitted to renounce their peerages, and in 1965 the last hereditary peerage was awarded.[11]

A majority of the 556 peerages created in the period 1901–57 went to former MPs, most of whom are included in the 'other' category in Table 7.3. A number of these MPs had interests in business, and Table 7.3 shows a breakdown of the business backgrounds of the twentieth-century peers. A major category includes those from industry, especially shipping, textiles and steel.

TABLE 7.3   *Background of new peers (1901–57)*

Background	Number
Industry	91
Law	91
Land	46
Rentiers and directors	42
Finance	27
Newspapers	12
Commerce	12
Other	235
Total	556

Source: from Guttsman (1963) table 11, p. 122.

The financial and commercial categories together account for almost as many new peers as do the landowners, though many of those classified as lawyers or 'directors' will have had interests in manufacturing, commerce or finance. Whilst such classifications are somewhat arbitrary, it is clear that the peerage has come to represent the business class as a whole rather than simply its landed segment. More particularly it encompasses the politically active members of the business class, since many of those who were not MPs were prominent party activists or supporters.

Outside the peerage are the important categories of baronet and knight. Many of the nineteenth-century industrialists were made baronets rather than barons, and the size of the baronetage increased rapidly. Many other baronets are the descendants of or are themselves backbench MPs and Lord Mayors. A decline in the number of baronet creations occurred in 1946–51 when the Labour government refused to create any new baronets except those traditionally accorded to retiring Lord Mayors of London. Although the succeeding Conservative governments reversed this policy, no baronets have been created since 1964. The ending of what are essentially hereditary knighthoods thus coincided with the virtual ending of hereditary peerages.[12] The title of 'knight', therefore, is the sole remaining non-peerage title, and there are essentially three categories of knighthood. Knighthoods in the old-established Orders are now virtually reserved for members of the peerage who are close to the royal family, and the number of such knighthoods is extremely small.[13] Knighthoods in the Order of the British Empire are normally reserved for higher civil servants, military officers and others in the public sector; whilst the title of knight bachelor is most commonly used for people from business.

It can be said that the predominant tendency of at least the post-war period has been towards the creation of a two-tier system of titular honours. The two tiers are knights and life peers, with there being fairly clear criteria for 'promotion' from one to the other. A knighthood is now the normal award for those prominent in business and for their counterparts in the civil and military services, and can normally be expected at a certain stage of their careers. Life peerages tend to be awarded to those knights who have shown themselves to be solid and reliable supports of the state and who it is desired to bring into the political arena on a more formal basis. This system of titular honours, and its massive tail of lesser honours such as CBEs and OBEs, is firmly grounded in what has survived of the gentlemanly meaning system of the nineteenth century. This meaning system is itself an integral part of a framework of traditional ideas which encompasses much of British life. At the heart of this system of ideas is the institution of the monarchy, which brings to a focus the political activities of the state and the criteria of social status which legitimate those activities.[14] In order for the monarchy to play its role in legitimation it is necessary that its links with the status system be continually put into evidence through the normal round of court activities (royal visits, state openings of parliament, etc.) and through periodic royal celebrations such as coronations, jubilees and weddings.

A useful analysis of the importance of the coronation and other royal ceremonials has been given by Shils and Young, who employ Durkheimian ideas to see such occasions as ritualised affirmations of the values which underpin British society and constitute its moral order.[15] They see the royal family as symbolising the family in general, and they go on to interpret specific features of the coronation service as symbols of different aspects of the value consensus. Whilst their detailed symbol interpretation may be questioned, a more fundamental criticism concerns the underlying assumptions of value consensus and value consistency which are to be found in their argument.[16] Their central assumptions are that all members of British society assent equally to the same coherent set of values and that these values are a necessary, and possibly sufficient, condition of social integration. Whilst it must be recognised that no such moral consensus has ever existed in Britain, much of the Shils and Young view can be accepted if it is taken as applying to the *dominant* meaning system which legitimates the system of stratification. Inequalities are accepted by people in a factual and not a moral way, just as they accept the weather – there is apparently nothing that the person in the street can do about it.[17] These inequalities, however, are justified by those who are privileged in terms of particular vocabularies of motive, and those who are less privileged will voice similar justifications when required to make some general statement about their perceptions of stratification. The importance of the monarchy to the system of titular honours is that it reinforces the ideas of 'public service' and 'merit' in the allocation of honours and so provides a vocabulary of motive which can be employed in public contexts to legitimate inequality. The significance of such rituals as coronations and royal weddings lies in the fact that they are occasions on which this vocabulary of motive can be concretised and rehearsed in front of a national audience, so making it all the more acceptable as a way of justifying inequalities.

The old-boy network

The business class as a whole is characterised by a high degree of social cohesion, the main supports of this cohesion being its system of kinship and its educational experience. The kinship system is marked by a high degree of homogamy. In part this is due to the fact that those who interact frequently with one another in business circles and other formal contexts are more likely to choose marriage partners from among the families of those with whom they interact than they are to choose from other social circles. This reinforces the segregation of the business class from other classes, transforming it from a mere social category into a group of intermarrying families. This is furthered by more conscious family strategies pursued by members of the business class. The cultural and material practices aimed at perpetuating the family name and increasing the family property result, as an unintended consequence, in the perpetuation of a homogamous privileged class. Within the business class there is to be found a dominant status group within which the level of homogamy is even higher. In this status group the perpetuation of the family name and tradition is of particular significance, as is securing access to political power. This status group – the establishment – emerged as an important social and political force during the nineteenth century, and has been seen as a central element in the 'antique' or 'patrician' character of the British state.[18] Attempts by members of the establishment to marry off their children to those who are eligible socially, economically and politically guarantee the perpetuation of a homogamous and intensive kinship network.[19] Commenting on this fact, Sampson remarks that such a kinship tree is the basis for a high degree of informality in the numerous social contacts which it involves:

It would be wrong . . . to see this tree as the result of a dynastic plot, whereby old families deliberately ally themselves to future prime ministers: nor is there a secret wand which dukes can wave, which puts their sons-in-law into the cabinet. . . . The importance of the tree, in fact, is not so much the power it confers, as the access and system of communication – a common background and attitude, a common language and trust, reinforced by Eton, Oxbridge, and country house life, which leads one member to prefer another.[20]

The establishment has been defined as 'a body of people, acting, consciously or subconsciously, together, holding no official posts through which they exercise their power but nevertheless exercising a great influence on national policy'.[21] That is to say that whatever formal power its members may or may not have, the establishment has a considerable amount of informal power and influence. This influence is based upon its role as a means of opinion formation: it facilitates communication among those who are familiar with one another, share a common social background and meet in numerous formal and informal contexts. Henry Fairlie – reputedly the originator of the word 'establishment' – has argued that 'The idea of the Establishment is concerned less with the actual exercise of power than with the established bodies of prevailing opinion which powerfully, and not always openly, influence its exercise.'[22]

The establishment is not simply a group of people; it is a group of people allied around certain social institutions. These institutions are the Conservative party, the Church of England, the public schools and ancient univiersities, the legal profession and the Guards regiments; and the life-style of establishment members has traditionally been expressed in the 'season' of social activities in London, the gentlemen's clubs and country-house life. The dominant status group can be termed 'an establishment' so as to bring out the 'assumption of the attributes of a state church by certain powerful institutions and people'.[23] In its informal aspect the establishment is the 'old-boy network', the system of social contacts which stem from family and education. Such contacts 'are maintained largely in an informal manner by membership of the London clubs, by the social round of dinners and parties as well as, more formally, in business meetings and at official events'.[24] The contacts which constitute this informal network of social relationships are important in the determination of the life chances of those who go through the public school and Oxbridge system. Their contacts 'both facilitate their careers and enable them to have more influence in the posts where they eventually land'.[25]

The significance of a public school and Oxbridge education lies not so much in any enhanced educational attainments which students might earn as in the part which it plays in the structuration of the establishment. This structuration occurs in the two dimensions of integration and recruitment.[26] The integrative role of the public schools concerns their ability to mould the ideas and outlook of their pupils and to ensure frequent and easy interaction among them. Their role in recruitment relates to their importance in determining the degree of social closure in positions of privilege. The system of sponsored mobility ensures that those who already have positions of privilege are those who determine the qualifications required for recruitment to these same positions.[27] Without any deliberate intention to bias patterns of recruitment, those who have the appropriate qualifications 'just happen' to be the products of the public schools. The Nuffield mobility study has shown that those from the business class and the higher levels of the service class tend to obtain a similar level of educational qualifications regardless of whether they go to a grammar school or a public school. Almost regardless of schooling they achieve those cultural assets which are important conditions for entry into top jobs.[28] The generalised social assets of social background and life-style which ensure the attainment of these cultural assets are not, however, sufficient for entry to these jobs. Entry is enhanced by the possession of those particular opportunities within a social milieu which involve the mobilisation of contacts, friendship and kinship. It is these particularised social assets – summed up in the phrase 'old-boy network' – which are monopolised by the public school boys and are relatively less available to the products of the grammar schools.[29]

The ethos of the public schools, an ethos which has trickled down to the major grammar schools, legitimates the structure of life chances with which they are associated. The privileges and interests of the dominant status group, and of the wider business class, are justified in terms of notions of service and the common good which derive from the nineteenth-century gentleman ideal. As Vaizey has argued,

The public schools train people to accept the cultural norms which they exist to perpetuate. . . . As a result, whole numbers of people walk about convinced that they are wearing themselves to the bone for the public good; they are really walking about keeping the Establishment going.[30]

The public school ethos justifies the privileges enjoyed by members of the business class. This social class, with the establishment as its leading edge, is able to perpetuate its privileges and is able to justify this to its own members in terms of a vocabulary of motive which legitimates its position in relation to the members of other classes.

The Nuffield mobility study discovered that 6.5 per cent of their respondents in a national sample had attended public or direct-grant schools. Within the service class alone, between 15 and 35 per cent of people attended public schools: 15 per cent at the lower levels and 35 per cent at the upper levels.[31] There were too few members of the business class in their sample to get any assessment of participation rates, but it is clear that the proportion from public schools was high.[32] It nevertheless remains the case that a number of people from the business class have gone through the grammar-school system. Looked at from a different point of view it is possible to examine the class composition of the public schools. Two-thirds of the boys from public schools and a half of the boys from the direct-grant schools were service class or business class.[33] It is clear that business-class children who attend the public or direct-grant schools come into contact with a large number of service-class children, and with a reasonable number from the lower levels of the stratification system. The Clarendon schools[34] are relatively more exclusive in their recruitment, with a greater proportion of children from the business class. Perhaps the most important consequence of these patterns of recruitment is that many of those children from the service class who achieve intergenerational or career mobility into the business class have been 'primed' for their new positions by their public school education and the social contacts which they made during their school days.

A further important finding of the Nuffield study was that those who lack the generalised social assets of social background and life-style may nevertheless achieve equivalent educational assets as those who do, if they are able to gain entry to a lesser public school rather than a grammar school. Through the lesser public schools they are able to acquire certain of the required cultural assets for entry to top jobs. Since the number of top jobs has been increasing faster than the growth in the size of the business class, there are inevitably openings for those who have the appropriate generalised social assets without the particularised assets embodied in the old-boy network, and for those from the lower levels who have simply the educational assets. It may be surmised that those from the service class who are relatively impoverished in social assets will tend to enter the newer, expanding sectors of the economy, and that they will be concentrated among those who have been designated internal capitalists. Once in such positions of privilege, such people have opportunities to accumulate the assets in which they are deficient. They are thereby able to further their own careers and – more importantly – to smooth the entry of their own children into similar positions.

The public schools and the ancient universities are crucial mechanisms for the integration and recruitment of both the establishment and the wider business class. They maintain a high level of closure in access to positions of privilege, and they ensure the assimilation of those newcomers who have necessarily to be granted entry. Directly through their 'old boys', and indirectly through the influence which they exert on the older grammar schools, they bring about a social and cultural unity among those who possess superior life chances. In the monopoly sector of the economy; in parliament, government, the military and para-military forces, and the civil service; in the church and the legal profession; and in the various bodies and agencies which bridge the gap between the state and the economy are to be found people with a similar social and cultural background and a similar set of life chances. Within and between these various occupational milieux, intragenerational and intergenerational mobility is frequent. It is with a description of these milieux and the connections between them that the rest of this section will be concerned.

For most of this century government has been dominated by the Conservative party; and over that period the Conservative party has been dominated by the products of the public schools. Table 7.4 shows that the proportion of public school MPs on the Conservative benches dropped immediately after 1950 from 83 per cent to 70 per cent and fluctuated between 75 and 80 per cent after

TABLE 7.4   *Educational background of Conservative MPs*
(1945–74)

Education	Numbers of MPs at each election									
	1945	1950	1951	1955	1959	1964	1966	1970	1974a	1974b
Eton	55	77	75	75	70	66	56	62	54	47
All public	169	240	216	264	274	232	199	243	222	206
Oxford	62	94	99	106	104	66	80	93	89	76
Cambridge	46	62	68	74	79	88	64	75	76	76
All universities	131	187	199	217	219	190	169	208	198	186
Total no. of Conservative MPs	213	297	320	343	365	301	253	330	297	277

Note: the two entries for 1974 relate to the two elections of that year.

Source: adapted from Mellors (1978) table 4.2 on pp. 41–4, and table 4.4 on p. 48.

1955. Within this figure the role of Eton has been particularly great, though the proportion has fallen from 26 per cent to 17 per cent. Whilst the proportion of all boys attending public schools is extremely low, three-quarters of all Conservative MPs in the post-war period were public school boys. Similarly, over 50 per cent of Conservative MPs attended Oxford or Cambridge colleges: and the proportion of Oxbridge MPs was actually higher in 1974 than in 1945. Almost a half of all Conservative MPs in the post-war period have followed the public school and Oxbridge route. The public school MPs tend to have the safest seats and to form a core of long-serving Conservative MPs whose numbers are periodically enlarged by the arrival at Westminster of non-public school, non-Oxbridge men when the party wins sufficient marginal seats to attain power. For this reason those from the public schools are likely to be the more established and influential MPs. Other things being equal, they are more likely to attain ministerial posts. At this level, and especially in the Cabinet, the products of Eton and Harrow have been particularly prominent.

In the period 1901–57 a total of 317 MPs moved on to the House of Lords (included in the total in Table 7.3). Allowing for inheritance of titles and for MPs who died in office, about one-fifth of MPs could expect to end their careers with a peerage. Of these 317 peers, 180 had been backbench MPs and 137 had been ministers. Given the small number of ministers – 89 ministers out of 635 MPs in 1980 – it is clear that the chance of attaining a peerage is greater for those who reach ministerial posts.[35] The normal grade of peerage for a minister or backbencher is a barony, nowadays a life peerage, and backbenchers have also qualified for the lesser titles of baronet and knight. Those who have held senior posts as Leader of the House or Home Secretary, and those who have been Speaker have traditionally been able to expect a viscountcy; and a Prime Minister has usually been able to claim an earldom.[36] As well as a peerage being a reward at the end of a political career, it can be used in the time-honoured way for building up a bloc of support in the Lords – though the declining power of the Lords makes this less necessary than in the past. More usually a peerage can be a short cut to a parliamentary career, obviating the need for selection and election in a parliamentary constituency.

A major branch of the state in which the upper levels are dominated by public school boys is the civil service. For much of the nineteenth century recruitment to the civil service continued to show traces of the old patronage system. Each department handled its own recruitment and civil servants were often dependent upon political patrons. It was only in the 1870s that a unified Permanent Civil Service was established with recruitment based on a competitive entrance examination. This reform enabled the civil service as a body to develop an autonomous power base for itself. Whilst politicians had only a temporary tenure of office, the civil servants were *permanent* officials who were no longer dependent upon the support of their ministers. Whilst this autonomy certainly created the possibility for an 'impartial' civil service, it also created the possibility for civil servants to evolve their own policy preferences and to pursue their own interests in opposition to those of the government. This is not, of course, to say that they will corruptly pursue their personal pecuniary interests. Rather, their independent power base makes it possible for civil servants to evolve a collective interest in policy stability and smooth operating procedures which would conflict with the attempts of radical politicians to change the direction of state policy. It has been argued that this constitutes an inbuilt conservatism which reinforces Conservative policies and counteracts Labour policies.[37]

The Treasury has been dominant within the administration, one of its Permanent Secretaries being the head of the civil service. Through this control over personnel and its more general control over departmental expenditure the Treasury is able to structure administrative action and practices in other departments of the state. For this reason, the balance of power between politicians and civil servants within the Treasury is all-important. Some of the implications of this will be taken up in the next section.

The number of senior civil servants is about 1,000, though only 150 or so hold the important ranks of Assistant Secretary or above. Kelsall has shown that the proportion of the latter who had been to public or private schools fell from 71 per cent in 1939 to 60 per cent in 1950. According to Halsey and Crewe a total of 63 per cent had attended public, private or direct-grant schools. By contrast, the proportion of top civil servants who attended Oxford or Cambridge fluctuated only between 60 and 66 per cent over this same period.[38] The higher the level, the more exclusive is the pattern of recruitment. Four-fifths of Under Secretaries and above in 1939 were from public schools, and in 1960 and 1970 the proportion had fallen to two-thirds. The proportion of Permanent Secretaries from public schools fell from just over two-thirds in 1900–19 to just over one-half in 1945–63.[39] Similarly, within the high-status diplomatic corps the public school and Oxbridge men predominated. Over the period 1900–50, 92 per cent of ambassadors to major countries were from the public schools with one-third from Eton alone. In the 1960s and 1970s the proportion of public school ambassadors had fallen only slightly to four-fifths.[40] These figures show an apparent decline in the importance of the public schools, with most of the drop being taken up by the direct-grant grammar schools. Since the mid-1970s, following the hostile actions of the Labour government, many of the grant-aided grammar schools have gone fully independent and so the proportion of public school civil servants might be expected to rise once more. Boyd has, however, questioned the reality of the trend towards greater openness, claiming that the figures are distorted by the relaxation of normal recruiting procedures for the war-time intake. Boyd suggests that the situation may now be returning to normal as the people recruited after the war begin to reach the top posts.[41]

Those who enter the top rungs of the civil service hierarchy, therefore, tend to come from the exclusive educational background which is characteristic of the business class. Their integration into this class, and into its dominant status group, is furthered by the operation of the honours system. Although the Order of the British Empire is the normal order for civil servants, those in the Foreign Office and the diplomatic service normally receive honours in the Order of St Michael and St George. Honours below the level of CBE are used in a relatively non-discriminating way, but the CBE (or CMG) itself is awarded more or less automatically on promotion to the level of Assistant Secretary. Under Secretaries can expect a Commandership in the more prestigious Order of the Bath (CB), whilst those who are promoted to Deputy Secretary are well-placed for a knighthood (either KBE or KCMG). At the top of the civil service hierarchy a Permanent Secretary will be 'promoted' to a knighthood in the Order of the Bath (KCB), and those who continue to give service at this level might become superior knights grand cross (GBE).[42] This articulation of the honours system with career promotion makes it a highly effective mechanism of social control. There is sufficient uncertainty about the receipt of an honour for the system to create a climate of conformity. Furthermore, by accepting the system of meanings which are embedded in the honours, civil servants are assenting to the whole hierarchy of status. Those members of the business class who choose to enter the civil service will find that the system of promotion and honours which awaits them reinforces their commitment to the ideas and values to which they have already been exposed at school and university. It is this set of social meanings which legitimates the structure of unequal life chances from which these people benefit.

This pattern of recruitment whereby those who enter a profession are engaged both in a process which materially supports the privileged life chances of themselves and their fellow class members *and* in a process which legitimates these privileges is an equally marked characteristic of the military and para-military services of the state. The military and the police are the obvious forces of surveillance, discipline and repression through which the state attempts to ensure that its powers are not undermined by those it regards as its enemies. In this they are aided by the secret services, which operate in more clandestine ways to the same end. From the late nineteenth century the army was transformed by a

series of reforms which changed the formal patterns of recruitment
and grouped together the old battalions into county regiments.
Recruitment to the officer corps was controlled by an examination
similar to that introduced for the civil service. This same process of
formalisation and bureaucratisation also led to the ending of the
dual system of regimental and brevet ranks whereby an officer
performing a subordinate technical role in a regiment might be
accorded the status of a higher brevet rank. Competitive entry into
Sandhurst and Woolwich colleges and then into the officer corps
was the normal pattern of recruitment, though some men were
commissioned from the universities and a few were promoted from
the lower ranks. After the second world war an attempt was made
at initiating a form of 'scientific selection' involving character
assessment by a selection board. Many administrative functions
have been transferred upwards from the regiments to the divisions
into which they are grouped. The process of centralisation
significantly increased the number of staff posts for senior officers
who carried out the day-to-day tasks of operational administration
at Division, District and Ministry level. It is at the Ministry of
Defence that the army generals are joined by their equivalents in
the naval and air forces to liaise with the ministers and civil servants
in the formulation of defence policy.[43] Table 7.5 shows the
numbers of top officers in each of the three military services.[44]

TABLE 7.5   *Top military officers (1980)*

Rank	Number	
General	10	
Lieutenant-General	8	
Major-General	78	
Total army		96
Admiral	5	
Vice-Admiral	15	
Rear-Admiral	45	
Total navy		65
Air Chief Marshal	6	
Air Marshal	11	
Air Vice-Marshal	39	
Total air force		56
Total		217

Source: calculated from *Whitaker's Almanack*.

Prior to the introduction of army selection boards the use of a competitive entry examination favoured those who came from the public schools because of the predominance of these schools in education up to the age of 18. These schools had the resources and the desire to prepare their pupils for the necessary examination.[45] The selection boards were introduced in an attempt to open up recruitment to the officer corps, but they have in fact involved a continuation of the old pattern. From 1900 to 1939 the proportion of entrants to Sandhurst who had been educated at public or private schools increased. After the second world war the proportion from grammar schools increased somewhat, and by 1960 had risen to 23.2 per cent.[46] At the senior levels of the officer corps, though, the situation was different. Among those holding the top ranks of general or lieutenant-general (see Table 7.6) the proportion of public school boys increased from one-third in 1897

TABLE 7.6   *Educational background of top army officers (1897–1971)*

Education	Number of officers					
	1897	1913	1926	1939	1959	1971
Major boarding school	17	29	31	33	21	24
Other public school	6	5	6	4	8	5
Private	17	12	5	6	0	0
Other	23	12	6	2	7	3
Total	63	58	48	45	36	32

Note: the figures relate to the ranks of lieutenant-general and above.

Source: adapted from Otley (1973) table 4 on p. 198, and table 8 on p. 199.

to three-quarters in 1926, four-fifths in 1939 and 1959 and nine-tenths in 1971. Indeed, the figure for 1971 was the highest in the whole of the 160-year period studied by Otley. There seems to be an unconscious selection of those who possess the gentlemanly leadership qualities which are already possessed by those who are doing the selecting.[47] As Miliband has argued:

Those who control and determine selection and promotion . . . are likely to carry in their minds a particular image of how a high ranking civil servant or military officer ought to think, speak, behave and react; and that image will be drawn in terms of the class to which they belong.[48]

That class is, of course, the business class; and the people who have the desired qualities of leadership and who epitomise that class image are, of course, the products of the public schools. Without any consciously intended bias the established old boys sponsor the recruitment of each new generation of old boys.

Although the army has been extensively studied, there have been few investigations of the navy or the air force. In one of the few studies Boyd discovered that the proportion of former public school boys among naval officers of rear-admiral rank or above increased from one-fifth in 1960 to one-third in 1970. The corresponding figures for RAF officers of rank air vice-marshal and above show an increase from one-half to two-thirds. Both the navy and the air force, therefore, showed a rise in the number of public school officers, with the figures for the navy rising to four-fifths in both 1960 and 1970 if Dartmouth is counted alongside the public schools.[49] These figures are pointers to the continuing monopolisation which the business class is able to exercise over the higher levels of the officer corps in each of the three services. Nowhere is this more true than in the army regiments comprising what used to be known as the Household Brigade. Colloquially known as the 'Guards', regiments such as the Coldstreams and Grenadiers have the highest status within the army. There are between 500 and 600 Guards officers, and they are far more likely to be drawn from the establishment than is the case for the rest of the officer corps. Indeed, the military section of the establishment might fairly be taken to include the general officers together with many officers from the Guards and Cavalry regiments.[50]

The police force has never constituted a particularly popular occupational milieu for members of the business class, only the Chief Constables showing any tendency to be recruited from this class. This is not the case in the allied Security Service or the Secret Service. Until the end of the nineteenth century secret intelligence was organised on a largely amateur basis with control exercised by leading politicians through networks of peripatetic agents and informers. This began to change at about the same time that the army was reorganised: in 1909 the Security Service (MI5) was set up, and in 1911 the Secret Intelligence Service (SIS) was formed.[51]

MI5 is responsible for internal security and at its lower levels is closely linked with the Special Branch of the Metropolitan Police and its equivalents in the provincial forces. At the higher levels of the organisation its top officials are directly responsible to the Home Secretary and the Prime Minister and they move easily around the world of the top civil servants. SIS is responsible for the collection of secret information from foreign countries. It is nominally responsible to the Foreign Office and both in London and abroad its top officials are in close contact with top civil servants in that department and the Diplomatic Service as well as maintaining liaison with military intelligence and the Ministry of Defence.[52] Recruitment to both MI5 and SIS was initially on an exclusively gentlemanly basis through the old-boy network. This was partly a requirement of secret work, depending as it does on the ability of agents to trust one another: and who could better be trusted than one's associates from school and university and those whose family were well-known to one's own. In part the pattern of recruitment was simply a consequence of the search for 'suitable' professions by those from a gentlemanly background. Although the second world war saw a lessening of the amateur characteristics of secret intelligence-gathering, recruitment to the higher echelons continues to be monopolised by the business class – though, for obvious reasons, there is no systematic information on the social background of senior members of the intelligence profession.[53]

The scions of the privileged classes have monopolised the military profession from the time that it became established as an integral part of the national state. The same is true of the church and the law, which have provided profitable sources of income for the younger sons of the great families and have acted as essential adjuncts of the state's social control functions of legitimation and discipline. Whilst the declining salience of religion in British life and the increasing bureaucratisation of the church have perhaps restricted the power and influence of the Church of England in modern Britain, it remains the established church and, as such, retains an important role in state ceremonials. There were, in 1980, 144 Church of England bishops, of whom the 26 most senior sit in the House of Lords.[54] The bishops, still appointed by the Prime Minister and the Patronage Secretary, stand at the head of a formal hierarchy in which many important managerial functions have been delegated to the numerous deans, provosts and archdeacons. The legal profession does not have this hierarchical structure, though the judicial bench remains the position of highest status in the profession and the members of the judiciary are themselves formed into a hierarchy of superior and subordinate courts. The number of top judges is similar to the number of Church of England bishops: in 1980 there were 136 people holding the most senior judicial appointments (see Table 7.7). Those judges who are required to sit in the House of Lords to enable it to fill its role as a Court of Law have, since 1850, been accorded peerages for life. The House of Lords does, of course, include many other former lawyers and judges among its membership, just as it includes former churchmen who have received peerages in their own right.

TABLE 7.7   *The senior judiciary (1980)*

	Number
Law Lords	13
High Court	95
Scottish Court of Session	21
Northern Ireland Supreme Court	7
Total	136

Note: with the Law Lords are counted the Lord High Chancellor, the Master of the Rolls and the Lord Chief Justice of England. The Court of Appeal is counted with the High Court.

Source: calculated from *Whitaker's Almanack*.

Both the law and the church show a high degree of self-recruitment, showing the existence of church families and lawyer families. Those who fill the senior posts within the professions tend to be recruited from the business class, and especially from its dominant status group. In the years 1900–9 there were 43 per cent of judges whose fathers had been in the legal profession and 18 per cent whose fathers or uncles had been judges. By the period 1960–9 both of these figures had increased: 52 per cent of judges had lawyer fathers and 29 per cent had fathers or uncles who were judges. In terms of their general patterns of recruitment the judiciary of the 1960s and 1970s had four-fifths of its members drawn from the public schools, with 39 per cent of judges in 1963 coming from Eton, Winchester, Harrow and Rugby alone. In the same year 18 per cent of judges were the sons or close relatives of peers.[55] For the period 1947–70 it has been found that a consistent two-thirds of bishops were public school products, though the proportion of Oxbridge bishops declined slightly from nine-tenths in 1920–39 to four-fifths in 1960-70. Bishops remain a university-based group, but the proportion of university men among the clergy as a whole has decreased. This has led to a greater educational separation of the episcopacy from the parochial clergy. At the same time the tendency for bishops to come from church families has increased to a current level of over one-half.[56]

Within the business world itself the same patterns of gentlemanly recruitment are to be observed. The previous chapter has shown that business leaders tend to be drawn from the wealthiest levels of society and that the inheritance of wealth plays a crucial role in the perpetuation of business fortunes. Among the business leaders there is a high degree of self-recruitment, and the top positions tend to be monopolised by members of the establishment. Erickson's widely cited study of intergenerational mobility among steel executives suggests that there may have been a move towards relatively greater openness. Erickson's study shows that the proportion of steel executives whose fathers were major landowners declined towards the end of the nineteenth century and has since remained at a level of between 7 and 10 per cent. The main group of steel executives consisted of those whose fathers had come from a business background, though she shows that the proportion declined from 55 per cent in the period 1905–25 to 34 per cent in 1953.[57] Although the proportion of steel executives drawn from the professions may have increased, the main increase was in those who came from clerical and skilled manual backgrounds. Erickson argues that the decline in the proportion coming from a background of business leadership is mainly due to the failure of sons to take up positions in family firms. During the inter-war years, she argues, the heirs of these family businesses found more congenial career lines available to them and so began to abdicate from control in their own firms.[58] Further light is thrown on this by two other discoveries from Erickson's research: the proportion of steel executives from public schools remained constant at about one-third, and the proportion of Oxbridge executives increased from 15 per cent in 1905–25 to 21 per cent in 1935–47. These figures suggest that a gentlemanly education was important for the second- and third-generation steelmen who remained in the industry and for the financiers who dominated the boards of the steel companies in the inter-war years.[59] That is, the entrepreneurial capitalists and finance capitalists continued to follow the public school and Oxbridge route, though Erickson gives no information on how important this route might be for those internal capitalists who enter business leadership from outside the ranks of the business class.

Erickson's findings are drawn from one particular industry and relate to those who are actively involved in management; they have less relevance to the question of the social background of other participants in business leadership. In particular, the finance capitalists whose interests spread across the monopoly sector as a whole are not covered by the research. Fortunately, a number of recent studies have concentrated their attention on precisely these groups. Whitley has shown that one-half of the directors of the largest industrial companies in 1970 were former public school boys, with one-sixth coming from Eton alone. Among financial companies it was found that about one-half of the directors of clearing banks and large insurance companies in 1957 came from six major public schools, with one-third from Eton alone. Among clearing-bank directors of 1970 three-quarters were public school products: one in three from Eton and one in ten from Winchester. Between one-half and three-quarters of bank directors had graduated from Oxford or Cambridge.[60] The most recent figures on the social origins of business leaders, presented in Table 7.8, seem to show that the proportion of directors of top companies coming from a background of 'substantial property or wealth'[61] has declined over the period 1906–70 for both industrial and financial companies. An important qualification to be made about these figures, however, is that those whose fathers were in the professions were classified as being of upper-middle-class origins. In view of the monopolisation of the higher levels of the older professions by members of the business class, this is an important qualification. This is particularly so in the light of the authors' comment on the table: 'Most of the change is accounted for by the increase in the percentage of directors . . . drawn from "upper middle class" backgrounds: particularly important here is a rise in the proportion of those whose fathers were in professional occupations.'[62] Whilst only 6 or 7 per cent of directors were from such a background in 1906, fully a quarter were in 1970. Indeed, the total of 'upper-class' and upper-middle-class origins over the period shows virtually no decline at all. Clearly, any alteration in the openness of recruitment to positions of business leadership must be far less than the figures in Table 7.8 suggest.

TABLE 7.8   *Social origins of business leaders (1906–70)*

	%o from propertied and wealthy background					
	1906	1920	1946	1952	1960	1970
Top 50 industrials	62	61	53	48	50	39
Top 30 financials	78	73	71	68	69	55

Note: in the original source the figure for financial companies in 1952 was incorrectly given as 48. This has been corrected above.

Source: adapted from Giddens and Stanworth (1978) table 4–6, p. 219.

It has been argued that the business class has exercised a high degree of closure over recruitment to a number of privileged occupations, and that members of the establishment have been able to monopolise those positions of greatest privilege through the mechanisms of sponsored mobility. The business class, despite the diversity in occupations followed by its members, has been able to achieve a high degree of unity and cohesion because of the amount of circulation that takes place between positions of privilege. Mobility between the various class situations, both intergenerationally and intragenerationally, has been frequent enough to counteract any tendency towards the formation of distinct class fractions. Although there are to be found church families, army families, political families and business families, there is sufficient circulation to prevent the formation of separate groups. Whilst this is true for the business class as a whole, it is particularly true for the establishment. Members of the establishment have been able to perpetuate its position as a group with an extremely high degree of social solidarity.[63] Table 7.9 shows the occupations of Conservative MPs prior to their election. The fact that many of these occupations are continued concurrently with membership of the House of Commons is a further source of solidarity between the various positions of privilege. It can be seen that the largest groups of Conservative MPs in 1945 were those

TABLE 7.9 *Occupational background of Conservative MPs (1945–74)*

Occupation	Numbers of MPs at each election									
	1945	1950	1951	1955	1959	1964	1966	1970	1974a	1974b
Barrister	37	51	55	60	66	58	48	50	50	47
Solicitor	4	10	11	11	12	13	13	13	11	9
Civil service	3	2	2	1	1	0	0	0	1	1
Diplomatic service	8	11	12	14	14	17	14	12	11	8
Military	30	30	31	36	30	20	11	12	4	4
Director	67	100	109	113	122	85	74	94	83	81
Banking and finance	1	4	2	2	3	3	4	7	13	13
Commerce and insurance	7	8	10	14	17	13	9	13	11	9
Farmer, landowner	25	28	32	30	36	36	34	35	28	22
Other	31	53	56	62	64	56	46	94	85	83
Total	213	297	320	343	365	301	253	330	297	277

Note: the two entries for 1974 relate to the two elections of that year.

Source: adapted from Mellors (1978) table 5–2, pp. 62–6.

from the law, the armed forces, business and the land. By 1974 the number of military MPs had fallen away considerably, even after allowing for the inflation of the figures in the immediate post-war period by those who were commissioned for war service. The law, business and industry all held their positions over the thirty-year period, indicating that the social composition of the Conservative party has altered only very slightly. It is perhaps particularly significant that two-thirds of Conservative MPs in the 1970s held a business directorship at the time they sat in the House.[64]

The solidarity and cohesion of the business class has depended on the extent to which it could maintain its social distinctiveness. Members of the business class have, however, increasingly tended to eschew the language of class division in formulating images of their own social positions. Instead, they have projected a view of themselves as part of an extensive 'middle class'.[65] Such a claim is made realistic by the formal position of business executives and directors at the head of managerial hierarchies, and by the absence of any obvious distinctions between those professional employees who do and those who do not come from a background of wealth and privilege. Unequal life chances are, in many respects, invisible; and this invisibility lends plausibility to the image of a continuous and hierarchical middle class. The business class, then, has a degree of social anonymity: it no longer sees itself and is no longer seen by others as constituting a distinct social class. Business class and service class appear to merge into a unified middle class. As Giddens has argued, the decline of conspicuous consumption means that 'the wealthy now maintain a much lower profile'.[66] Although it makes sense to speak of a partial normative convergence between business class and service class, there remains a crucial economic and relational differentiation between them – and the survival of the establishment involves the survival of distinctive normative standards and a distinct life-style. Centred on the honours system and its gentlemanly values, this meaning system is a crucial aspect of social legitimation. The hierarchical character of the system of honours, leading from the peerage through the knightage to the 'officers' and 'members' of the Order of the British Empire, overlays the formal hierarchies of authority which permeate modern British society. In this way the norms of the establishment are an important condition for the plausibility of the image of a hierarchical middle class. The social anonymity of the business class is, paradoxically, enhanced by the survival of the gentlemanly meaning system. The relational differentiation of the business class from the service class is apparent in the myriad contexts of informal interaction, in patterns of intermarriage, and in political and leisure activities. The life-style of the establishment constitutes a paradigm of social behaviour for other members of the business class. Those who are outside the established social circles may follow the precepts of this paradigm because they aspire to the higher social status with which it is associated, or they may simply accept the activities it enjoins as being normal features of a civilised life-style. The tendency for members of the business class to live in half-timbered houses in areas commonly referred to as the 'stockbroker belt' or to live in carefully modernised cottages in 'rural' areas, their preference for private education and private health care, and their regular involvement in such sporting activities as golf, racing, shooting and hunting are all reflections of the salience of the established life-style.

The life-style of the nineteenth-century establishment had been based on the country house and the London season, and both of these persisted until well into the middle of the twentieth century. The rising value of agricultural land after the second world war and the continued development of supplementary sources of income enabled landowners to retain their country houses and perhaps also a London house or flat, though many landed gentlemen sold their country houses and moved into farmhouses or estate cottages. At the same time the life of the country gentleman or the gentleman farmer remained a popular option for those who worked in commerce or industry. In central London areas such as Belgravia retain their cachet of social exclusiveness and are magnets for the wealthier members of the business class. For example, 50 of the residents of some 120 houses in Eaton Square in 1976 were listed in *Who's Who*.[67] Although the extravagant 'jet-set' life-style of the wealthy members of the entertainment world is of marginal importance to the establishment as a whole, an impressive round of balls and other social occasions continue to fill the summer months of June and July. But the traditions of the London season, like many of the country houses, are progressively decaying. Court presentation of well-connected young ladies ended in 1958, the Queen Charlotte Ball surviving for a further twenty years without royal sponsorship. Entry to London Society is now gained through inclusion on 'The List' of about 150 debutantes compiled each year by the editor of *The Tatler*. Similarly, Royal Ascot, Henley and Wimbledon, like autumn grouse-shooting parties, are pale reflections of what they have been in former years. These social activities derived their importance from the role they played in class structuration, and Giddens has claimed that this is still the case. Ascot and the grouse moor continue to function, albeit in an attenuated way, 'because they help establish and maintain the personal contacts and the kinship ties upon which the existence of a propertied class depends'.[68] One institution which has frequently been seen as a bastion of the old-boy network of personal contacts is the London club, where bonds of friendship and informality are supposed to have been cultivated.

Entry to the London gentlemen's clubs has always been through a formal and explicit process of sponsorship, with large entry fees and annual subscriptions to back up their exclusivity. They have offered accommodation for country members, dining and drinking facilities, and congenial surroundings for the transaction of business and political matters. It is in the latter respect that greatest attention has been paid to them by commentators.[69] Pall Mall, the heart of London's clubland, has been depicted as a venue for political conspiracy and business intrigue. However true such claims may be, the more important function of the clubs has undoubtedly been to encourage that informality in business and political contacts which has been the essential counterpart of the more formal features of the old-boy network.[70] Those who join a club can be sure of meeting people from a similar social background to themselves and who they may meet in other business, political and professional contexts. Those who do not join a club will find themselves that much more isolated from the contacts and connections which might be of use to them or to members of their families. Taking the largest industrial and financial companies together, it has been found that 28 per cent of directors were members of nine major clubs, with the individual entrepreneurs being the least clubbable of all.[71] Club membership has, however, been of declining importance since the 1950s. Giddens and Stanworth have shown that 57 per cent of the directors of the top companies they studied were members of major London clubs in 1906, with the level dropping to 51 per cent in the 1950s and 1960s and to an all-time low of 35 per cent in 1970.[72] Clubs continue to be convenient lunch-time drinking places, but they are far less popular and far less likely to be centres of discussion and intrigue. The smaller clubs may be important for particular cliques, for example the gambling clubs, but the large clubs have lost much of their importance in the cultivation of informality.

The old-boy network continues to exist and to have important social consequences, but its informal mode of operation has increasingly been supplemented by more formal methods of recruitment and political representation. Despite its decline in the post-war period, however, the establishment remains an important social force. Guttsman has argued that in so far as the establishment continues to monopolise positions at the higher levels of the political system and to assist their children to reach similar positions they constitute the core of a 'ruling class'.[73] The establishment, unlike the eighteenth-century oligarchy, does not constitute a totally separate political grouping; it is simply the dominant status group within the business class:

From a strongly endogamous group, whose individual 'houses' drew their support largely from immovable property of which the head of the family was only the temporary custodian, it has grown into a section of the population much less closely interlinked by ties of marriage and based very frequently on widely dispersed and more transient industrial and commercial property and varied economic interests.[74]

It would be wrong to depict the business class as totally closed to outsiders. The evidence presented here and in the previous chapter has shown that this is not the case. Whilst members of the business class are able to pass on their own privileges to their children, the growth in size of the occupational groups which they have traditionally monopolised has necessitated relatively high rates of recruitment from other sectors of society. As a result, many newcomers are to be found in the fringes of the business class, and together with others who reach high managerial and professional positions they may be able to secure access to the business class for their children. It is difficult to judge the full extent of such openness at the upper levels, since studies of those reaching the peaks of their careers in the 1960s and 1970s are concerned with people who were educated before the second world war and whose fathers were educated before the first world war. The new entrants to the business class are still likely to have followed the public school and Oxbridge route and so are likely to be endowed with the appropriate habits of class behaviour, but they are far less likely to owe their positions to the operation of the old-boy network. Educational assets and technical expertise are increasingly prominent factors in executive recruitment and in recruitment to the professions. Any changes in rates of upward mobility into the business class may not yet be apparent in the available statistics. The relative decline of the establishment and the possibility of increased openness mean that the traditional means of representing the interests of the business class within the political system are likely to prove increasingly inadequate.

The establishment and corporatist politics

Analyses of the distribution of power in British society have tended to be cast in terms of either an 'elite' approach or a 'decision-making' approach. The much over-worked notion of an elite[75] has been used to point to the supposed fact that all those at the head of the various formal and informal institutional hierarchies coalesce to form a unified and all-pervasive ruling class which effectively dominates British political and economic life. On the other hand, the decision-making perspective holds that it is wrong to equate 'position' with 'power'. It is argued that power may only be studied through detailed research into processes of decision-making within particular institutions. The location of power is always an empirical question.[76] In recent years the 'instrumentalism' of these approaches has been countered by 'structuralist' perspectives which emphasise that the power of individuals and groups is constrained by the structures in which they are located and that such structures may exercise an independent influence over the social process.[77] I wish to suggest that rather than being alternative explanatory theories, these various approaches are complementary to one another. The 'elite' approach stresses the mechanisms of sponsorship, informality, institutional overlap, and social solidarity which are specific to the practices of the establishment. By contrast the 'decision-making' approach is far more relevant to the procedures followed within the bureaucracies of the state and the large enterprises, and to the parliamentary lobbying carried out by organised interest groups. Finally, the structuralist approach emphasises the limitations imposed on both the establishment and interest groups by the general structure of the state and economy in which they are constrained to operate.

At the same time that the debates between these various approaches came to a head[78] there was an increased interest in the concept of 'corporatism'. This concept was taken up and elaborated in an attempt to come to grips with important social changes which were under way in the 1960s. Theories of corporatism have tended to draw on many of the arguments of the decision-making and structuralist approaches, and it can be argued that their increasing relevance in opposition to 'elite' approaches reflects the relative decline in the position of the establishment which has been documented in the previous section. Underlying the emergence of corporatist ideas and practice has been the move towards collectivism. The latter refers to the tendency for the interests of capital and labour to be expressed through organised groups and associations. Interests are collectively organised and collectively pursued within an alignment of state and economy which is fundamentally different from that which prevailed during the late nineteenth and the early twentieth century. The state has adopted an increasingly interventionist role and undertakes the task of the 'efficient' management of social resources. In following this more purposive strategy it is necessary that those who man the state should be able to arrive at some conception of the direction of state activity. In the past the interests of the dominant class were translated into state policy by virtue of the presence of members of this class within the state and by the informal practices of the establishment. The increasingly collectivised organisation of interests and the increasing power of the labour movement have necessitated the adoption of more formal practices, of which corporatism has been the most-discussed variant. Corporatism, then, can be defined as

> a system of interest representation in which the constituent units are organised into a limited number of singular, compulsory, non-competitive, hierarchically ordered and functionally differentiated categories, recognised or licensed (if not created) by the state and granted a deliberate representational monopoly within their respective categories in exchange for observing certain controls on their selection of leaders and articulation of demands and supports.[79]

Although the prominent manufacturers had gradually been assimilated into the establishment, the increased power and autonomy of provincial industrial areas created strains which the establishment found it difficult to cope with. As a mode of interest representation, the establishment depended upon the restriction of key decision-making powers to relatively limited social circles. The growth in the number of large enterprises, the increasing bureaucratisation of corporate decision-making and the relative isolation of provincial industrialists from the London-based establishment combined to produce important centres of power outside the dominant status group. Cities such as Birmingham, where the nineteenth-century electoral principle had its roots, became the focii for the collective organisation of capital. The first really important umbrella organisation for the representation of capitalist interests was the Engineering Employers Federation, formed in 1896. This was the most important of the new types of employers' organisations aimed at countering the growing strength of organised labour. The fact that capital was not sufficiently concentrated to support strong national associations is apparent in the fact that the EEF was limited to one industry.[80] In the years leading up to the first world war a number of regional organisations were set up, but it was only during the war that attempts to form such organisations coincided with greater economic concentration and state intervention. In the years 1916 to 1919 three important 'peak' organisations were formed, including the Federation of British Industry. Although the government found it useful to operate through such organisations – and to play one off against another – they never achieved sufficient authority over their members and were never fully co-opted into the structure of the state. What emerged, therefore, was not corporatism but 'pluralism', a system which Middlemas has characterised as involving a 'corporate bias'.[81] Governments could draw upon the existence of such organisations when it suited them, but policy was more usually formulated through the personnel and practices of the establishment.

Post-war governments withdrew from the interventionist practices of the Lloyd George coalition, but the industrial problems of the 1920s and the economic collapse of 1929 stimulated a growth in government intervention during the 1930s. The Bank of England, in conjunction with the Treasury, became the main arm of a state-sponsored programme of reconstruction. The Bank, still privately owned, co-ordinated the efforts of the clearing banks which had been forced to intervene in corporate affairs in order to protect their loans and overdrafts to ailing enterprises. Where the government became more directly involved, it preferred to operate through trade associations rather than through the FBI.[82] Although this trend considerably enhanced the power of national business organisations, there was still no real attempt to regularise their constitutional position. A number of prominent industrialists and politicians did advocate more formal corporatist policies, involving a return to old Tory principles of the benevolent use of state power, but these ideas had little influence.[83] Of particular importance was the attempt to involve trades unions in the evolving structure of political power. The main moves in this direction occurred after 1926 when the unions were losing membership and their power was weakening. It was not a case of government co-opting a powerful group, but of an attempt to co-opt the union movement at a time of weakness so as to legitimate the dominant business/government axis of power through ·the mythology of tripartism.[84]

Beer has summarised the pluralism of the 1920s and 1930s as follows:

> Associations among producers were greatly encouraged and were brought into regular contact with government. In this structure of 'quasi-corporatism', the relationship was neither one of business pressure groups dictating to government nor of government agencies planning the activities of business. Decisions were made, rather, in a process of bargaining and negotiation.[85]

That is to say that business organisations undertook the role of voluntary brokers between business and government. In playing this role they adopted new techniques of 'lobbying' to influence government.[86] This role was considerably altered during the second world war, when the government reimposed the type of direct controls which had been used in the previous war. The post-war Labour government extended these controls and introduced all the institutional mechanisms of effective economic planning. A whole range of advisers, directors and controllers with large staffs supervised particular sectors of the economy. The personnel were drawn from the major companies and trade associations, which often continued to pay them whilst they were on secondment. This pattern generated a high level of interchange of personnel, information and resources between business and the various agencies and ministries.[87] The Labour government also nationalised the Bank of England and the coal, electricity, gas, telegraph and transport industries, all being sectors of the economy where government or municipal regulation had a long history. In this way some earlier corporatist practices were drawn fully into the orbit of the state.[88] The planning and regulatory mechanisms introduced by the Labour government, though, were directed towards the short-term objective of relieving particular shortages; and once this was achieved the mechanisms were gradually dismantled.

Following its electoral success in 1951 the Conservative party retained much of the structure left by the Labour government. In particular, 'Keynesian' economic techniques were extended and refined as a support of the mixed economy and welfare state. Keynesianism is essentially a system of economic control which operates through the mechanisms of the market. With its emphasis on technique and rationality, its success depended upon the ability of the government to sustain the idea that economic policy is not a 'political' matter but a technical affair to be managed by experts. The central procedure of such a policy was demand management: by expanding or contracting the level of demand in the economy it was possible to influence such things as the level of employment and the rate of economic growth with the minimum of interference in autonomous economic mechanisms.[89] But no policy can be simply 'technical'; there are always implicit or explicit goals to be identified. The key point about Keynesianism was that the experts who were to manage economic policy were the civil servants and officials of the Treasury and the Bank of England.[90] Keynesianism was managed by members of the establishment, since these branches of the state and the financial companies of the City of London were at the heart of that social group. It was within the establishment that the ends of economic policy were formulated and clarified; and it was through the time-honoured mechanisms of informal consultations and personal contacts that this policy was supported. This was, of course, an uneasy combination, since the Keynesian principles of technique and rationality ran counter to the gentlemanly principles of particularism and informality.[91]

Towards the end of the 1950s a number of factors contrived to undermine the Keynesian polity. The worsening position of Britain in the world economy undermined the ability of the economy to sustain an upward path of economic growth, and aggressive foreign competition stimulated a domestic company take-over boom. At the same time the increased power of the labour movement destroyed the consensus upon which Keynesianism had depended. The power of organised labour had gradually built up during the 1950s and put an increasing strain upon the limited corporatist practices which had been introduced.[92] The concurrent weakening of the establishment meant that the evolving corporatist system found it increasingly difficult to rely upon the support which the establishment had originally provided. It was for these reasons that a number of prominent politicians and businessmen began to argue for the introduction of newer and more effective mechanisms of corporatist interest representation. As Schmitter has argued

the more the modern state comes to serve as the indispensable and authoritative guarantor of capitalism by expanding its regulative and integrative tasks, the more it finds that it needs the professional expertise, specialised information, prior aggregation of opinion, contractual capability and deferred participatory legitimacy which only [corporatism] . . . can provide.[93]

Moves towards planning were initiated by the Macmillan government and led to the formation of the National Economic Development Council and the reform of the Treasury in 1962. With the Labour government of 1964 the pace of these changes was hastened by the creation of the Department of Economic Affairs, the Ministry of Technology and the Industrial Reorganization Corporation. In 1965 the Confederation of British Industry was formed with the encouragement of the government and joined the Trades Union Congress in regular tripartite discussions. These new organisations and agencies were explicitly aimed at planning and industrial reconstruction and remained separate from the Treasury, which retained control over short-term economic policy.[94] This 'disarticulation' of the state apparatus precluded any coherent economic strategy. The 1960s, then, saw a number of new corporatist institutions and practices, but a truly corporatist policy was not pursued. The demise of some of these new organisations and their replacement with yet others gives a great deal of truth to Jessop's claim that the 1970s produced only a 'relatively ineffective system of tripartite discussions among incompletely incorporated and fragmented peak organisations and representatives'.[95]

The establishment now retains only an attenuated form of its old social role. Whilst it may still be considered as a dominant status group within the business class, its economic and political role has been fundamentally altered. As a mode of interest representation the establishment has declined in significance as new corporatist institutions and practices have arisen. The pace of decline was increased when the levels of economic concentration, product diversification and internationalisation reached their post-war levels. The finance capitalists who have emerged as an important group within the business class are the key agents in the corporatist practices whose pace of economic evolution increased so rapidly in the post-war period. These finance capitalists are co-opted onto the councils, agencies and regulatory bodies formed by the state, and they are active in strengthening such organisations as the CBI in its role as the collective voice of the monopoly sector of the economy. The ability of the business class to secure the political conditions of its own structuration, to perpetuate its own privileges, depends on whether the finance capitalists are able to consolidate the trend towards a corporatist mode of interest representation.

This book has traced the development of the modern business class as a transmutation of the various upper classes which preceded it in history. The upper classes in Britain have undergone many transmutations during the period described in this book, each transformation being related to determinate forms of state and economy. The superior life chances of the feudal baronage had to be perpetuated through the direct and frequent use of coercive measures, but the business class is able to perpetuate its position through more routine and less obvious means. The business class depends for its privileges on the operation of 'impersonal' mechanisms of class structuration. The dynamics of the modern capitalist economy are such that those who head the major business enterprises reproduce their own class privileges, and those of their fellow class members, at the same time that they determine the pace and pattern of economic production. The business class remains a propertied class, but its personal wealth is buttressed by the complex structure of 'institutional' ownership which now encompasses so much of the economy. This structure of economic relations is fundamental to the maintenance of the privileges of the business class. Transformations in the state and the economy have been both causes and consequences of the rise and decline of the various upper classes which have played their part in British social development. The future of today's upper class is dependent upon the prospects of the contemporary political economy – but that is another story.

Notes to Chapter 7

1. See, for example, Guttsman (1963) and Aaronovitch (1961). See also Bottomore (1964), Parry (1969) and Giddens (1974).
2. Giddens (1973) p. 286.
3. This brief summary draws on the extended arguments of O'Connor (1973) and Habermas (1973).

4. See also Habermas (1979).
5. This committee was set up in the 1920s following a scandal over the sale of honours.
6. See Richards (1963).
7. The chief honours tout at this time was Maundy Gregory. See Macmillan (1954).
8. Knight bachelor is the lowest grade of knighthood and does not involve membership of a particular Order of knighthood.
9. See Hanham (1960) p. 279, and Sampson (1965) p. 341.
10. Prior to this time Scottish peers elected some of their number to represent them in the Lords.
11. Although it is still possible to create hereditary peerages, none have in fact been created since Lord Margadale in 1965. It is clear that governments will now only use this option under exceptional circumstances.
12. It should be noted that although *new* hereditary titles are no longer being created, existing holders can continue to pass on their titles to their descendants. It will, therefore, be a very long time before demographic factors could lead to the total disappearance of hereditary title-holders.
13. Certain exceptions to this will be discussed later in the chapter. Full details on the history and current position of the various types of title can be found in any recent volume of *Debrett's Peerage and Baronetage*. See also Perrott (1968), Sutherland (1968) and Bence-Jones and Montgomery-Massingberd (1979).
14. See the discussion of Bagehot on the 'dignified' and 'efficient' aspects of the Victorian state in Chapter 5.
15. Shils and Young (1953).
16. See Birnbaum (1955) and Miliband (1969).
17. See Mann (1970), and Blackburn and Stewart (1975).
18. See Nairn (1977), Nairn (1979) and Thompson (1965).
19. See the kinship diagrams given in Lupton and Wilson (1959).
20. Sampson (1962) p. 20.
21. Hollis (1959) p. 171.
22. Fairlie (1959) p. 202. Fairlie is reputed to have introduced the word in 1955 in the context of the Burgess and Maclean espionage cover-up.
23. Thomas (1959) p. 20.
24. Parry (1969) p. 87.
25. Blondel (1963) p. 243. See also Rex (1974).
26. See Giddens (1974) p. 120, and Miliband (1969) pp. 65–6.
27. Turner (1960).
28. Halsey *et al.* (1980). See also Parkin (1979) pp. 54, 62–3.
29. See Bourdieu and Saint-Martin (1978).
30. Vaizey (1959) p. 36. See also Gathorne-Hardy (1977) and Wakeford (1969).
31. Halsey *et al.* (1980) table 4.8, p. 60.
32. In 1953 over 90 per cent of top income recipients were paying fees for their children's education. See Vaizey (1959) p. 26.

33. Halsey *et al.* (1980) table 4.5, p. 53.
34. Charterhouse, Eton, Harrow, Merchant Taylors', Rugby, St Pauls, Shrewsbury, Westminster and Winchester.
35. Guttsman (1963) table 11, p. 122; Guttsman (1974) p. 25.
36. Even before the virtual ending of hereditary titles this right had not been exercised since Eden became Lord Avon.
37. See Kellner and Crowther-Hunt (1980) and Balogh (1959).
38. Kelsall (1955); Halsey and Crewe (1969); Boyd (1973) pp. 50ff.
39. See Harris and Garcia (1966); Giddens and Stanworth (1978) p. 215.
40. Boyd (1973) pp. 53, 88ff.
41. Boyd (1973). See also Kelsall (1974).
42. The three Orders discussed here each have three top levels of Commander, Knight and Knight Grand Cross. These are abbreviated as follows: CBE, KBE, GBE (Order of the British Empire); CMG, KCMG, GCMG (Order of St Michael and St George); CB, KCB, GCB (Order of the Bath). On civil servants and honours see Sampson (1965).
43. See Stanhope (1979) and Otley (1973).
44. In addition to the officers included in the table various honorific ranks were as follows: nine field-marshals, eight admirals of the fleet and nine marshals of the Royal Air Force.
45. Otley (1973) p. 194.
46. Op. cit., table 5 on p. 198, and table 3 on p. 197.
47. See Salaman and Thompson (1978). See also Giddens and Stanworth (1978); Abrams (1962); Otley (1966).
48. Miliband (1969) p. 59.
49. Boyd (1973).
50. See Sampson (1965) and Raven (1959).
51. The names of these organisations have changed a number of times, and I here use the modern names. The SIS is sometimes known popularly as MI6.
52. An overview of the development of the secret services can be found in Deacon (1980) and Bunyan (1977).
53. Some insight can be gained from a close study of the honours lists and biographical directories. Directors-General of the two secret services are the formal counterparts of the civil servants and military officers who qualify for knighthoods, and so a knighted civil servant who is unusually secretive about his official post is a likely candidate for the head of one of these services.
54. This total is made up of 45 assistant bishops, 56 suffragan bishops, 41 diocesan bishops, and two archbishops. There were, in addition, 6 bishops in the church in Wales. The Scottish established church is presbyterian and so has a totally different structure.
55. See Giddens and Stanworth (1978); Boyd (1973) pp. 80ff.
56. See Thompson (1974) p. 201; Morgan (1969); Sampson (1965); Boyd (1973) p. 57.
57. Erickson (1959) table 2, p. 12.
58. Ibid. p. 21.

59. Ibid. pp. 33, 37.
60. See Lupton and Wilson (1959); Boyd (1973) pp. 80ff; Whitley (1974) p. 76.
61. Giddens and Stanworth (1978) p. 247 n. 32. This group are termed 'upper class'.
62. Ibid. p. 220.
63. For a general review of studies of such circulation see Perkin (1978).
64. See also Guttsman (1963); Guttsman (1974) table 6–7, p. 34; Johnson (1973).
65. See Fidler (1981).
66. Giddens (1976).
67. Thomas (1979).
68. Giddens (1976) p. 66. See also Giddens (1979b).
69. For a discussion of the London clubs see Perrot (1969), Sampson (1965) and Lejeune (1979).
70. Lupton and Wilson (1959) pp. 187, 192.
71. See Whitley (1974) and Channon (1979).
72. Giddens and Stanworth (1978) p. 247.
73. Guttsman (1963) pp. 355–6.
74. Ibid. p. 134.
75. For reasons discussed in Chapter 5 I do not myself think it useful to employ the word 'elite'. I use it here simply to designate a particular research tradition.
76. The various issues have been thoroughly aired by the contributors to Stanworth and Giddens (1974). See also Bottomore (1964) and Parry (1969).
77. See Lukes (1974).
78. See in particular the debate between Miliband and Poulantzas in Urry and Wakeford (1973).
79. Schmitter (1974) p. 13. See also Panitch (1979), Crouch (1979), Strinati (1979), Winkler (1977) and Beer (1965).
80. See Brady (1943) p. 157; Blank (1973) p. 12; Whigham (1973). For a discussion of the earlier chambers of commerce see Ilersic and Liddle (1960).
81. See Middlemas (1979) p. 373. The term 'pluralism' is introduced by Schmitter (1974) to characterise this looser and less hierarchical system of interest representation; it is not used in the sense commonly found in American political science to characterise a 'democratic' political system.
82. See McEachern (1980) on the role of the Iron and Steel Federation.
83. Carpenter (1976). See also Gamble (1974), Harris (1972) and Budd (1978).
84. I am grateful to Dominic Strinati for discussions on this point.
85. Beer (1965) p. 297.
86. See Finer (1955), (1956) and (1958).
87. See Westergaard and Resler (1975) p. 202; Brady (1943) pp. 182ff.
88. The iron and steel industry was nationalised late in the life of the government and was soon denationalised by the Conservatives.

89. See Shonfield (1965) p. 101.
90. See Brittan (1964) and Longstreth (1979).
91. Skidelsky (1979) pp. 63–4; Jessop (1980).
92. See Skidelsky (1979) pp. 69–70.
93. Schmitter (1974) p. 27.
94. See Shonfield (1965), Jessop (1980) and Grant and Marsh (1977).
95. Jessop (1980) p. 54.

Bibliography

In all cases the date of first appearance follows the author's name. Occasionally an additional date appears after the publisher's name, and refers to an English language edition or a particular reprint.

Aaronovitch, S. (1961) *The Ruling Class* (London: Lawrence & Wishart).
Abrams, P. (1962) 'Democracy, Technology and the Retired British Officer', in Huntingdon (1962).
Abrams, P. (ed.) (1978) *Work, Urbanism and Inequality* (London: Weidenfeld & Nicolson).
'A Citizen' (1938) *The City Today*, New Fabian Research Bureau, Pamphlet 38 (London: Gollancz).
Acton Society (1956) *Managerial Succession* (London: Acton Society Trust).
Aldcroft, D. (1964) 'The Entrepreneur and the British Economy, 1870–1914', *Economic History Review*, vol. 17.
Amin, S. (1975) 'Toward a Structural Crisis of World Capitalism', *Socialist Revolution*, vol. 23.
Anderson, P. (1964) 'Origins of the Present Crisis', in Anderson and Blackburn (1965).
Anderson, P. (1974a) *Passages from Antiquity to Feudalism* (London: New Left Books).
Anderson, P. (1974b) *Lineages of the Absolutist State* (London: New Left Books).
Anderson, P. and Blackburn, R. (eds) (1965) *Towards Socialism* (London: Fontana).
Ardant, G. (1975) 'Financial Policy and Economic Infrastructure of Modern States and Nations', in Tilly (1975).
Ashley, M. (1952) *England in the Seventeenth Century* (Harmondsworth: Penguin).
Ashton, R. (1979) *The City and the Court, 1603–1643* (Cambridge: Cambridge University Press).
Aston, T. (ed.) (1965) *Crisis in Europe, 1560–1660* (London: Routledge & Kegan Paul).
Atkinson, A. B. (1973) *Unequal Shares* (Harmondsworth: Penguin).
Atkinson, A. B. (1975) *The Economics of Inequality* (London: Oxford University Press).

Atkinson, A. B. and Harrison, A. J. (1978) *Distribution of Personal Wealth in Britain* (Cambridge: Cambridge University Press).

Aydelotte, W. O. (1962) 'The Business Interests of the Gentry in the Parliament of 1841–47', in Barber and Barber (1965).

Bagehot, W. (1867) *The English Constitution* (London: Fontana, 1963).

Balogh, T. (1959) 'The Apotheosis of the Dilettante', in Thomas (1959).

Barbalet, J. M. (1980) 'Principles of Stratification in Max Weber: An Interpretation and Critique', *British Journal of Sociology*, vol. 31.

Barber, B. and Barber, E. G. (eds) (1965) *European Social Class: Stability and Change* (New York: Macmillan Co.).

Barlow, F. (1955) *The Feudal Kingdom of England, 1042–1216* (London: Longmans Green).

Barnett, C. (1969) 'The Education of Military Elites', in Wilkinson (1969).

Barnett, C. (1970) *Britain and Her Army, 1509–1970* (Harmondsworth: Allen Lane).

Barnett, C. (1972) *The Collapse of British Power* (London: Eyre Methuen).

Bateman, J. (1883) *The Great Landowners of Great Britain* (Leicester University Press, 1971).

Bechhofer, F., *et al.* (1978) 'Structure, Consciousness, and Action: A Sociological Profile of the British Middle Class', *British Journal of Sociology*, vol. 29.

Becker, J. F. (1971) 'On the Monopoly Theory of Monopoly Capitalism', *Science and Society*, vol. 35.

Becker, J. F. (1973) 'Class Structure and Conflict in the Managerial Phase', *Science and Society*, vol. 37.

Bédarida, F. (1976) *A Social History of England, 1851–1975* (London: Methuen, 1979).

Bell, C. and Newby, H. (1974) 'Capitalist Farmers in the British Class Structure', *Sociologia Ruralis*, vol. 14.

Bence-Jones, M. and Montgomery-Massingberd, H. (1979) *The British Aristocracy* (London: Constable).

Bendix, R. (1956) *Work and Authority in Industry* (New York: Wiley).

Bendix, R. (1964) *Nation-Building and Citizenship* (New York: Wiley).

Bendix, R. (1978) *Kings or Peoples* (Berkeley: University of California Press).

Berkowitz, S. (1978) 'The Determination of Enterprise Groupings through Combined Ownership and Directorship Ties', *Social Networks*, vol. 1.

Berle, A. A. and Means, G. C. (1932) *The Modern Corporation and Private Property* (New York: Macmillan Co.).

Bermant, C. (1971) *The Cousinhood* (London: Eyre & Spottiswoode).

Best, G. (1971) *Mid-Victorian Britain* (London: Weidenfeld & Nicolson).

Bindoff, S. T. (1950) *Tudor England* (Harmondsworth: Penguin).

Birnbaum, N. (1955) 'Monarchs and Sociologists', *Sociological Review*, vol. 3.

Birnie, A. (1935) *An Economic History of the British Isles* (London: Methuen, 1965).

Blackburn, R. M. and Stewart A. (1975) 'The Stability of Structural Inequality', *Sociological Review*, vol. 23.

Blank, S. (1973) *Industry and Government in Britain* (Farnborough: Saxon House).

Bloch, M. (1940) *Feudal Society* (London: Routledge & Kegan Paul, 1961).

Blondel, J. (1963) *Voters, Parties and Leaders* (Harmondsworth: Penguin).

Bolton, J. L. (1980) *The Medieval English Economy, 1150–1500* (London: Dent).

Bonfield, L. (1979) 'Marriage Settlements and the "Rise of the Great Estates": Their Demographic Aspects', *Economic History Review*, vol. 32.

Bottomore, T. B. (1964) *Elites in Society* (Harmondsworth: Penguin, 1966).

Bottomore, T. B. and Rubel, M. (1956) *Karl Marx: Selected Writings* (Harmondsworth: Penguin, 1963).

Bourdieu, P. (1971) 'Cultural Reproduction and Social Reproduction', in Brown (1973).

Bourdieu, P. and Saint-Martin, M. de (1978) 'Le Patronat' (The Directorate), *Actes de la Recherche en Sciences Sociales*, vol. 20/21.

Boyd, D. (1973) *Elites and their Education* (London: NFER).

Brady, R. A. (1943) *Business as a System of Power* (New York: Columbia University Press).

Braun, R. (1975) 'Taxation, Sociopolitical Structure, and State-Building', in Tilly (1975).

Brenner, R. (1977a) 'Agrarian Class Structure and Economic Development in Pre-Industrial Europe', *Past and Present*, vol. 76.

Brenner, R. (1977b) 'The Origins of Capitalist Development', *New Left Review*, no. 104.

Brewer, J. (1976) *Party Ideology and Popular Politics at the Accession of George III* (Cambridge: Cambridge University Press).

Briggs, A. (1963) *Victorian Cities* (Harmondsworth: Penguin, 1968).

Brittan, S. (1964) *The Treasury Under the Tories* (Harmondsworth: Penguin).

Bromley, J. S. and Kossman, E. H. (eds) (1960) *Britain and the Netherlands* (London: Chatto & Windus).

Brown, R. (ed.) (1973) *Knowledge, Education, and Cultural Change* (London: Tavistock).

Budd, A. (1978) *The Politics of Economic Planning* (London: Fontana).

Bulmer-Thomas, I. (1965) *The Growth of the British Party System*, vol. 1 (London: Baker).

Bunyan, T. (1977) *The History and Practice of the Political Police in Britain* (London: Quartet).

Burnham, J. (1941) *The Managerial Revolution* (Harmondsworth: Penguin, 1945).

Bury, J. B. (ed.) *Cambridge Medieval History*, vol. 3 (Cambridge: Cambridge University Press).

194 *Bibliography*

Cannadine, D. (1980) *Lords and Landlords* (Leicester University Press).
Carchedi, G. (1975) 'On the Economic Identification of Social Classes', in Carchedi (1977).
Carchedi, G. (1977) *On the Economic Identification of Social Classes* (London: Routledge & Kegan Paul).
Carpenter, L. R. (1976) 'Corporatism in Britain', *Journal of Contemporary History*, vol. 11.
Carus-Wilson, E. M. (1954) *Medieval Merchant Venturers* (London: Methuen).
Chambers, J. D. and Mingay, G. E. (1966) *The Agricultural Revolution, 1750–1880* (London: Batsford).
Checkland, S. G. (1964) *The Rise of Industrial Society in England, 1815–1885* (London: Longman).
Checkland, S. G. (1975) *Scottish Banking: A History* (Glasgow: Collins).
Cipolla, C. M. (1973) *The Fontana Economic History of Europe*, vol. 4(1) (London: Fontana).
Clapham, J. H. (1938) *An Economic History of Modern Britain*, vol. III: *1887–1929* (Cambridge: Cambridge University Press).
Clark, G. K. (1962) *The Making of Victorian Britain* (London: Methuen).
Clay, C. (1974) 'Marriage, Inheritance, and the Rise of Large Estates in England', *Economic History Review*, 2nd Series, vol. 27.
Cole, G. D. H. (1955) *Studies in Class Structure* (London: Routledge & Kegan Paul).
Coleman, D. C. (1973) 'Gentlemen and Players', *Economic History Review*, vol. 26.
Coleman, D. C. (1975) *Industry in Tudor and Stuart England* (London: Macmillan).
Corrigan, P. (ed.) (1980) *Capitalism, State Formation and Marxist Theory* (London: Quartet).
Crewe, I. (ed.) (1974) *Elites in Western Democracy* (London: Croom Helm).
Critchley, J. (1978) *Feudalism* (London: Allen & Unwin).
Crouch, C. (1979) 'The State, Capital, and Liberal Democracy', in Crouch (1979).
Crouch, C. (ed.) (1979) *State and Economy in Contemporary Capitalism* (London: Croom Helm).
Crozier, D. (1965) 'Kinship and Occupational Succession', *Sociological Review*, vol. 13.
Dahrendorf, R. (1957) *Class and Class Conflict in Industrial Society* (London: Routledge & Kegan Paul, 1959).
Dahrendorf, R. (1979) *Life Chances* (London: Weidenfeld & Nicolson).
Dandeker, C. (1978) 'Patronage and Bureaucratic Control', *British Journal of Sociology*, vol. 29.
Dangerfield, G. (1936) *The Strange Death of Liberal England* (London: Constable).
Davidoff, L. (1973) *The Best Circles* (London: Croom Helm).
Deacon, R. (1980) *A History of British Secret Service* (London: Granada).
Deane, P. (1969) 'Great Britain', in Cipolla (1973b).

Denholm-Young, N. (1969) *Country Gentry in the Fourteenth Century* (Oxford: Clarendon Press).

Devine, T. M. (1971) 'Glasgow Colonial Merchants and Land, 1770–1815', in Ward and Wilson (1971).

Devine, T. M. (1975) *The Tobacco Lords* (Edinburgh: Donald).

Diamond Commission (1975) *Royal Commission on the Distribution of Income and Wealth* (London: HMSO).

Dockray, K. R. (1979) 'Japan and England in the Fifteenth Century', in Ross (1979).

Duby, G. (1962) *Rural Economy and Country Life in the Medieval West* (London: Edward Arnold, 1968).

Elias, N. (1939a) *The Civilizing Process*, vol. I (Oxford: Blackwell, 1978).

Elias, N. (1939b) *Über den Prozess der Zivilisation, Zweiter Band* (Frankfurt: Suhrkamp, 1977).

Elton, G. R. (1953) *The Tudor Revolution in Government* (Cambridge: Cambridge University Press).

Erickson, C. (1959) *British Industrialists: Steel and Hosiery, 1850–1950* (Cambridge University Press).

Fairlie, H. (1959) 'The BBC', in Thomas, (1959).

Fidler, J. (1981) *The British Business Elite* (London: Routledge & Kegan Paul).

Field, F. (ed.) (1979) *The Wealth Report* (London: Routledge & Kegan Paul).

Finer, S. (1955) 'The Political Power of Private Capital', part I, *Sociological Review*, vol. 3.

Finer, S. (1956) 'The Political Power of Private Capital', part II, *Sociological Review*, vol. 4.

Finer, S. (1958) *Anonymous Empire* (London: Pall Mall, 1966).

Finer, S. (1975) 'State- and Nation-Building in Europe: The Rise of the Military', in Tilly (1975).

Foster, J. (1974) *Class Struggle and the Industrial Revolution* (London: Weidenfeld & Nicolson).

Fourquin, G. (1970) *Lordship and Feudalism in the Middle Ages* (London: Allen & Unwin, 1976).

Fraser, D. (1976) *Urban Politics in Victorian England* (Leicester Univesity Press).

Fulton Commission (1969) *The Civil Service* (London: HMSO).

Gamble, A. (1974) *The Conservative Nation* (London: Routledge & Kegan Paul).

Ganshoff, F. L. (1944) *Feudalism* (London: Longmans Green, 1952).

Gathorne-Hardy, J. (1977) *The Public School Phenomenon* (London: Hodder & Stoughton).

Gerth, H. H. and Mills, C. W. (eds) (1948) *From Max Weber* (London: Routledge & Kegan Paul).

Gerth, H. H. and Mills, C. W. (1954) *Character and Social Structure* (London: Routledge & Kegan Paul).

Giddens, A. (1973) *The Class Structure of the Advanced Societies* (London: Hutchinson).

Giddens, A. (1974) 'Elites in the British Class Structure', in Stanworth and Giddens (1974).

Giddens, A. (1976) 'The Rich', *New Society*, 14 Oct.

Giddens, A. (1979a) *Central Problems in Social Theory* (London: Macmillan).

Giddens, A. (1979b) 'An Anatomy of the British Ruling Class', *New Society*, 4 Oct.

Giddens, A. and Mackenzie, G. (eds) (1981) *Class and the Division of Labour* (Cambridge: Cambridge University Press).

Giddens, A. and Stanworth, P. (1978) 'Elites and Privilege', in Abrams (1978).

Girouard, M. (1978) *Life in the English Country House* (New Haven: Yale University Press).

Glenerster, H. and Pryke, R. (1964) 'The Public Schools', in Urry and Wakeford (1973).

Goldthorpe, J. (1980) *Social Mobility and Class Structure* (Oxford: Clarendon Press).

Goldthorpe, J. H. and Bevan, P. (1977) 'The Study of Social Stratification in Great Britain, 1946–1976', *Social Science Information*, vol. 16.

Goodwin, A. (ed.) (1962) *The European Nobility in the Eighteenth Century*, 2nd ed. (London: A. & C. Black).

Gourvish, T. R. (1980) *Railways and the British Economy, 1830–1914* (London: Macmillan).

Grant, W. and Marsh, D. (1977) *The Confederation of British Industry* (London: Hodder & Stoughton).

Grassby, R. (1970a) 'English Merchant Capitalism in the Late Seventeenth Century: The Components of Business Fortunes', *Past and Present*, vol. 46.

Grassby, R. (1970b) 'The Personal Wealth of the Business Community in Seventeenth Century England', *Economic History Review*, vol. 32.

Guttsman, W. L. (1963) *The British Political Elite* (London: MacGibbon & Kee).

Guttsman, W. L. (1974) 'The British Political Elite and the Class Structure', in Stanworth and Giddens (1974).

Habakkuk, J. (1939) 'English Landownership, 1680–1740', *Economic History Review*, vol. 10.

Habakkuk, J. (1950) 'Marriage Settlements in the Eighteenth Century', *Transactions of the Royal Historical Society*, 4th Series, vol. 32.

Habakkuk, J. (1953) 'The Economic Functions of English Landowners in the 17th and 18th Centuries', *Explorations in Entrepreneurial History*, vol. 6.

Habakkuk, J. (1960) 'The English Land Market in the Eighteenth Century', in Bromley and Kossman (1960).

Habakkuk, J. (1962) 'England', in Goodwin (1962).

Habermas, J. (1973) *Legitimation Crisis* (London: Heinemann, 1976).

Habermas, J. (1979) 'Conservatism and Capitalist Crisis' (Interview), *New Left Review*, no. 115.

Halévy, E. (1913) *England in 1815* (London: Benn, 1924).

Halsey, A. H. and Crewe, I. (1969) 'Surveys and Investigations: Social Survey of the Civil Service', in Fulton Commission (1969).

Halsey, A. H., *et al.* (1980) *Origins and Destinations* (Oxford: Clarendon Press).

Hanham, H. J. (1959) *Elections and Party Management* (London: Longmans Green).

Hanham, H. J. (1960) 'The Sale of Honours in Late Victorian England', *Victorian Studies*, vol. 3.

Hannah, L. (1976) *The Rise of the Corporate Economy* (London: Methuen).

Harbury, C. D. and Hitchens, D. M. W. N. (1979) *Inheritance and Wealth Inequality in Britain* (London: Allen & Unwin).

Harries-Jenkins, G. (1977) *The Army in Victorian Society* (London: Routledge & Kegan Paul).

Harris, J. S. and Garcia, T. U. (1966) 'The Permanent Secretaries: Britain's Top Administrators', *Public Administration Review*, vol. 26.

Harris, N. (1972) *Competition and the Corporate Society* (London: Methuen).

Harrison, J. F. C. (1971) *The Early Victorians* (London: Weidenfeld & Nicolson).

Heath, A. (1981) *Social Mobility* (London: Fontana).

Heers, J. (1974) *Family Clans in the Middle Ages* (Amsterdam: North-Holland Publishing, 1977).

Hexter, J. H. (1950) 'The Myth of the Middle Class in Tudor England', in Barber and Barber (1965).

Hexter, J. H. (1958) 'The Military Decline of the Aristocracy', in Stone (1965).

Hilferding, R. (1910) *Finance Capital* (London: Routledge & Kegan Paul, 1981).

Hill, C. (1958) *Puritanism and Revolution* (London: Secker & Warburg).

Hill, C. (1967) *Reformation to Industrial Revolution* (Harmondsworth: Penguin, 1969).

Hilton, R. (1975) *The English Peasantry in the Late Middle Ages* (Oxford: Clarendon Press).

Hilton, R. (1976) 'Introduction', in Hilton (ed.) (1976).

Hilton, R. (ed.) (1976) *The Transition From Feudalism to Capitalism* (London: Routledge & Kegan Paul).

Hindess, B. and Hirst, P. Q. (1975) *Pre-Capitalist Modes of Production* (London: Routledge & Kegan Paul).

Hobsbawm, E. J. (1954) 'The Crisis of the Seventeenth Century', in Aston (1965).

Hobsbawm, E. J. (1962) *The Age of Revolution: Europe 1789–1848* (London: Sphere, 1977).

Hobsbawm, E. J. (1968) *Industry and Empire* (London: Pelican, 1969).

Hobsbawm, E. J. (1975) *The Age of Capital, 1848–1875* (London: Sphere, 1977).

Hollingsworth, T. H. (1964) 'The Demography of the British Peerage', supplement to *Population Studies*, vo, 18.

Hollis, C. (1959) 'Parliament and the Establishment', in Thomas (1959).

Holmes, G. A. (1957) *The Estates of the Higher Nobility in Fourteenth Century England* (Cambridge: Cambridge University Press).

Huntingdon, S. P. (ed.) (1962) *Changing Patterns of Military Politics* (New York: Free Press).

Ilersic, A. R. and Liddle, P. F. B. (1960) *Parliament of Commerce* (London: Newman & Neame).

James, M. E. (1974) *Family, Lineage, and Civil Society* (Oxford: Clarendon Press).

James, M. E. (1978) 'English Politics and the Concept of Honour, 1485–1642', supplement to *Past and Present.*

Jenkins, M. (ed.) (1980) *Daily Mail Year Book, 1981* (London: Harmsworth Publications).

Jessop, B. (1980) 'The Transformation of the State in Post-war Britain', in Scase (1980).

Johnson, R. W. (1973) 'The British Political Elite, 1955–1972', *European Journal of Sociology*, vol. 14.

Kamenka, E. and Neale, R. S. (eds) (1975) *Feudalism, Capitalism and Beyond* (London: Edward Arnold).

Kellner, P. and Crowther-Hunt, N. (1980) *The Civil Servants: An Inquiry into Britain's Ruling Class* (London: Macdonald).

Kelsall, R. K. (1955) *Higher Civil Servants in Britain* (London: Routledge & Kegan Paul).

Kelsall, R. K. (1974) 'Recruitment to the Civil Service: How Has the Pattern Changed?', in Stanworth and Giddens (1974).

Lander, J. R. (1965) *The Wars of the Roses* (London: Secker & Warburg).

Lander, J. R. (1969) *Conflict and Stability in Fifteenth Century England* (London: Hutchinson).

Lander, J. R. (1976) *Crown and Nobility, 1450–1509* (London: Edward Arnold).

Landes, D. S. (1969) *The Unbound Prometheus* (Cambridge: Cambridge University Press).

Laslett, P. (1971) *The World We Have Lost*, 2nd ed. (London: Methuen).

Lederer, E. (1912) 'The Problem of the Modern Salaried Employee', chs 2 and 3 of *Die Privatangestellten in der modernen Wirtschaftentwicklung*, translated and published by Columbia University (New York: 1937).

Lederer, E. and Marschak, J. (1926) 'The New Middle Class', article translated and published by Columbia University (New York: 1937).

Leggatt, T. (1978) 'Managers in Industry: Their Background and Education', *Sociological Review*, vol. 26.

Lejeune, A. (1979) *The Gentlemen's Clubs of London* (London: Macdonald & Janes).

Levine, J. H. (1978) 'The Theory of Bank Control', *Social Science Quarterly*, vol. 58.

Lockwood, D. (1956) 'Some Remarks on "The Social System" ', *British Journal of Sociology*, vol. 7.

Longstreth, F. (1979) 'The City, Industry and the State', in Crouch (1979).

Loyn, H. R. (1962) *Anglo-Saxon England and the Norman Conquest* (London: Longman).

Lukes, S. (1974) *Power: A Radical View* (London: Macmillan).

Lupton, T. and Wilson, C. S. (1959) 'The Social Background and Connections of Top Decision-Makers', *The Manchester School*, vol. 27.

McCahill, M. W. (1981) 'Peerage Creations and the Changing Character of the British Nobility', *English Historical Review*, vol. 96.

McCloskey, D. N. (1973) *Economic Maturity and Entrepreneurial Decline* (Cambridge, Mass.: Harvard University Press).

McEachern, D. (1980) *A Class Against Itself* (Cambridge: Cambridge University Press).

McEwan, J. (1977) *Who Owns Scotland?* (Edinburgh: EUSPB).

McFarlane, K. B. (1936) 'England: The Lancastrian Kings, 1399–1461', in Bury (1936).

McFarlane, K. B. (1973) *The Nobility of Later Medieval England* (Oxford: Clarendon Press).

Macfarlane, A. (1978) *The Origins of English Individualism* (Oxford: Blackwell).

Macmillan, G. (1954) *Honours For Sale* (London: Richards Press).

Macpherson, C. B. (1973a) 'A Political Theory of Property', in Macpherson (1973b).

Macpherson, C. B. (1973b) *Democratic Theory* (London: Oxford University Press).

Mann, M. (1970) 'The Social Cohesion of Liberal Democracy' *American Sociological Review*, vol. 35.

Manning, B. (1956) 'The Nobles, The People and the Constitution', in Aston (1965).

Mariolis, P. (1978) 'Type of Corporation, Size of Firm, and Interlocking Directorates', *Social Science Quarterly*, vol. 58.

Marriott, O. (1967) *The Property Boom* (London: Hamish Hamilton).

Marshall, G. (1980) *Presbyteries and Profits* (London: Oxford University Press).

Marshall, T. H. (1953) 'The Nature and Determinants of Social Status', in Marshall (1963).

Marshall, T. H. (1963) *Sociology at the Crossroads* (London: Heinemann).

Marx, K. (1852a) 'The Elections – Tories and Whigs', in Bottomore and Rubel (1956).

Marx, K. (1852b) 'The Chartists', in Bottomore and Rubel (1956).

Marx, K. (1866) 'Results of the Immediate Production Process', reprinted in Marx (1867).

Marx, K. (1867) *Capital*, vol. 1 (Harmondsworth: Penguin, 1976).

Marx, K. and Engels, F. (1848) *Communist Manifesto* (Harmondsworth: Penguin, 1967).

Massey, D. and Catalano, A. (1978) *Capital and Land* (London: Edward Arnold).

Mathias, P. (1957) 'The Social Structure in the Eighteenth Century', in Mathias (1979).

Mathias, P. (1969) *The First Industrial Nation* (London: Methuen).
Mathias, P. (1973) 'Capital, Credit and Enterprise in the Industrial Revolution', in Mathias (1979).
Mathias, P. (1979) *The Transformation of England* (London: Methuen).
Mathias, P. and Postan, M. M. (eds) (1978) *The Cambridge Economic History of Europe, VII: The Industrial Economies* (Cambridge: Cambridge University Press).
Mellors, C. (1978) *The British MP* (Farnborough: Saxon House).
Merrett, A. J. (1968) *Executive Remuneration in the United Kingdom* (London: Longmans Green).
Middlemas, K. (1979) *Politics in Industrial Society* (London: Deutsch).
Miliband, R. (1969) *The State in Capitalist Society* (London: Quartet, 1973).
Mills, C. W. (1956) *The Power Elite* (New York: Oxford University Press).
Mingay, G. E. (1963) *English Landed Society in the Eighteenth Century* (London: Routledge & Kegan Paul).
Mingay, G. E. (1976a) *The Gentry* (London: Longman).
Mingay, G. E. (1976b) *Rural Life in Victorian England* (London: Futura, 1979).
Minns, R. (1980) *Pension Funds and British Capitalism* (London: Heinemann).
Mintz, B. and Schwartz, M. (1980) 'The Structure of Power in American Business', unpublished paper (Stoneybrook: SUNY).
Mintz, B. and Schwartz, M. (1981) 'The Structure of Intercorporate Unity in American Business', *Social Problems*, vol. 28.
Montgomery-Massingberd, H. (1976) *Burke's Family Index* (London: Burke's Peerage).
Moore, B. (1966) *Social Origins of Dictatorship and Democracy* (Harmondsworth: Allen Lane, 1967).
Moore, D. C. (1976) *The Politics of Deference* (Hassocks: Harvester).
Morgan, D. H. J. (1969) 'The Social and Educational Background of Anglican Bishops', *British Journal of Sociology*, vol. 20.
Mousnier, R. (1969) *Social Hierarchies* (London: Croom Helm, 1973).
Myers, A. R. (1952) *England in the Late Middle Ages* (Harmondsworth: Penguin, 1976).
Nairn, T. (1977) 'The Twilight of the British State', *New Left Review*, no. 101-2.
Nairn, T. (1979) 'The Future of Britain's Crisis', *New Left Review*, no. 113-14.
Namier, L. B. (1928) *The Structure of Politics at the Accession of George III* (London: Macmillan, 1957).
Namier, L. B. (1930) *England in the Age of the American Revolution* (London: Macmillan).
Neale, J. E. (1949) *The Elizabethan House of Commons* (London: Cape).
Neale, R. S. (1968) 'Class and Class Consciousness in Early Nineteenth Century England', in Neale (1972).
Neale, R. S. (1972) *Class and Ideology in the Nineteenth Century* (London: Routledge & Kegan Paul).

Neale, R. S. (1975a) 'The Bourgeoisie, Historically, Has Played a Most Revolutionary Part', in Kamenka and Neale (1975).
Neale, R. S. (1975b) 'Property, Law, and the Transition From Feudalism to Capitalism', in Kamenka and Neale (1975).
Newby, H. (1975) 'The Deferential Dialectic', *Comparative Studies in Society and History*, vol. 17.
Newby, H. (1979) *Green and Pleasant Land?* (London: Hutchinson).
Newby, H., *et al.* (1978) *Property, Paternalism, and Power* (London: Hutchinson).
Nichols, T. (1969) *Ownership, Control, and Ideology* (London: Allen & Unwin).
Nicolaus, M. (1967) 'Proletariat and Middle Class in Marx', *Studies on the Left*, vol. 7.
O'Connor, J. (1973) *The Fiscal Crisis of the State* (New York: St Martins Press).
Offe, C. (1970) *Industry and Inequality* (London: Edward Arnold, 1976).
Ossowski, S. (1957) *Class Structure in the Social Consciousness* (London: Routledge & Kegan Paul, 1963).
Otley, C. B. (1966) 'The Public Schools and the Army', in Urry and Wakeford (1973).
Otley, C. B. (1973) 'The Educational Background of British Army Officers', *Sociology*, vol. 7.
Painter, S. (1943) *Studies in the History of the English Feudal Barony* (Baltimore: John Hopkins University Press).
Painter, S. (1951a) *Medieval Society* (New York: Cornell University Press).
Panitch, L. (1979) 'The Development of Corporatism in Liberal Democracies', in Schmitter and Lehmbruch (1979).
Parkin, F. (1979) *Marxism and Class Theory* (London: Tavistock).
Parry, G. (1969) *Political Elites* (London: Allen & Unwin).
Parsons, T. (1937) *The Structure of Social Action* (Glencoe: Free Press).
Parsons, T. (1940a) 'An Analytical Approach to the Theory of Social Stratification', in Parsons (1954).
Parsons, T. (1940b) 'The Motivation of Economic Activities', in Parsons (1954).
Parsons, T. (1953) 'A Revised Analytical Approach to the Theory of Social Stratification', in Parsons (1954).
Parsons, T. (1954) *Essays in Sociological Theory* (Glencoe: Free Press).
Parsons, T. (1970) 'Equality and Inequality in Modern Society – or Social Stratification Revisited', *Sociological Inquiry*, vol. 40.
Payne, P. L. (1967) 'The Emergence of the Large-Scale Company in Great Britain, 1870–1914', *Economic History Review*, vol. 20.
Payne, P. L. (1974) *British Entrepreneurship in the Nineteenth Century* (London: Macmillan).
Payne, P. L. (1978) 'Industrial Entrepreneurship and Management in Great Britain', in Mathias and Postan (1978).
Perkin, H. (1969) *The Origins of Modern English Society, 1780–1880*, (London: Routledge & Kegan Paul).

Perkin, H. (1978) 'The Recruitment of Elites in British Society Since 1800', *Journal of Social History*, vol. 12.

Perrott, R. (1968) *The Aristocrats* (London: Weidenfeld & Nicolson).

Pine, L. G. (1963) *The Story of Heraldry*, rev. ed. (London: Country Life).

Plumb, J. H. (1950) *England in the Eighteenth Century* (Harmondsworth: Penguin).

Plumb, J. H. (1967) *The Growth of Political Stability in England, 1675–1725* (London: Macmillan).

Poggi, G. (1978) *The Development of the Modern State* (London: Hutchinson).

Polanyi, G. and Wood, J. B. (1974) *How Much Inequality?* (London: Institute of Economic Affairs).

Pollard, S. (1965) *The Genesis of Modern Management* (London: Edward Arnold).

Postan, M. M. (1966) 'England', in *Cambridge Economic History of Europe*, vol. 1 (Cambridge: Cambridge University Press, 1966).

Postan, M. M. (1972) *The Medieval Economy and Society* (Harmondsworth: Penguin, 1975).

Poulantzas, N. (1974) *Classes in Contemporary Capitalism* (London: New Left Books, 1975).

Power, E. (1933) 'The Wool Trade in the Fifteenth Century', in Power and Postan (1933).

Power, E. (1941) *The Wool Trade* (London: Oxford University Press).

Power, E. and Postan, M. M. (eds) (1933) *Studies in English Trade in the Fifteenth Century* (London: Routledge & Kegan Paul).

Prais, S. J. (1976) *The Evolution of Giant Firms in Britain* (Cambridge: Cambridge University Press).

Pumphrey, R. (1959) 'The Introduction of Industrialists into the British Peerage', *American Historical Review*, vol. 65.

Raven, S. (1959) 'Perish By the Sword', in Thomas (1959).

Razzell, P. E. (1963) 'Social Origins of Officers in the Indian and British Home Army', *British Journal of Sociology*, vol. 14.

Return (1874a) *Return of Owners of Land, 1872–3* (England and Wales), Parliamentary Papers, 1874, LXXII, parts I and II.

Return (1874b) *Return of Owners of Land* (Scotland), Parliamentary Papers, 1874, LXXII, part III.

Return (1876) *Return of Owners of Land* (Ireland), Parliamentary Papers, 1876, LXXX.

Rex, J. (1961) *Key Problems of Sociological Theory* (London: Routledge & Kegan Paul).

Rex, J. (1974) 'Capitalism, Elites, and the Ruling Class', in Stanworth and Giddens (1974).

Richards, P. G. (1963) *Patronage in British Government* (London: Allen & Unwin).

Richards, P. (1980) 'State Formation and Class Struggle, 1832–48', in Corrigan (1980).

Rose, D., *et al.* (1977) 'Land Tenure and Official Statistics: A Research Note', *Journal of Agricultural Economics*, vol. 28.
Rosenthal, J. T. (1976) *Nobles and the Noble Life, 1295–1500* (London: Allen & Unwin).
Ross, C. (ed.) (1979) *Patronage, Pedigree, and Power* (Gloucester: Sutton).
Rowse, A. L. (1950) *The England of Elizabeth* (London: Macmillan).
Rubinstein, W. D. (1974a) 'Men of Property: Some Aspects of Occupation, Inheritance, and Power Among Top British Wealth Holders', in Stanworth and Giddens (1974).
Rubinstein, W. D. (1974b) 'British Millionaires, 1809–1949', *Bulletin of the Institute of Historical Research*, vol. 48.
Rubinstein, W. D. (1976) 'Wealth, Elites and the Class Structure of Modern Britain', *Past and Present*, vol. 70.
Rubinstein, W. D. (1977) 'The Victorian Middle Classes: Wealth, Occupation, and Geography', *Economic History Review*, vol. 30.
Rubinstein, W. D. (1980) 'Modern Britain', in Rubinstein (ed.) (1980).
Rubinstein, W. D. (ed.) (1980) *Wealth and the Wealthy in the Modern World* (London: Croom Helm).
Rubinstein, W. D. (1981) *Men of Property* (London: Croom Helm).
Rudé, G. (1972) *Europe in the Eighteenth Century* (London: Weidenfeld & Nicolson).
Salaman, G. and Thompson, K. (1978) 'Class Culture and the Persistence of an Elite: The Case of Army Officer Selection', *Sociological Review*, vol. 26.
Sampson, A. (1962) *Anatomy of Britain* (London: Hodder & Stoughton).
Sampson, A. (1965) *Anatomy of Britain Today* (London: Hodder & Stoughton).
Sandelson, V. (1959) 'The Confidence Trick', in Thomas (1959).
Scase, R. (ed.) (1977) *Industrial Society: Class, Cleavage and Control* (London: Allen & Unwin).
Scase, R. (ed.) (1980) *The State in Western Europe* (London: Croom Helm).
Schaffer, G. (1939) *Riches and Poverty* (London: Gollancz).
Schmitter, P. C. (1974) 'Still the Century of Corporatism', in Schmitter and Lehmbruch (1979).
Schmitter, P. C. and Lehmbruch, G. (eds) (1979) *Trends Towards Corporatist Intermediation* (London: Sage).
Scott, J. P. (1979) *Corporations, Classes, and Capitalism* (London: Hutchinson).
Scott, J. P. (1981) 'Property and Control: Some Remarks on the British Propertied Class', in Giddens and Mackenzie (1981).
Scott, J. P. and Hughes, M. D. (1980) *The Anatomy of Scottish Capital* (London: Croom Helm).
Scott-Thomson, G. (1923) *Lords Lieutenant in the Sixteenth Century* (London: Longmans Green).
Shils, E. and Young, M. (1953) 'The Meaning of the Coronation', *Sociological Review*, vol. 1.

Shonfield, A. (1965) *Modern Capitalism* (Oxford University Press).
Skidelsky, R. (1979) 'The Decline of Keynesian Politics', in Crouch (1979).
Slater, M. (1976) 'Marriage in an Upper-Gentry Family in Seventeenth Century England', *Past and Present*, vol. 72.
Smout, T. C. (1968) 'The Glasgow Merchant Community in the Seventeenth Century', *Scottish Historical Review*, vol. 47.
Sombart, W. (1913) *The Quintessence of Capitalism* (London: Fisher Unwin, 1915).
Soref, M. (1976) 'Social Class and a Division of Labour Within the Corporate Elite', *Sociological Quarterly*, vol. 17.
Soref, M. (1980) 'The Finance Capitalists', in Zeitlin (1980).
Spring, D. (1963 *The English Landed Estate in the Nineteenth Century: Its Administration* (Baltimore: Johns Hopkins University Press).
Spring, D. (1971) 'English Landowners and Nineteenth Century Industrialism', in Ward and Wilson (1971).
Spring, D. (1977) 'Landed Elites Compared', in Spring (ed.) (1977).
Spring, D. (ed.) (1977) *European Landed Elites in the Nineteenth Century* (Baltimore: Johns Hopkins University Press).
Stanhope, H. (1979) *The Soldiers* (London: Hamish Hamilton).
Stanworth, P. (1974) 'Property, Class and the Corporate Elite', in Crewe (1974).
Stanworth, P. and Giddens, A. (eds) (1974) *Elites and Power in British Society* (Cambridge: Cambridge University Press).
Stenton, D. M. (1951) *English Society in the Early Middle Ages* (Harmondsworth: Penguin).
Stenton, F. M. (1961) *The First Century of English Feudalism* (Oxford: Clarendon Press).
Stephenson, C. (1942) *Medieval Feudalism* (New York: Cornell University Press).
Stone, L. (ed.) (1965) *Social Change and Revolution in England* (London: Longman).
Stone, L. (1967) *The Crisis of the Aristocracy, 1558–1641*, abridged ed. (Oxford: Clarendon Press).
Stone, L. (1972) *The Causes of the English Revolution* (London: Routledge & Kegan Paul).
Stone, L. (1979) *The Family, Sex and Marriage in England, 1500–1800*, abridged ed. (Harmondsworth: Penguin).
Strayer, J. R. (1965) *Feudalism* (Princeton, N.J.: Van Nostrand).
Strayer, J. R. (1971) *Medieval Statecraft and the Perspectives of History* (New Jersey: Princeton University Press).
Strinati, D. (1979) 'Capitalism, the State and Industrial Relations', in Crouch (1979).
Sutherland, D. (1968) *The Landowners* (London: Blond).
Tawney, R. H. (1912) *The Agrarian Problem in the Sixteenth Century* (London: Longmans Green).
Tawney, R. H. (1926) *Religion and the Rise of Capitalism* (Harmondsworth: Penguin, 1938).

Tawney, R. H. (1941) 'The Rise of the Gentry', in Stone (1965).

Thomas, D. (1972) 'The Social Origins of Marriage Partners of the British Peerage in the Eighteenth and Nineteenth Centuries', *Population Studies*, vol. 26.

Thomas, A. B. (1978) 'The British Business Elite: The Case of the Retail Sector', *Sociological Review*, vol. 26.

Thomas, C. (1979) 'Family and Kinship in Eaton Square', in Field (1979).

Thomas, H. (1959) 'The Establishment and Society', in Thomas (1959).

Thomas, H. (ed.) (1959) *The Establishment* (London: Blond).

Thompson, E. P. (1963) *The Making of the English Working Class* (Harmondsworth: Penguin).

Thompson, E. P. (1965) 'The Peculiarities of the English', in Thompson (1978a).

Thompson, E. P. (1978a) *The Poverty of Theory* (London: Merlin Press).

Thompson, E. P. (1978b) 'Eighteenth Century English Society: Class Struggle Without Class', *Social History*, vol. 3.

Thompson, F. M. L. (1963) *English Landed Society in the Nineteenth Century* (London: Routledge & Kegan Paul).

Thompson, F. M. L. (1977) 'Britain', in Spring (ed.) (1977).

Thompson, K. (1974) 'Church of England Bishops as an Elite', in Stanworth and Giddens (1974).

Thomson, D. (1950) *England in the Nineteenth Century* (Harmondsworth: Penguin).

Thrupp, S. L. (1948) *The Merchant Class of Medieval London, 1300–1500* (Chicago: Chicago University Press).

Tilly, C. (ed.) (1975) *The Formation of National States in Western Europe* (New Jersey: Princeton University Press).

Townsend, P. (1979) *Poverty in the United Kingdom* (Harmondsworth: Penguin).

Trevor-Roper, H. R. (1953) 'The Decline of the Mere Gentry', in Stone (1965).

Trevor-Roper, H. R. (1959) 'The Economic Crisis of the Seventeenth Century', in Aston (1965).

Trumbach, R. (1978) *The Rise of the Egalitarian Family* (New York: Academic Press).

Turner, R. H. (1960) 'Sponsored and Contest Mobility and the School System', *American Sociological Review*, vol. 25.

Urry, J. (1973) 'Towards a Structural Theory of the Middle Classes', *Acta Sociologica*, vol. 16.

Urry, J. and Wakeford, J. (eds) (1973) *Power in Britain* (London: Heinemann).

Useem, M. (1978) 'The Inner Group of the American Capitalist Class', *Social Problems*, vol. 25.

Useem, M. (1980) 'Corporations and the Corporate Elite', *Annual Review of Sociology*, vol. 6.

Useem, M. (1981) 'Corporate and Class-Wide Principles of Organisation in Business Politics in America and Britain', paper to EGOS Conference, York.

Vaizey, J. (1959) 'The Public Schools', in Thomas (1959).
Veblen, T. (1899) *The Theory of the Leisure Class* (New York: Mentor, 1953).
Vincent, J. R. (1966) *The Formation of the British Liberal Party, 1857–1868* (Hassocks: Harvester, 1976).
Wagner, A. R. (1972) *English Genealogy*, 2nd ed. (Oxford: Clarendon Press).
Wagner, A. R. (1975) *Pedigree and Progress* (London: Phillimore).
Wakeford, J. (1969) *The Cloistered Elite* (London: Macmillan).
Wallerstein, I. (1974a) *The Modern World System* (New York: Academic Press).
Wallerstein, I. (1974b) 'The Rise and Future Demise of the World Capitalist System', *Comparative Studies in Society and History*, vol. 16.
Wallerstein, I. (1980) *The Modern World System, II* (New York: Academic Press).
Ward, J. T. and Wilson, R. G. (eds) (1971) *Land and Industry* (Newton Abbot: David & Charles).
Weber, M. (1904–6) *The Protestant Ethic and the Spirit of Capitalism* (London: Allen & Unwin, 1930).
Weber, M. (1910) 'Class, Status, and Party', in Gerth and Mills (1948).
Weber, M. (1913) 'The Social Psychology of the World Religions', in Gerth and Mills (1948).
Weber, M. (1916–17) 'India: The Brahman and the Castes', in Gerth and Mills (1948).
Weber, M. (1918–20) 'Social Stratification and Class Structure', in *The Theory of Social and Economic Organisation* (Glencoe: Free Press, 1947).
Weber, M. (1920) *Economy and Society* (New York: Bedminster Press, 1968).
Wedgwood, J. (1929) *The Economics of Inheritance* (Harmondsworth: Penguin, 1939).
West, F. J. (1975) 'On the Ruins of Feudalism – Capitalism?', in Kamenka and Neale (1975).
Westergaard, J. H. and Resler, H. (1975) *Class in a Capitalist Society* (London: Heinemann).
Whitley, R. (1973) 'Commonalities and Connections Among Directors of Large Financial Institutions', *Sociological Review*, vol. 21.
Whitley, R. (1974) 'The City and Industry', in Stanworth and Giddens (1974).
Wigham, E. (1973) *The Power to Manage* (London: Macmillan).
Wilkinson, R. (1964) *The Prefects: British Leadership and the Public School Tradition* (London: Oxford University Press).
Wilkinson, R. (ed.) (1966) *Governing Elites* (New York: Oxford University Press).
Williams, C. H. (1936) 'England: The Yorkist Kings, 1461–1485', in Bury (1936).
Wilson, C. (1965a) *England's Apprenticeship, 1603–1763* (London: Longman).

Wilson, C. (1965b) 'Economy and Society in Late Victorian Britain', *Economic History Review*, vol. 18.

Winkler, J. T. (1977) 'The Corporatist Economy: Theory and Administration', in Scase (1977).

Wright, E. O. (1978) *Class, Crisis, and the State* (London: New Left Books).

Wright, J. F. (1979) *Britain in the Age of Economic Management* (London: Oxford University Press).

Zeitlin, M. (1980) 'On Classes, Class Conflict, and the State: An Introductory Note', in Zeitlin (ed.) (1980).

Zeitlin, M. (ed.) (1980) *Classes, Class Conflict, and the State* (Cambridge, Mass.: Winthrop).

Zeitlin, M., *et al.* (1976) 'Class Segments: Agrarian Property and Political Leadership in the Capitalist Class of Chile', *American Sociological Review*, vol. 41.

Index

agricultural revolution 35–6, 41, 46
agriculture 10, 17, 19, 44, 85, 133, 135, 176
  capitalist 17, 20, 26, 34–5
  commercialisation of 13, 17, 19
  see also agricultural revolution
Anderson, P. 8, 51
army see military service
Atkinson, A. B. 116–17

Bagehot, W. 99
Bank of England 53, 79, 80, 111n, 182, 183, 184
banks 43, 45, 46, 62, 71, 79–80, 83, 89, 100–1, 111n, 132–3, 173
  relation to industry 69, 79, 132–3
  spheres of influence 139, 142–4
baronets 39, 50, 58, 61, 100, 102, 106, 109, 154, 156, 164
barons and baronies 15–17, 22, 28, 29, 33n, 50, 155, 164
Bédarida, F. 116
Beer, S. 182
Bendix, R. 75, 95
Birmingham 82, 95, 98, 103, 181
bishops see church
Bloch, M. 8
bourgeoisie 14–15, 16, 20–2, 23, 24, 30, 34, 51
Boyd, D. 165, 169
Bristol 32n, 42
Burnham, J. 128
business class 114–15, 124ff, 130ff, 141, 149, 158, 160ff
business enterprise 71ff, 88, 125ff, 131ff, 150, 186

capital 19, 21, 37–8, 39, 41–2, 45, 68ff, 73, 81, 115, 125, 131, 141, 142, 180–1
  market for 42–3, 44, 45, 71
capitalism 10, 21, 51, 72
capitalist spirit 72, 75, 129
church 25, 46, 49, 55, 66n, 89, 159
  and landownership 35, 86, 138
  recruitment 20, 108, 124, 170–1
  see also Nonconformism
civil service 124, 152, 164–6
civil war 48, 51–3, 65n
class and class situation 1ff, 9, 12–13, 16, 36, 69, 73, 78, 88, 95, 129, 174
  fractions and segments of 5, 43, 63, 80, 85, 95, 96, 144, 174
  see also business class; middle class; social class; working class
class consciousness 4, 5–6
closure 4, 7, 55, 160, 174
clubs 63, 99, 103, 110, 142, 159, 177–8
Cole, G. D. H. 47
Coleman, D. C. 93
commercial class 34, 42ff, 63, 78, 80, 90, 96, 109
Commons, House of 25–6, 51, 56, 57–8, 95, 100–1, 109
  see also members of parliament
company, joint stock 41, 69, 79, 83, 88–9, 111n, 114, 148n
  see also business enterprise
Conservative Party 99, 100, 102–4, 105, 154, 156, 159, 162–3, 174–5, 183

constellation of interests, control through 139, 140
control and ownership 37, 81, 89, 127–8, 139–40
corporatism 180ff
country party 51
court 27–8, 31, 49, 51, 63, 91, 157, 177
court party 51–3, 54, 57
credit *see* capital
Crewe, I. 165
cultural assets 55, 63, 160

Dahrendorf, R. 5
Davidoff, L. 90
deference 51, 92–3, 100
Deputy Lieutenants 26
directors 85, 101, 124, 126ff, 138, 140–1, 178
dukes 29–30, 33n, 39, 50, 60, 154

earls 29, 33n, 50, 151, 153–4
economic concentration 83–4, 115, 131–2, 141, 149
see also monopoly sector
economy, as distinct sphere of action 7, 12–13, 34, 150
electoralism 98–9, 104
see also parties
Elias, N. 28
elite, notion of 1, 98, 112n, 179–80
elitism 97ff, 103
enclosure *see* agricultural revolution
Engels, F. 1
entrepreneurial capitalists 70, 72, 75, 83, 125, 126–7, 135–7, 139, 145, 172
see also family firms
entrepreneurial decline 93–4
Erickson, C. 90, 136, 172–3
establishment 104ff, 113n, 149, 158ff, 180ff
estate, as stratification concept 2, 4–5, 6

estates, landed 16–17, 36ff, 60, 62, 82–3, 139
management of 17–18, 36, 39, 41, 46, 80–1, 85
and strict settlement 40–1
see also family strategies
executives 90, 124, 125, 126ff, 136, 140, 141, 146n, 172
see also internal capitalists

Fairlie, H. 159
family firms and family control 69ff, 84–5, 94, 123, 130, 135–7, 139–40, 172
family strategies 18, 23–4, 29, 39–41, 45–6, 62, 81–2, 94, 118–19, 136, 158
see also kinship; marriage
farmers, capitalist 19, 36, 38–9, 44, 47, 63, 76, 80–1, 102, 139, 146n
feudal relations 6ff, 13, 14, 17, 28, 31, 32n, 186
fief 8, 13, 15, 16
finance capitalists 125, 126–7, 137, 140–3, 172, 185–6
financiers 42, 43, 56, 78, 83, 123, 137
and modern enterprise 126–7, 172
Foster, J. 68, 97

genealogy 31, 49, 91
see also heralds
gentleman, concept of 29–30, 49–50, 58–9, 84, 92, 97, 104, 151, 157, 172
life-style of 62–3, 90, 91, 94
gentry, landed 21, 24, 25–6, 29–30, 34ff, 46–7, 49, 51–3, 91, 98
Giddens, A. 176, 177, 178
gilds 14
Glasgow 42, 95, 98
Glorious Revolution 53
Guttsman, W. 178

Habermas, J. 64n, 99
Halévy, E. 38, 56, 58, 63, 96

Halsey, A. H.　165
Harbury, C. D.　119, 121
Harrison, A. J.　116–17
heralds　30
　see also genealogy
Hilferding, R.　133
Hill, C.　52, 57
Hindess, B.　9
Hirst, P. Q.　9
Hitchens, D. M. W. N.　119, 121
honour　2–3, 4, 8, 27ff, 49, 55,
　58, 60
　honours system　28–30, 151–4,
　156–7, 176
　sales of honours　50, 152, 187n

income　40, 41, 46–7, 86–7, 89,
　115ff
　see also wealth
industrial revolution　68–9, 74,
　76, 93
inequality　*see* income; life
　chances; wealth
inheritance　18, 29, 40, 46, 119–
　20, 130
　see also wealth
interests　5–6, 9, 98, 105, 126–7,
　142, 180–1
internal capitalists　125, 126–7,
　140, 145, 172
international trade　13, 15, 20,
　42, 67, 78
Irish peerages　59, 60, 66n

Jessop, B.　185
judges　*see* lawyers
Justices of the Peace　26, 97, 108

Keynesianism　150, 183–4
kinship　4, 18, 20–1, 40, 45, 47,
　57, 70, 80, 124, 141, 153–4,
　158, 160
　see also family strategies
knight service　8–9
knighthood　16, 28, 59–60, 106,
　109–10, 122, 156, 164, 166
　creations of　61, 109–10
　title of　29, 50, 61

Labour Party　154, 156, 165,
　183ff
labour process　14–15, 44, 73–5,
　88, 129–30
landed class　34, 39–40, 44, 61,
　62, 63, 67, 78, 86, 93, 96ff,
　114, 135, 149, 151
landowners　5, 7, 9, 16, 29–30,
　31n, 35, 44–6, 52, 76, 79,
　81–3, 85, 89, 95, 98, 100, 105,
　109, 121, 124–5, 133–5,
　138–9, 145
　see also estate; gentry; magnates
landownership, statistics on　16,
　21, 35, 37, 39, 85–7, 134
law and legal forms　4, 7, 8, 9,
　20, 30, 40, 69, 79
lawyers　46, 47, 49, 55, 58, 62,
　71, 83, 100, 106, 159, 171–2
　and land　45, 89
　recruitment　124
legitimation　3, 4, 8, 24, 64n, 75,
　99, 150ff, 176
　problems of state　48–9, 51,
　151
leisure　27–8, 62, 94
Liberal Party　102–4, 105
life chances　2, 3, 5, 7, 12–13,
　14, 22, 107, 124, 125, 160,
　162, 166, 175, 186
life peerages　155, 156, 164
life-style　3, 5, 10, 14, 27–8, 30,
　49, 61, 82, 104, 160, 176
　see also gentleman
Liverpool　42, 82, 95
London　14, 20, 32n, 34, 63, 71,
　82, 181
　City of　23, 42, 52, 69, 78, 79–
　80, 96, 102, 123, 132, 133,
　137
　'Society' in　62–3, 90, 159,
　176–7
Lord Lieutenant　26, 108
Lords, House of　25, 52, 60,
　100–1, 163, 170

McCloskey, D. N.　94
McEwan, J.　134

magnates, landed 14, 17ff, 22, 23–5, 28, 29–30, 34ff, 43, 52, 54, 56, 57–8, 60, 98
managers 36, 39, 70, 74, 81, 88, 128–30, 138
see also executives
Manchester 69, 95, 97, 98, 102
manufacturers, capitalist 14, 22, 41, 44, 67ff, 71ff, 78, 87, 90, 93, 95, 96, 98ff, 114, 123
market and market relations 7, 12, 14, 19, 22, 43, 55, 71, 74
growth of 17, 38
market situation 2, 12–14, 114, 126
see also international trade
marquesses 29, 33n, 50, 60, 151, 154
marriage 18, 40, 41, 45, 47, 55, 70, 82, 89, 158
see also family strategies
Marx, K. and Marxian theory 1, 19, 74, 87, 102
Mathias, P. 70
members of parliament (MPs) 57, 96, 103, 105–7, 152, 154–5, 156, 162–4, 174–5
merchants 14–15, 17, 20–1, 30, 34, 38, 42ff, 49, 51–3, 58, 67–8, 69, 72, 76, 78, 79, 80, 87, 89, 95, 96–7
companies of 15, 42
see also bourgeoisie; financiers
middle class 58, 88, 175–6
Middlemas, K. 182
Miliband, R. 168
military service 8, 24–5, 31, 45, 46, 52, 58, 61, 101–2, 105, 154, 166–9
in feudalism 7, 22, 28
recruitment 102, 108, 167–8, 169
Mills, C. Wright 114
Mingay, G. E. 40, 41, 47
ministers 100, 105, 163–4
minority control 127–8, 136, 140, 148n

mobility 4, 43, 45, 47, 49, 160, 161, 174, 179
see also patronage
monarchy 7, 8, 18–19, 22ff, 28–9, 56–7, 96
finances of 20, 22ff, 48ff
and landownership 8, 16, 18, 21, 26, 34–5, 86
and legitimation 24, 28, 99–100, 151–2, 157
see also court
monopoly sector 123ff, 132–3, 141, 144
motive, vocabulary of 153, 157–8, 161

Nairn, T. 54
Namier, L. 56, 57–8
nobility *see* gentry; magnates; peerage
Nonconformism 70–1, 75, 104
see also Protestant ethic; Quakers
Norman society 7, 11n, 15, 22, 33n
normative order 2–3, 27, 176
see also legitimation

'old corruption' 53ff, 98
Otley, C. B. 168
'Oxbridge' 92, 93, 107, 108, 159ff

parliament 25, 48, 51–3, 56ff, 96, 98, 100, 102
parliamentary management 26, 56, 58, 60
see also Commons, House of; Lords, House of
Parsons, T. 2–3, 11n, 55
parties
definition of 6
modern emergence of 57, 58, 99, 103–4
see also Conservative Party; country party; court party; electoralism; Labour Party; Liberal Party; Tories; Whigs

patronage   52, 53, 55–8, 103, 107, 109
peerage   21, 29, 33n, 47, 49–51, 58–61, 87, 90, 99, 101–2, 106, 109, 122, 134, 163–4
Perkin, H.   62, 87
Perrott, R.   134
Plumb, J. H.   39, 53, 54
police   26, 166, 169
politics   7, 12, 24, 28, 31, 34, 43, 51, 55ff, 60, 62, 76, 84, 94, 96ff, 149, 162–4
possession   2, 8, 9, 15, 19, 37, 73
Postan, M. M.   16, 17
prestige   2, 49, 50–1, 55
property   7, 18, 37, 55, 114, 130
   see also possession
Protestant ethic   72
public schools   91–3, 95, 107–8, 159ff

Quakers   70, 72
   cousinhood   70–1
   see also Nonconformism

railways   69, 82, 83, 100–1, 131
relations of production   7, 8, 9, 17, 19, 21–2, 36–7, 72–4
rentiers   21, 34ff, 47, 69, 72, 80, 114
representation   98ff
Rex, J. A.   6
Rubinstein, W. D.   87, 121

Sampson, A.   158
Saxon England   11n, 33n
Schmitter, P.   184
Scotland   57, 65n, 66n, 79, 80, 86, 91, 111n, 132, 134–5, 155, 188n
'season'   see London, 'Society' in
secret services   166, 169–70
serfs   5, 8, 9–10, 16, 19
shareholders   83, 111n, 124, 126ff, 130, 136, 140
   institutional   130ff, 137–9, 140, 143, 149, 186
Shils, E.   157

social assets   45–6, 55, 63, 107, 160, 161
social class   4, 8, 10, 78, 95, 175
social order   4
Sombart, W.   129
Spring, D.   81
Stamp, J.   115
Stanworth, P.   178
state   22, 25, 30, 34, 42, 54, 99, 105, 126, 151, 158
   fiscal problems   48ff, 150
   formation of   22, 25, 27
   intervention   139, 150–1, 180–5
   see also corporatism; legitimation; monarchy
status and status situation   2–3, 5, 10, 11n, 14, 18, 21, 29–30, 49–50, 52, 58, 61–2, 90, 95, 97, 123, 149, 151, 158, 185
   see also honour; prestige
Stone, L.   51
strategic control   81, 89, 114, 123ff, 141
stratification   1–2, 157
   see also class; estate; social order; status
stratum   see stratification
Stuart state   48ff, 58

Thompson, E. P.   44, 54
titles and ranks   28–30, 49–50, 105–6, 151ff, 187n
   see also entries for main titles
Tories   53, 54, 56, 58, 96–7, 98–9, 182
towns   14, 45, 63
   and bourgeoisie   14
   growth of   13
   in nineteenth century   82
Townsend, P.   116–19
trades unions   104, 126, 182–3
traditionalism   72, 75, 150–1, 157
Tudor state   19, 25–6, 30–1, 34, 50

Vaizey, J.   160
vassalage   8
Veblen, T.   27–8, 62

Vincent, J. R.   104
violence   7, 8, 25, 30
viscounts   29, 33n, 50, 153,
     154–5

wage labour   15, 19, 72–4, 80
   see also working class
war   23
   wars of the roses   23–4, 32n
   see also civil war
wealth   2, 42–3, 61, 88, 114,

115ff, 124
   see also income
Weber, M.   2ff, 12, 72, 129
Wedgwood, J.   115–16, 121
Whigs   53, 54ff, 96–7, 99, 102,
     105
Whitley, R.   173
wool trade   15, 17, 20, 44
working class   73–4, 76, 105

yeomen   19, 32n, 35, 38, 49
Young, M.   157